Library of
Davidson College

Computer Models
in the Social Sciences

WINTHROP COMPUTER SYSTEMS SERIES
Gerald M. Weinberg, *editor*

COATS AND PARKIN
Computer Models in the Social Sciences

CONWAY AND GRIES
Primer on Structural Programming Using PL/I, PL/C, and PL/CT

CONWAY, GRIES, AND WORTMAN
Introduction to Structured Programming Using PL/I and SP/k

CONWAY, GRIES, AND ZIMMERMAN
A Primer on PASCAL

CONWAY
A Primer on Disciplined Programming Using PL/I, PL/CS, and PL/CT

EASLEY
Primer for Small Systems Management

FINKENAUR
COBOL for Students: A Programming Primer

GELLER AND FREEDMAN
Structured Programming in APL

GILB
Software Metrics

GILB AND WEINBERG
Humanized Input: Techniques for Reliable Keyed Input

WEINBERG, WRIGHT, GOETZ, AND KAUFFMAN
High Level COBOL Programming

FUTURE TITLES

ECKHOUSE AND SPIER
Guide to Programming

GREENFIELD
The Architecture of Microcomputers

LINES
Minicomputer Systems

POOCH
Simulation

SHNEIDERMAN
Human Factors in Computer and Information Systems

TOPPING
Simula Programming

WILCOX
Introduction to Compiler Construction

Computer Models
in the Social Sciences

Robert B. Coats

Andrew Parkin
Leicester Polytechnic
England

Foreword by
Gerald M. Weinberg

Winthrop Publishers, Inc.
Cambridge, Massachusetts

Library of Congress Cataloging in Publication Data

Coats, R B
    Computer models in the social sciences.

    Includes bibliographies and index.
    1.   Social sciences — Data processing. 2.   Social sciences — Mathematical models. I.   Parkin, Andrew, joint author. II.   Title.
H61.C5   300'.28'54   77-10895
ISBN 0-87626-167-5

300.18
C652c

© R. B. Coats and A. Parkin 1977

Published by
Edward Arnold (Publishers) Ltd.,
25 Hill Street, London W1X 8LL

Published in the U.S. by
Winthrop Publishers, Inc.
17 Dunster Street
Cambridge, Massachusetts 02138

All rights reserved. No part of this book may be reproduced in any form or by any means without permission in writing from the publisher. Printed in the United States of America.

10 9 8 7 6 5 4 3 2 1

Cover graphic by Roger Vilder
from the series *Variations with 9 Squares (1971)*
Courtesy of Galerie Gilles Gheerbrant, Montreal

Cover design by Harold Pattek

80-7852

Contents

Foreword   ix

Preface   xi

1 **Models in the Social Sciences**   1
A discussion of some philosophical issues. The role of models in scientific method.

2 **Computer Models**   9
Some fundamental concepts of stochastic models. How a computer model differs from other models.

3 **Designing a Computer Model**   26
The building blocks of models on a queuing process. When will Erewhon airport need a new runway?

4 **Experiments with Computer Models**   50
Data gathering, testing, sensitivity analysis. How sure are you about that runway?

5 **The Variety of Computer Models**   73
Computer-model applications in the social sciences. Bibliography of modern social-science models.

6 **A Computer Model of Memory** 93
   An explanation of human memory processes based on a network data structure.

7 **Bed Usage in a Hospital Surgical Suite** 126
   How many recovery beds should be provided by Deaconness Hospital?

8 **An Educational Economic Model** 151
   A simulated Keynesian macroeconomy.

   Appendix A — Statistical Concepts 164

   Appendix B — Computer Concepts 168

   Appendix C — EDSIM Subroutines 171

   Glossary 179

   Index 182

Foreword

Being the spouse of an anthropologist, I meet dozens of social scientists in the course of a typical year. I tag along to a few professional meetings. At cocktail parties given in honor of distinguished visitors, I get free drinks. During the dreadful annual cycle of faculty job interviews, I get dragged into the whirlpool of social events. I always try, in these situations, to palm myself off as a mere "faculty spouse," but all too often I'm introduced as someone who is "in computers" or "in systems."

Once the beans are spilled, it's only a matter of a negative exponential waiting time before I get the question: "Can you recommend a good book on simulation - one that a poor social scientist can understand?" Until recently, the answer has always been something like "Um, huh, oh, uhhhn, well . . . NO." Now, thanks to Coats and Parkin, my social life among the social scientists has taken a significant turn for the better.

In the six months since I got my hands on their manuscript, I've used it to help seven anthropologists, three sociologists, two geographers, one and one-half historians, and one-half of a political scientist.

I've become, in fact, the life of parties - even when there are biologists, chemists, and physicists present. I've given five graduate students terrific boosts on their theses. I have a waiting list of computer scientists eager to improve their own social lives - and to teach that super simulation course they've always wanted to give to the great unwashed masses.

In short, Coats and Parkin have made a wonderful difference in my life - which is why I pursued them until permission was given to put their lovely book in our *Winthrop Computer Systems Series*. Of course, now that it's published in the United States, my postage and copying bills will be reduced, but my reasons are not *entirely* selfish. I can't be the *only* person "in computers" or "in systems" who's married to a social scientist. And perhaps there are other computer people or systems people who, though not tied to the social, biological, or *whatever* science by affectional bonds have some sort of relationship with the "outsiders."

Perhaps you have a sister or a cousin or an aunt who is heavily involved in simulation - or ought to be. Perhaps you're tired of queuing up at your barbers' shop and would like to encourage them to make a little simulation study of their operation. Perhaps your department head would give you a well-deserved merit increase if you would only teach that service course in simulation - the course that's never quite made it over the Hill of Acceptability into the Valley of Greatness.

Or perhaps you, yourself, have always had a gnawing fear that there was more to simulation than writing programs in GPSS, DYNAMO, CSMP, GASP, SIMSCRIPT, SIMPL, SIMULA, ALGOL, or, heaven forbid, FORTRAN. Perhaps you, too, have been yearning for a text that teaches the WHY behind the HOW of simulation, and teaches in a style and language that ordinary human beings, scientists of all colors, business people, and even computer scientists can understand. If so, it's with the greatest pleasure that I introduce you to *Computer Models in the Social Sciences*. I'm sure you'll become great friends - even if it doesn't improve your social life as much as it did mine.

Gerald M. Weinberg

Preface

Our aim is to arouse your interest in the potential of computer models in explaining or predicting social phenomena; to explain to you in plain terms how such models can be built; to instruct you, if you wish, in some practical methods of designing and testing these models; and to give you leads to further information should you wish to extend your knowledge or skills.

In writing this book, few problems have taxed us more than this: what assumptions can we make about our readers and how can we organize the book to suit their different backgrounds? The notes that follow state our assumptions and the structure that has resulted.

May we first dispel any idea you may have that in order to understand things to do with computers you must be something of a mathematician? We are not sure about the origins of this common misconception - could it be because mathematicians played such an important part in the development of early computers? Could it be because of the spectacular feats of mathematics which have been achieved with the aid of computers? Or could it be that most people's early learning about computers came from their mathematics teacher who, naturally, drew his examples from the area he was most familiar with? Whatever the reason, let us assure you that to understand this book you need only simple algebra, a little statistics and an alert mind. Quite a large part of the book can be understood without the first two of these.

The statistical concepts used are: probability, randomness, frequency, histogram, distributions of the normal, negative exponential and uniform types, sampling from a distribution. If histograms and distributions are new to you, you will find a precis explanation in Appendix A.

We have assumed you have an appreciation of computers but little or no practical experience. The key concepts here are: program, instruction, memory, loop, branch or jump, subroutine. For readers with less knowledge than we have assumed, a very brief description of these is supplied in Appendix B. We hope the text will be sufficiently novel still to maintain the interest of readers with more computing knowledge that we have assumed.

xii Preface

The particular techniques we introduce are used in a variety of places in the book and the reader may feel disappointed that there is no summary at the end which consolidates them. We find ourselves unable to summarize a collection of disparate techniques - perhaps the most useful thing we can do is list right here the techniques we describe and where they are used: processes involving sequential choices practically throughout, and sequential choices over time particularly in Chapters 3 and 4 and the hospital model of Chapter 7; stochasticity, sampling and the summation of distributions are used in Chapters 2, 3, 4 and 7 as well as the models of Smith and Vertinsky, and our suggested continuation of Reisman's experiments, in Chapter 5; the idea of discrete events is in Chapters 3, 4, and 7 and the similar notion of a threshold variable is in Smith's model in Chapter 5; the computer representation of a graphic network by a linked list, and the use of a push-down stack, are introduced in the memory model of Chapter 6; interactive models in Chapters 6 and 8; feedback through a time lag in Vertinsky's model in Chapter 5 and the macroeconomic model in Chapter 8; Greist's model in Chapter 5 is based on Bayesian statistics; solving a model based on a system of simultaneous equations is described in Chapter 8; and a number of other tricks pop up here or there.

We must apologize to readers who find the particular methods or models described do not immediately relate to their specific discipline: we can only hope that the knowledge of a technique may suggest a model - if not now, perhaps later. Certainly we find it difficult to imagine any system which could not - at least in principle - be modelled using the basic techniques we present here.

The book is organized as follows:

    Chapters 1 to 4 - explanation
    Chapters 5 to 8 - examples

The first four chapters are concerned with the purpose of computer models and some of the principles used in designing and constructing them. Chapter 1 may safely be skipped by readers with no interest in philosophical discussion or who consider this a digression from the important practicalities.

Chapter 5 is a survey which tries to describe the wider uses of models in the social sciences. The subsequent chapters are each concerned with a more detailed examination of an example model drawn from the work of researchers in a variety of fields. A small part of the model analyses is in the form of technical notes aimed at those readers who have programmed a computer in the FORTRAN programming language. The general reader will, obviously, skip over these pages, but if such a reader later feels inspired to try building a computer model without assistance from a trained programmer, he could tackle this by learning FORTRAN from one of the many books or training courses available and then returning to a consideration of the **skipped** passages. Additional notes for readers with FORTRAN experience are provided in Appendix C.

We have not made any serious attempt to give references in the subject area treated by a particular example model - if you wish to follow up one of these, the original work cites its source references and a citation index in your library will help you find any later work done on the model. What we have done is to collect together the titles of a number of interesting computer models in a bibliography at the end of Chapter 5, and we hope some of these will be useful to you.

We hope you do not expect too much from us. We cannot teach you how to easily conceive good models, for instance - if we could we would gladly make you into an instant Galileo or Newton. Moreover, although we hope to lead you gently, we have sought to add a dose of realism to the simplicity of our examples, to avoid oversimplification which may be misleading. We have come across some descriptions of computer models which are so simple that we are at a loss to understand why a computer was used at all, unless it was to impress the innocent reader. Generally, using a computer becomes worthwhile only when analyzing a system of some complexity which cannot easily be analyzed in more conventional ways. Practical techniques of analyzing complex systems is, perhaps, the unifying theme of the various parts of this book.

Acknowledgements

Our special thanks to Patricia Siddall, of Leicester Polytechnic Library, for her skillful and stalwart search for models to go in the bibliography.

We are also grateful to all the following for assistance, encouragement or a permission:

Nature-Times News Service;
Donald A. Norman, Professor and Chair, Department of Psychology, University of California, San Diego;
Sage Publications, Inc., publishers of *Simulation and Games*;
The Society for Computer Simulation (Simulation Councils, Inc.), publishers of *Simulation*;
William B. Stronge, Associate Professor of Economics, Florida Atlantic University;
Daniela Weinberg, Professor of Anthropology, University of Nebraska.

Computer Models
in the Social Sciences

1 Models in the Social Sciences

Introduction

A short while ago, one of the authors of this book set out to read a dozen or so books written on scientific method as applied to the social sciences. In his naivety, he thought he would obtain from this exercise a collection of rules or dicta which he could point to and say, 'It is the consensus of opinion of social scientists that these are the methods to apply in social inquiry.'

He had not got very far before he realized that he had plunged into a hot-bed of debate of which he was previously unaware. The issues ranged from philosophical ones (what is truth?) through self-examination (are the social sciences Sciences?, i.e. is the method of the natural sciences applicable to the social sciences?) to practical ones (e.g. how can we obtain an observed fact without the experimenter influencing his subject?).

In all this literature, he found the word *model* cropped up but rarely and the words *computer model* even less frequently. The first amazed him, for it had been his opinion that the concept of a model was fundamental to reaching a view on matters such as truth and explanation. The second was less surprising, since computers are a new invention and their potential in other applications has been more readily apparent than their possible uses in the explanation of social phenomena.

It was from this experience that the idea came to write a book, for social scientists, on the construction and use of computer models. Before that theme is developed, though, we feel it desirable to express some personal opinions on the place of models in general in the social scientist's quest for knowledge. We feel we can best do this by offering our own interpretation of some of the issues under debate.

Is social science a Science?

Let us argue from the less evident end in order to develop our point. We suppose the argument *ad hominem* is just about the most ascientific method one can imagine. The argument *ad hominem* is one where the proponent, without showing any experimental evidence, puts forward his case in the expectation that it will appeal to the prejudices or existing opinions of the listener. Arguments *ad hominem* are found everywhere, perhaps no more abundantly than in management literature distilling the wisdom of practising managers, usually propped up by examples or anecdotes. Of course, *an* example can be found in support of nearly *any* point. We are not arguing that such works are value-less for this reason - far from it, as we shall see later.

If we argue to you that there is no God, we will not have to talk for long if you are an atheist. If you are a believer, though, we will have a rough ride, probably without success even if we were to bring a scientific method into our case. If you listened at all, you would subject our method to a level of critical examination which it almost certainly would not stand. We

2 Computer Models

might produce examples to show we did not find a God when we looked for him, while you might produce examples of events that could only have been wrought by a God. Atheism would be our prejudice, believing would be yours.

In debating the existence of a deity as an example we have, of course, chosen a case where views are usually deep-rooted - people do not have to believe in everything with the same conviction as they might believe in the existence or non-existence of God. But people hold more or less belief on many matters, particularly to account for those phenomena which confront them daily. Many such beliefs are founded on culture or tradition, and our point is that there is a culture and tradition enveloping scientists - natural or social - in the same way as any other group. A physicist will have a hard time proving something that no other physicist is willing to believe, but if he attempts to prove something which is already embodied in, or is a natural corollary to, existing beliefs, his path will be comparatively easy. Every day, experiments are made which produce results contradicting this or that law, but it is rarely that the law itself is seriously questioned in consequence. Rather, the experiment will be called into question (and this is a proper course), but experiments which support the established doctrines are perhaps not subjected to the same degree of critical examination. Another way of putting this view is that, even in the natural sciences, experiments are confounded by the observer.

Our theme is that all arguments are, at root, arguments *ad hominem*. Objectivity is impossible in a human being. Truth is founded on belief; belief is founded on confidence; confidence is founded on the explanatory and predictive capacity of models. To the extent that there is nothing else in this chain, the truth and the model are identities - there is no room in this scheme of things for an absolute or 'extra-human' truth.

Scientific method tests the models and influences our confidence.

Objectivity and subjectivity

Let us take *objective* to mean *based exclusively on observation, without being influenced in any way by prejudice or existing opinion.* (We should at this stage raise the issue of whether or not observation itself is or can be objective in the sense of being totally external to mind, but any discussion in that direction can only reinforce our case. We would be content to accept observation as purely external, if only because it does not affect our argument much one way or the other. As it happens, our personal model does not concede that observation - or anything - is external to mind, but it plays the role of an assumptive truth on which the human system works, rather as a mathematician's preliminary definitions allow him to construct an abstract algebra. The analogy with the mathematician is not complete, however, for the human system suffers from the complication that observations are unlimited and one observation can be modified in the light of others, rather like correcting the readings of an instrument for instrument error.)

It is our opinion that all facts are subjective, but we do not want to conclude that the concept of objectivity is without value. In our personal model of scientific method, subjectivity is a continuous variable bounded by two extreme values, unity and zero. At unity, subjectivity would be complete, i.e. the fact could be shown to rest on no observation whatsoever or whensoever, purely a product of the mind. At zero, subjectivity would be totally absent, the fact would rest entirely on correct observation. Our variable of subjectivity can infinitely approach either of these extremes, but cannot quite attain them. Objectivity is the limiting case at the lower bound. We cannot reach it; we can only approach it more closely.

Confidence

One writer described as 'insidious' the view that 'all knowledge is relative and the search for absolute truth without hope.' Where does truth lie in our scheme?

Our answer is that truth has little place in it, and neither does falsehood. Concepts of truth and falsity do not arise - they have no need to arise. If you asked us to *define* 'true' (in this context), we would say it is a word used to describe the attainment of a high degree of confidence in a model; but, since the degree of confidence is not explicit when the word is used, it is not a very precise descriptor.

This confidence is another important variable. Like subjectivity, we see it as a continuous spectrum with bounds of unity and zero. Unity, absolute confidence, cannot quite be attained. However many times you repeat an experiment, you can never show that the *next* repeat will produce the same result, because you cannot be absolutely sure until you have done it. You may have a very high degree of confidence but you cannot have (literally) absolute confidence. Some mind, somewhere, some day may be absolutely confident that his sun will rise tomorrow, only to be wrong. Similar arguments apply to absolute lack of confidence, except that here we would want to adjust the ordinary meaning of the phrase so that zero confidence is the antithesis of unit confidence, i.e. a model with zero confidence does not at all explain the phenomena and predicts them with only chance success, while a model with confidence of unity perfectly explains and always predicts the phenomena.

Statisticians have given us a scale with which to quantify confidence - the scale of probability - and other tools which influence it - measures of variance. A view which some writers seem to hold is that confidence exists only if you can quantify it on the scale, or that the experiment with no quantified confidence declared is somehow less scientific than one which has it. Can that be correct? Confidence is, surely, a subjective variable that existed long before there was a scale to measure it. Furthermore, quantification of some aspects of a model using the statistician's precise concept of confidence can be misleading if it draws attention away from other unquantified aspects which are fundamental to the overall judgement. For example, an opinion poll may quote 'confidence limits' which show how unlikely it is that the general population differs from the sample taken, but such limits account only for the statistical probabilities assuming that chance is the only factor that may have biased the result. Other factors such as the method of selecting the sample, the framing of the questions, the demeanour of the interviewer, etc., may have far more of a biasing influence than has chance and cannot be left out of the overall judgement of confidence just because they are unquantified.

We do not mean to suggest that quantification is not desirable, for we do believe the scientific tenet that the precise is to be preferred to the imprecise. What we are saying is that the seeker after precision must beware of illusory accuracy. Also, if you can subjectively reach an individual or collective view that this model inspires more confidence than that model (e.g. by demonstrating that that model has more, or more severe, deficiencies than this one) then we argue that progress towards truth has been made. There is an important caveat, though, for subjective judgements as well; the average human being seems to be prone to misjudgement, particularly of statistical likelihoods, when he relies solely on his intuition. Indeed, it is quite possible for a human being to make a series of judgements which, when taken together, prove logically inconsistent or irrational. This suggests that the intuitive judge should at least take steps to understand his own imperfections.

4 Computer Models

It may be that you cannot, or cannot easily, or cannot find the way to, or cannot with the resources you have available, quantify your confidence in a model. Such a position is reached more often, perhaps, in the social sciences than in the natural sciences. It should not follow that the model must be laughed out of court - if you have any confidence in it at all, it is properly kept until you find another model which inspires more confidence.

Subjectivity and confidence

It is tempting, at this stage, to try to link our two variables by suggesting that confidence varies inversely with subjectivity. Certainly, we think this is so in relation to one given model - if you reduce the subjectivity in the model and it retains the same explanatory and predictive powers, confidence in the model increases.

Between models of different things though, or different models of the same thing, unquantified confidence is hard to compare with quantified confidence. This leads us to make a tentative distinction between natural science and social science, which may be relevant to the discussion. A sociologist, say, builds models of human behaviour and he is a human being; an atomic physicist, say, builds models of atomic behaviour, but he is not an atom. Every human being is a walking encyclopaedia of conscious and unconscious models of human behaviour and could claim a privileged insight into the workings of the human because of his membership of the class; but every human being is not a walking encyclopaedia of models of atomic behaviour and no equivalent privilege could be claimed. If a sociologist finds a given model of human behaviour subjectively appealing, there may be good reason why his confidence in the model increases. The new model appeals because it fits in with extant models, or even because it *is* an extant model which had not hitherto been consciously expressed. His extant models are those which have survived a test of time: personal models which remain after some process of natural selection. They may not have been tested according to a scientific method, but they have, nonetheless, been subjected to *some* tests and to that extent are worth *some* confidence. If a new model cannot be subjected to scientific tests, that does not exclude confidence. The sociologist, in other words, may use his knowledge of himself to build models of others.

It may be that this is what makes poetry so alluring to us. The poet, it seems to us, is a master modeller whose appeal lies in good part in our recognition of his model as part of our own conscious or unconscious set. If we do not recognise the model, the poetry falls flat. Perhaps poetry is the archetype of the subjective scientific method we have been describing.

It is more difficult to see the models of the atomic physicist in quite the same light. There is little reason to suppose that he might have any extant or innate model which would give him insight into the workings of the atom before he first started studying the subject. Of course, the physicist develops personal models of atomic behaviour as his reading and experimentation progress, but are these models ever subjected to the same *quantity* of tests as his personal models of human behaviour, which are more or less continuously tested from the time he is born?

To summarize, we are saying that there is some argument that unquantified confidence that may exist in models in the social sciences is generally better founded than unquantified confidence that may exist in models in the natural sciences. Quantified confidence may be preferable to unquantified confidence, but unquantified confidence is an acceptable substitute until quantification can be done and the only alternative when quantification is impossible.

Explanation and causality

In our view, there is no end to the chain of causality. As Bacon put it in his *Maxims of Law*, discussing, we think, the legal doctrine of proximate cause, 'It were infinite for the law to consider the cause of causes and their impulsions one of another, therefore, it contenteth itself with the immediate cause and judgeth of acts by that, without looking to any further degree.' The immediate cause is not a happy concept for the researcher looking for precise antecedents to an event. If we were to ask you, 'What caused the Treaty of Rome to be signed?', we would hardly be satisfied if you replied, 'It was the action of a pen moving over the document' and left the room with an air of finality. (The law, of course, does not leave matters there, and modern definitions of proximate cause seek to distinguish the 'efficient' cause from that which is merely proximate in time. However, these definitions need interpretation in the light of the circumstances and to us imply the selection of a feature cause from a general background of causality.)

In the pursuit of knowledge, what we want is explanation, which we define as the provision of a model or part of a model which was missing from the questioner's existing set. We cannot be given the cause (i.e. all of the cause; we might be given *a* cause or some of the cause), but we can be given the explanation. It follows that explanations can be unique to the questioner. What is an explanation to one person may not be an explanation to another, who has different extant models. It is perhaps as well that people of a culture share largely the same models, otherwise science would be chaos.

Perhaps we should not have implied that explanations are finite. Maybe explanation, in the final analysis, is as infinite as cause, but at least explanation can answer the question to the satisfaction of the questioner - the mystery remains in the infinity of questions that can be asked.

The purpose of a model

It is our case that for many phenomena that affect an individual in his everyday affairs - and for many others that affect him only by arousing his curiosity - that individual needs a mental model of the phenomena. Many such models are formed quite unconsciously for a daily practical purpose. Such models need not be correct; in fact, one does not so much ask whether or not the model is correct as whether it adequately or inadequately fulfils its purpose. When we travel to work, we unconsciously use a flat-Earth model of the terrain, as we think most people do on their ordinary journeys. In estimating when we are to arrive, we do not take into account the increased distance we shall have to travel on account of the curvature of the Earth; in our imaginations we could see our office from home if it were not for the intervening hills, trees and haze. That such a flat-Earth model is adequate is easily demonstrated by the fact that people made local journeys for quite a while before Magellan cicumnavigated the world. Of course, the prediction of this model that we will fall off the edge when we reach the horizon is a limitation (not, as it happens, a particularly important one in this case since we would find we could never reach the horizon). Only when the model's limitations became important, as with a long sea voyage, would we then (consciously) choose a different model of the Earth for our journey.

We recall a phone-in radio broadcast in which a listener, anxious to prove the fallibility of scientists, made the point that 'scientists believed Newton for hundreds of years before Einstein proved him wrong.' It is hard to imagine a statement more inconsistent with the view we are putting.

6 Computer Models

Newton's model of the physical world was brilliantly 'right' when it was built, and is still 'right' to this day. The limitations it has are of consequence in only a minute proportion of its possible applications. Some sort of argument could even be raised that Newton's model is more 'right' than Einstein's, because it explains and predicts by building on the extant models of a large number of individuals, whereas Einstein's is useful only for a class of person with a minority set of extant models; but this argument would involve us in comparing the value of explanation and prediction for the ordinary educated man with the value of explanation and prediction for nuclear physicists and astronomers. We cannot make this value judgement, so we simply say that all models are 'right' when applied to a purpose for which they are useful. Only when you define the purpose of a model can you begin to argue that this model is more 'right' than that.

We do not think this suggestion is as far removed from classical scientific views as might at first appear. If we were to suggest that scientists want, as a common purpose of their models, that they should suffer from as few limitations as possible so that they tend towards universality of prediction (if not of explanation), perhaps we would be locating the place of scientific models in the class of all models. (To make this complete, we should also say that between equally powerful scientific models, the simpler is to be preferred to the more complex.) We hope that by putting matters this way we have exposed the value judgement implicit in science and shown the choice that may have to be made between universality of prediction and universality of explanation.

Scientific method

We see the rôle of scientific method as one of rigorous testing of models to increase or reduce confidence in their predictions, by exploring their limitations.

Although such methods may be rigorous, they cannot be perfect. A strictly controlled experiment is a philosophical impossibility, since two treatment conditions cannot occupy the same place at the same time. It may be that the chemist feels justified in assuming that his molecules will exhibit the same behaviour on one table top as another, or from one hour to another, but a social scientist cannot strictly allow himself similar assumptions, for it is common knowledge that human behaviour can change with time and environment.

The controlled experiment must be seen as another ideal concept, the variable being the degree of confounding that takes place. The less confounded experiment inspires more confidence than the more confounded experiment.

We suggest that in the social sciences confounding is often more difficult to avoid, or is at any rate more patent, than in the natural sciences. Even in the laboratory, a human subject (unlike a molecule, we assume) is at least aware that he is the subject of an experiment, even if he has been misled as to its purpose, and that knowledge might influence his behaviour. Outside the laboratory, the exposure to a large number of other factors is obvious and the degree of confounding may be very large.

Again, we suggest that just because an experiment is confounded there is no reason for rejecting the model under test. If the model is still the best available, that is progress. The proposition that social science is not scientific because all social experiements are confounded is defeatist; surely, the only way forward is to take one's best models and try to eliminate through ingenuity or patience such confounding factors as one can identify - if the model still holds water, it is worth more confidence than before. It seems to us that this is precisely what happens in the natural sciences, any difference being only one of the degree of initial confounding likely to be present.

Summary

We have tried to demonstrate the value of the concept of a model in truth and explanation and that objectivity, confidence and confounding of experiments are not black-and-white issues but variables that may take all shades of grey. It so happens that in many areas of the social sciences, the inquirer is more open to subjective inference, less able to quantify confidence and more easily confounds his experiments than his natural-science counterpart. This does not mean that the social scientist is unworthy of the title 'scientist'; at worst, it means only that he must be especially circumspect and that he may have to live with models that are difficult to test. While testing of the models is incomplete, the best model is still the best model.

The computer may be a tool which can help in the testing of models under more controlled conditions, or which can give insight into the working of a complex model, or which can be used to work a model of a process which may be too complex or tedious to work in any other way. These themes are developed in the subsequent chapters.

Further reading

There is a long history of philosophical debate in the social sciences, and the voluminous current literature indicates that the issues are not dead. We have tried twice to produce a short bibliography for the reader who wants to consider more of this subject, but we are not satisfied with either attempt. The first one had the classic material which could probably be uncontentiously included, but which would not reflect modern authors' viewpoints. The second tried to be more modern, but would probably be attacked from all sides for its lack of balance. We have decided that we prefer to let the reader decide his own strategy, if he wants to go down this path (after which exercise, we must forewarn, he may well feel he is coming out along the same route as in he went). The only other precautionary word we would offer is that the reader should not fight shy of some of the early classics of writers such as Popper, Russell, Ayer or Kuhn - these authors had a powerful command of language and are a good deal more understandable than many of the modern commentators.

There are plenty of introductory books to help; the reader need only inspect the library shelf. We have not found an introductory book which we felt gave a fair representation of ideas across the breadth of social science disciplines, schools of thought, and cultures, but in the British idiom an interesting book is Barker, P. (ed.), *The Social Sciences Today*, Edward Arnold, London, 1975 - a slim volume in which ten authors give a concise introduction to some of the values and literature of their disciplines.

If you do go down this path, you will be in need of refreshment when you come staggering back out of the fog. A taste of Ford, J., *Paradigms and Fairy Tales*, Routledge and Kegan Paul, London and Boston, 1975 (two volumes) may be reviving, or perhaps you will warm to the aggression of Andreski, S., *Social Sciences as Sorcery*, André Deutsch, London, 1972.

8 Computer Models

Postscript (reproduced with permission)

Science report
Physics: Fundamental law questioned

Dr Daniel Long, of Eastern Washington State College, has cast doubt in *Nature* on the inverse square law for gravity, which is close to the core of scientists' conception of the physical world. So fundamental is the inverse square law that he is likely to have an uphill struggle to persuade other physicists to take his ideas seriously.

For some years Dr Long has been drawing attention to the inadequate verification of the law of Newtonian gravitation, namely that the force between two bodies is proportional to the product of their masses and inversely proportional to the square of the distance separating their centres of mass.

Whereas astronomical observations have now largely confirmed the perturbations which Einstein's general relativity puts into the simple inverse square law at great distances, laboratory-scale tests at distances of a few tens of centimetres have not been done in any great number (the relativistic perturbations on the inverse square law would be trivial at such distances).

In an earlier study Dr Long accumulated such measurements of gravitational attraction as have been made in the laboratory (some of them from nineteenth-century experiments), and showed that they were not strikingly good evidence in favour of the inverse square law; in fact, a law in which there was a slight decrease in attraction at short ranges relative to the inverse square laws was a better fit to the data. He has now pursued that further by designing his own apparatus to measure those gravitational attractions.

The equipment is simple and closely resembles that used in earlier experiments. A thin suspended fibre supports a crossbar, from one side of which is suspended by threads a ball of mass 50 grams. On the other side of the crossbar is a small electrostatic plate mounted vertically and in the plane of the crossbar.

Heavy rings, weighing up to 50 kg can be brought close to the suspended ball; they will exert a small horizontal gravitational attraction roughly a hundred millionth of the vertical attraction of gravity. That horizontal force should cause a slight rotation of the crossbar, but it is counterbalanced by a force on the electrostatic plate on the other side of the crossbar. That force comes from a voltage applied between the plate and another plate nearby unattached to the suspended system. The size of the voltage is a measure of the gravitational attraction.

Dr Long found that a large 50kg ring at almost 30cm distance, and a small 1kg ring at 4cm distance which, according to the inverse square law, should have exerted the same attraction on the 50g ball failed to do so. The discrepancy, measured over repeated experiments, was a fraction of 1 per cent and is strikingly in agreement with the earlier observations. Dr Long proposes a small modification to the inverse square law.

In the covering letter which Dr Long sent to *Nature*, he accepts that the paper is controversial, "and in need of sympathetic treatment". Many physicists will reject the implications of the experiment out of hand as going against their intuition. Something, it will be asserted, must have been wrong with the experimental conditions.

That attitude has often been adopted in the past and, despite the mythology of science, has often been entirely justified. But the experiment is not very difficult to repeat, nor is it impossible to find another type of experiment to approach the question from a different angle. Who is going to try to prove Dr Long wrong?

By Nature-Times News Service.
Source: *Nature*, 260, 417 (1976).
© **Nature-Times News Service**, 1976.

2 Computer Models

A case study

The Ruritanian Sports and Social Club Committee was discussing its expenditure for the coming year. The debate was particularly pointed because, in the season just ended, payments had exceeded receipts from its two annual fund-raising events (the Gala Day and the Barbecue Dance) by a substantial amount.

'Look,' said the Membership Secretary, 'we can't possibly afford another year like the last - the members won't stand for it. We started the year with 25 000 Ruritanian dollars; we authorised expenditure on new buildings and equipment to the tune of $20 000; yet the Gala and Barbecue were such a wash-out that we netted only $5000, leaving us with a credit balance of a mere $10 000. We must make quite sure we don't make a loss this coming year, so we can build up our reserves again.'

The Treasurer looked thoughtful. 'What do you mean', he said, 'by *quite* sure? If you mean there must be absolutely no risk of a loss, then there is only one course of action open to us - we should not spend anything on new facilities next year. Indeed, to be strictly accurate, we should not even authorise the preliminary expenditure on the Gala and Barbecue - after all, it's on the cards that we could make a loss on both events. Look what happened this year at the Gala.'

'That's a bit thick, isn't it?', interposed the Events Organiser. 'The only reason we did so badly this year is that it poured with rain on both days. The chance of that happening two years running is so remote that we can ignore it.'

The Treasurer thought to himself, 'There's something wrong there. I don't see how this year's weather can affect next year's. The chance of bad weather next year must be the same, irrespective of what weather we had this year.' He opened his mouth to make this point but hesitated, wondering if the Events Organiser would understand him. Then he had a vision of an ensuing argument, a considerable detour from the matters in hand and an even more protracted meeting. He shut his mouth again.

The Membership Secretary ended the hiatus with a bland inconsistency. 'We can't have *no* expenditure next year - there would be uproar from the members if we failed to provide any new equipment at all. Then there's the repairs to the pavilion roof, a new filtration system for the swimming pool,...'; he went on with a long list which made it evident that there were ample outstanding projects to soak up whatever funds were made available.

'Then what you must decide', declared the Treasurer, 'is this: exactly what risk of loss is the club prepared to accept?'

There was silence for a moment, as nobody knew how to answer this question. 'I should have thought', said the Chairman, tentatively, 'that we want to be about 90 per cent sure that we will more than break even.'

'And accept a 10 per cent risk of loss?', queried the Events Organiser, doubtfully. 'I suppose we could afford a small loss, but I don't think we want more than, say, a one per cent risk of losing more than about $5000.'

'And I don't think we should accept any risk of a deficit as large as

10 Computer Models

$20 000', added the Treasurer, 'since we would never find large enough overdraft facilities to cover it and that would mean we would have to fold up completely. Now let me get this straight: the feeling of the committee is that the planned expenditure for next year should aim to give us a 90 per cent chance of making a profit. We are prepared to accept a small risk, one per cent, of making a loss of $5000 and no risk at all of making a loss greater than $20 000?' There were murmurs of assent. 'Of course', continued the Treasurer, 'the last constraint means we cannot contemplate more than $20 000 expenditure, for if we are avoiding any risk at all of a greater loss we must consider the very worst case, i.e. the possibility we will have no receipts.'

The Membership Secretary looked glum, but no one was prepared to counter this argument.

The Treasurer warmed to his analysis. 'It may be, when we dig deeper into the problem, that the expenditure which will give us a 90 per cent chance of making a profit is less than $20 000 - in which case we choose the lower expenditure, right? And if that expenditure gives us more than a one per cent chance of a $5000 loss, then we choose a still lower expenditure that will bring the risk down to one per cent?'

The Committee members fidgetted, many eyes on the clock, and nodded. 'Give me until the next meeting to think about it and I shall try to find the figure which meets these criteria', concluded the Treasurer.

The Chairman closed the meeting.

* * *

Considering the problem in the comfort of his study, the Treasurer was beginning to realize that his problem was not an easy one. He was not worried much by what was meant by 'a 90 per cent chance' of making a profit. His concept was that there was a certain level of expenditure which (if the same policy were applied every year thereafter and other circumstances did not materially alter) would tend, in the long run, to produce receipts exceeding payments in 90 per cent of the years. It did strike him that a very large number of years - more, perhaps, than his remaining years as Treasurer - might be needed before anyone could say whether his recommended figure had been right or wrong, but he found this more of an encouragement to continue than a philosophical obstacle.

No, his real problem was that the club had been running only five years and he did not have much past data to work on. From the preceding years' accounts, he constructed the chart shown in Fig. 2.1.

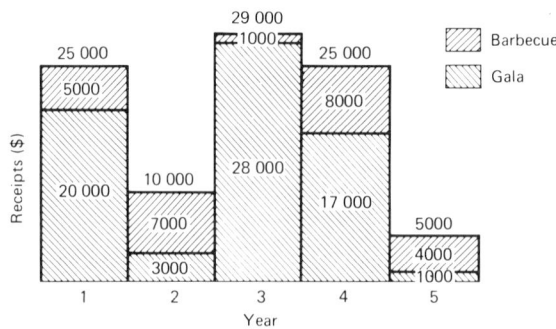

Fig. 2.1: The Treasurer's chart of the Club's receipts in the preceding five years, divided between the two events

The Treasurer was no statistician, but he did realize that he could not draw much conclusion from such a small sample which showed such large variations from year to year. He could, he supposed, take the average of these five years and declare that average to be his best bet for next year, but - quite apart from the question of the validity of doing such a thing with this sample - such a procedure would give him no information about the likelihood of any other outcome. Yet this was the information he needed if he was to solve his problem. The Treasurer decided he needed a fresh approach.

He was fully aware that Ruritania enjoyed an extraordinarily stable economy, currency and population and that Ruritanians were famous for their consistent habits. 'The only thing', he mused to himself, 'that can be affecting receipts from our annual events is the weather.' To test this hypothesis, he rang the Weather Bureau and asked for the rainfall figures during the time of the Gala (10 a.m. to 5 p.m.) and the Barbecue (8 p.m. to 1 a.m.) on the relevant dates in previous years. The Bureau gave him the following figures:

Year	Gala rainfall	Barbecue rainfall
1	1 mm	5 mm
2	12	1
3	0	21
4	2	0
5	17	8

Armed with these data, he plotted receipts against rainfall for each event, as shown in Fig. 2.2.

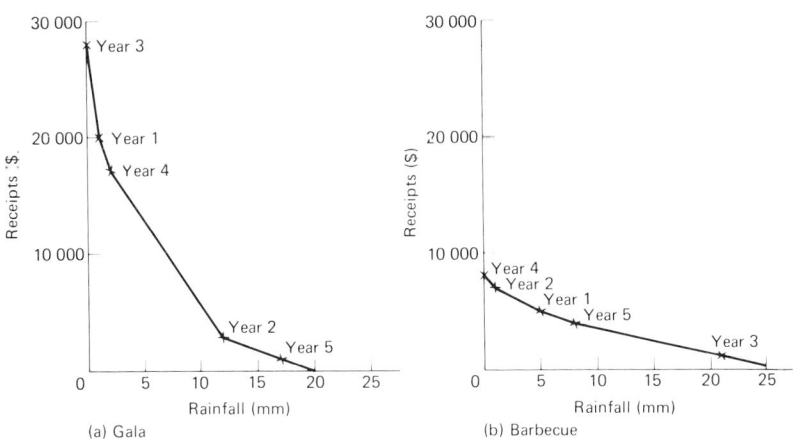

Fig. 2.2: Receipts from the stated event plotted against the rainfall during the event

The Treasurer found the consistent correlation between rainfall and receipts an encouragement to his hypothesis. He also found the difference

12 Computer Models

between the shape of the Gala curve and the shape of the Barbecue curve encouraging, for he knew that the Gala was entirely open-air while the Barbecue was partly covered and, if his rainfall hypothesis was correct, he would not expect Barbecue receipts to suffer as severely as those of the Gala when it rained.

Although there was clearly a strong correlation which he found subjectively convincing, it troubled the Treasurer that he was still dealing with only a small sample. He wondered if he ought to approach a trained statistician to establish an objective level of confidence in the relationship described by his graphs. 'It would be nice if he told me there was only a very small probability these relationships could have occurred by chance', he thought, 'but what if he said there was insufficient data to attribute much significance to the result? What would I do?' The Treasurer could not think of any alternative approach to analysing his problem and concluded that he would be obliged to use the relationship he had found, whatever the significance of it, if he wished to reach a decision at all. He made the pragmatic assumption that the relationships were reliable and described what could be expected in the coming year.

It was now becoming clear that if he could predict the rainfall on the days of the Gala and Barbecue in the coming year, he would be able to make a prediction of the total receipts. The Gala was scheduled for 1 July and the Barbecue for 27 August. Of course, there was no way he could determine the weather so far ahead but, if he could establish the rainfall pattern on those days in previous years, he would begin to have a pretty fair idea of the probabilities that could be expected.

He again contacted the Weather Bureau and asked them for the rainfall figures for 10 a.m. to 5 p.m. on every preceding 1 July and for 8 p.m. to 1 a.m. on every preceding 27 August. The Bureau's records went back 50 years and he was able to construct the histogram shown in Fig. 2.3 from the data they supplied.

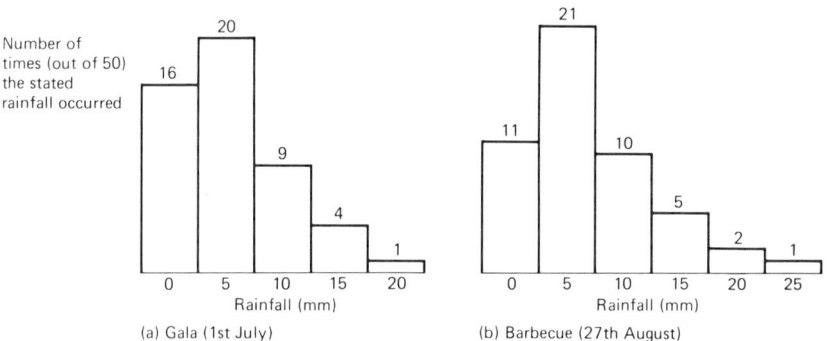

Fig. 2.3: Rainfall on 1 July and 27 August in the preceding fifty years

In constructing the histograms, he tallied each rainfall figure he had been given into the cell with a variate value closest to that figure.

The Treasurer began to get excited, for he realized that he could now start to make some statements about likely outcomes of the annual events. 'I can see there will be 20 chances in 50 that the rainfall on Gala Day will be 5 mm', he thought. 'Reading 5 mm rainfall off my rainfall-against-receipts graph, this will give receipts of approximately $13 000. Similarly, for example, I could state that there are five chances in 50 that the rainfall on the day of the Barbecue will be 15 mm, limiting receipts to about $2000. But how can I find the overall distribution of outcomes for the combined events?'

Being a practical person, he devised his own practical solution to this problem. First, he rewrote the rainfall histograms in the form of two tables, allocating a different range of integers to each rainfall variate value such that the inclusive range of numbers allocated was the same as the frequency of occurrence of that rainfall value (Table 2.1).

Rainfall in mm	(a) Allocated numbers for Gala (frequency in brackets)	(b) Allocated numbers for Barbecue (frequency in brackets)
0	1-16 (16)	1-11 (11)
5	17-36 (20)	12-32 (21)
10	37-45 (9)	33-42 (10)
15	46-49 (4)	43-47 (5)
20	50 (1)	48-49 (2)
25		50 (1)

Table 2.1: The ranges of numbers allocated by the Treasurer to each rainfall value for the stated events

Next he took a deck of 52 playing cards, removed two, and numbered the cards with the integers from 1 to 50, shuffling them well. 'I shall let these cards', he said to himself, 'be the God of the weather. If I wish to simulate what might happen in a particular year, I can choose a card at random by cutting the deck, find which range allocated for the Gala it falls in and pretend that the associated rainfall has occurred on Gala Day. Then I can shuffle the deck and repeat the process for the Barbecue Dance. From my graphs I can find out what the receipts would be and thus the total receipts for both events.

'I can repeat this process for as many trial years as I like until I feel I have sampled enough possible years to be able to describe reasonably accurately the frequency with which different total outcomes occur.'

After three hours of shuffling and cutting, he had constructed the table shown as Table 2.2. There was no particular reason why he stopped at 80 trials; he was just getting a bit tired and thought he'd done enough. He now continued to the last step, and constructed Table 2.3 by counting how many times a given total of receipts had occurred.

Total receipts ($)	Number of occurrences	Total receipts ($)	Number of occurrences
2500	1	15500	2
3200	1	16500	10
5500	2	18000	12
7000	5	21000	11
8500	2	29200	1
9500	4	30500	5
10000	1	31500	5
11000	2	33000	6
14000	4	36000	4
14200	2		80

Table 2.3: The Treasurer's results showing the number of occurrences of a given total receipts

14 Computer Models

Trial year	First card	Gala rain (mm)	Gala receipts ($)	Second card	Barbecue rain (mm)	Barbecue receipts ($)	Total receipts ($)
1	49	15	2000	19	5	5000	7000
2	8	0	28000	4	0	8000	36000
3	6	0	28000	44	15	2500	30500
4	35	5	13000	39	10	3500	16500
5	32	5	13000	35	10	3500	16500
6	13	0	28000	37	10	3500	31500
7	36	5	13000	33	10	3500	16500
8	30	5	13000	20	5	5000	18000
9	15	0	28000	42	10	3500	31500
10	44	10	6000	44	15	2500	8500
11	7	0	28000	43	15	2500	30500
12	41	10	6000	5	0	8000	14000
13	26	5	13000	21	5	5000	18000
14	46	15	2000	49	20	1200	3200
15	25	5	13000	49	20	1200	14200
16	35	5	13000	1	0	8000	21000
17	40	10	6000	4	0	8000	14000
18	19	5	13000	13	5	5000	18000
19	47	15	2000	34	10	3500	5500
20	10	0	28000	32	5	5000	33000
21	37	10	6000	31	5	5000	11000
22	22	5	13000	8	0	8000	21000
23	47	15	2000	25	5	5000	7000
24	30	5	13000	35	10	3500	16500
25	47	15	2000	21	5	5000	7000
26	22	5	13000	9	0	8000	21000
27	20	5	13000	30	5	5000	18000
28	10	0	28000	31	5	5000	33000
29	4	0	28000	49	20	1200	29200
30	10	0	28000	33	10	3500	31500
31	8	0	28000	20	5	5000	33000
32	4	0	28000	8	0	8000	36000
33	21	5	13000	12	5	5000	18000
34	34	5	13000	2	0	8000	21000
35	18	5	13000	36	10	3500	16500
36	17	5	13000	12	5	5000	18000
37	6	0	28000	45	15	2500	30500
38	38	10	6000	40	10	3500	9500
39	34	5	13000	49	20	1200	14200
40	32	5	13000	8	0	8000	21000
41	43	10	6000	45	15	2500	8500
42	38	10	6000	40	10	3500	9500
43	8	0	28000	40	10	3500	31500
44	25	5	13000	15	5	5000	18000
45	35	5	13000	43	15	2500	15500
46	1	0	28000	46	15	2500	30500
47	27	5	13000	27	5	5000	18000
48	34	5	13000	42	10	3500	16500
49	7	0	28000	9	0	8000	36000
50	20	5	13000	37	10	3500	16500
51	34	5	13000	36	10	3500	16500
52	28	5	13000	9	0	8000	21000
53	25	5	13000	40	10	3500	16500
54	24	5	13000	2	0	8000	21000
55	23	5	13000	4	0	8000	21000
56	15	0	28000	12	5	5000	33000
57	47	15	2000	6	0	8000	10000
58	50	20	0	43	15	2500	2500
59	48	15	2000	15	5	5000	7000
60	11	0	28000	9	0	8000	36000
61	35	5	13000	7	0	8000	21000
62	25	5	13000	31	5	5000	18000
63	7	0	28000	21	5	5000	33000
64	15	0	28000	36	10	3500	31500
65	19	5	13000	9	0	8000	21000
66	32	5	13000	23	5	5000	18000
67	43	10	6000	7	0	8000	14000
68	41	10	6000	36	10	3500	9500
69	25	5	13000	1	0	8000	21000
70	31	5	13000	43	15	2500	15500
71	29	5	13000	36	10	3500	16500
72	49	15	2000	22	5	5000	7000
73	12	0	28000	46	15	2500	30500
74	44	10	6000	15	5	5000	11000
75	21	5	13000	12	5	5000	18000
76	47	15	2000	36	10	3500	5500
77	9	0	28000	32	5	5000	33000
78	26	5	13000	13	5	5000	18000
79	41	10	6000	36	10	3500	9500
80	38	10	6000	1	0	8000	14000

Table 2.2: The Treasurer's results showing the two cards he drew for each year, and the rainfall and receipts each simulated

Using this table the Treasurer was able to draw the cumulative graph of receipts shown in Fig. 2.4. There are no receipts in excess of $36 000; there are four receipts in excess of $33 000 (those at $36 000); there are ten receipts in excess of $31 500 (the six at $33 000 and the four at $36 000); and so on. All 80 receipts are in excess of $0.

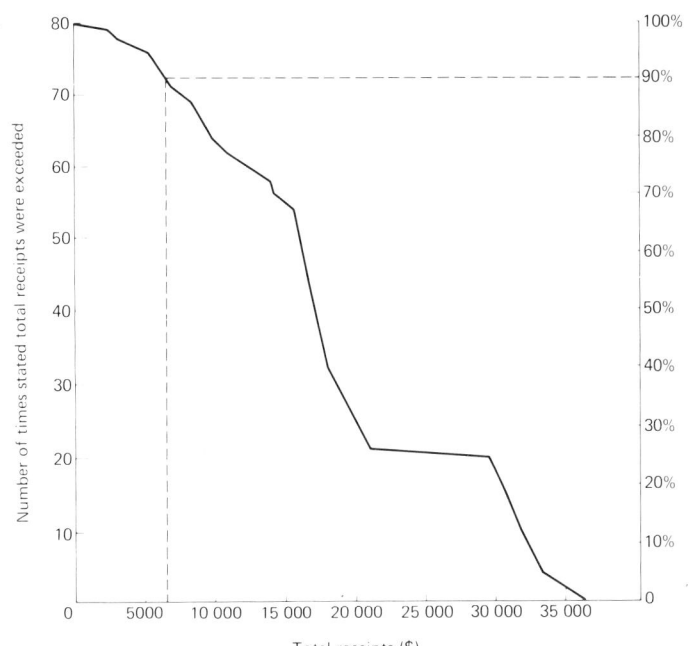

Fig. 2.4: *The Treasurer's cumulative graph of receipts from the combined events during the 80 trial years*

The Treasurer saw immediately that 90 per cent of the outcomes gave receipts of $6500 or more. So, if he recommended expenditure next year of $6500, he could assert that he was 90 per cent sure that income would at least equal expenditure. If he did recommend this figure, receipts would have to be as low as $1500 before a loss as large as $5000 was made. By looking at the $1500 receipts mark of his latest graph, he judged that the risk of getting receipts as low as this was less than one per cent. He decided to recommend expenditure of $6500 in the coming year.

* * *

The next day, the Treasurer bumped into his friend the Computer Programmer, who had an interest in computer models.
  'Hello there', said the Treasurer, 'I'm feeling rather pleased with myself today. I think this might interest you - here, let me show you.' He explained his problem and how he had solved it.
  'That is interesting', said the Programmer. 'You've tackled it in almost exactly the same way I would have done it on my computer. May I offer a few

16 Computer Models

criticisms of detail, though?'

'Go ahead.'

'Well', said the Programmer, thoughtfully, trying to find the right words, 'take a look first at your receipts-against-rainfall graph for the Gala. See how steep the slope is between the 0 and 10 mm rainfall marks? Yet the scale you have chosen for your rainfall histograms, 5 mm between each cell, is quite coarse and may have biased your results.'

'I don't quite follow you.'

'Let me take an extreme case to illustrate the principle. Suppose you had a receipts graph like this', here he sketched Fig. 2.5(a), 'and a rainfall histogram like this', he sketched Fig. 2.5(b).

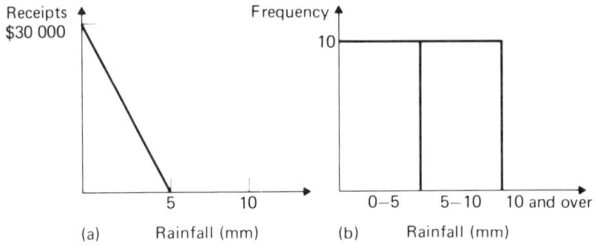

Fig. 2.5: *A hypothetical rainfall-against-receipts graph with a coarse-scaled histogram of rainfalls*

'You can see that if you were to sample the rainfall histogram, following the method you have already used, you would expect half your samples to come from the 0-5 mm range, which you could take as equivalent to 2.5 mm rainfall for reading off the receipts; while half would come from the 5-10 mm range, taken as equivalent to 7.5 mm.

'But when I redraw the rainfall histogram with a smaller cell interval like this', Fig. 2.6, 'you can see that a very different picture emerges. You can see straight away that the left half of the new histogram describes a skewness which wasn't apparent when the coarser scale was used. You would now expect half the samples to come from the 2.5-5 mm range, which you would take as 3.75 mm to read off the receipts - quite a different result. Of course, where the receipts graph is flatter, a coarse scale doesn't matter so much. If you consider the extreme case where the receipts graph is a horizontal line, you'll see that the coarseness of the scale cannot make any difference at all.'

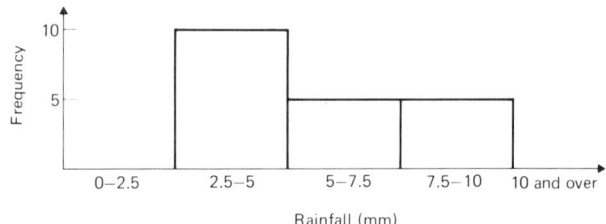

Fig. 2.6: *Drawing the histogram with a finer scale reveals something which was hidden by the coarse scale*

'Oh dear', said the Treasurer, 'I begin to see what you mean. Does that mean my results may be wrong?'

'Not at all', said the Programmer, cheerfully. 'In fact, if I may argue against myself for a moment, it probably didn't make any difference in your case even if the coarse scale did hide something which would be shown up by a finer scale. You see, the questions you were concerned to answer related only to the lower levels of receipt, where the graph is much flatter, whereas the coarse scale tends to affect only the higher receipts. If you had wanted to find out how often a particular high total of receipts occurred, or find the mean receipts, then there might have been bias.

'If I may continue in similar vein, you seem to have made a small error — but don't worry, this one doesn't make a difference either. I see that when you constructed your rainfall histograms you assigned a single variate value to each cell, and counted frequencies into the cell with the closest variate value. When you sampled the histograms, you read off from the receipts graph at the point of the variate value concerned. This procedure was fine — for example, the cell you labelled 5 mm really took values from 2.5 to 7.5 mm and it was a reasonable approximation to pick the central value, 5 mm, for looking up the receipts. But look at the first cell of the histogram, labelled 0 — because there's no such thing as negative rainfall, this cell takes only values between 0 and 2.5, so you should have read the receipts graph at the 1.25 mm value, not 0 as you did.'

'Oh yes', said the Treasurer, 'that was a mistake, wasn't it? But I suppose, since it only affected high receipt values, it luckily doesn't change the answers to my questions.'

'That's right. Actually, you often get a similar situation at the other end of a histogram — take a look at the last cell of your Barbecue rainfall histogram, which you'll see covers rainfalls between 22.5 and infinity. Heaven only knows which value you should choose to read off the receipts — but, fortunately, the receipts graph is so flat around that point that it isn't likely to make much difference.'

'I'm convinced', said the Treasurer. 'Is that all? I mean, can I be confident I have the right answer?'

'I'm afraid there is one other matter to be considered', frowned the Programmer, 'and this one is likely to be more important. You see, both your questions were concerned with an extreme end of the range of possible outcomes, i.e. the lowest receipts. If you look at your chart of outcomes, you will see that there was only one instance of total receipts amounting to $3000 or less — if, by chance, the fall of the cards had led to two or three more instances, this might have substantially coloured your view of the likelihood of very low receipts. Similarly, your conclusion about $6500 receipts being exceeded in 90 per cent of cases — if you look back at your original results you will see there are only four instances of receipts being less than $6500; two or three instances more or less might have led you to a different conclusion.'

'Mmm', said the Treasurer uncertainly, 'but surely my total of 80 trials was quite large. Wouldn't you expect that to give reasonably accurate results?'

'Not, I'm afraid, if you're making judgements based on events that occur only a very few times in your trials. Look, let's analyze your work a little. Now then, to complete your trials you had to generate 160 numbers at random in the range 1-50. If I were to divide that range into, say, five segments, i.e. 1-10, 11-20, 21-30, 31-40 and 41-50, we would expect about one fifth of the generated numbers, i.e. 32, to fall in each range, right? Of course, if *exactly* 32 fell in each range, I would be highly suspicious that you had cooked the results — I take it you didn't? So we must expect some variations which may have biased your particular trials. Now, let's see how serious these variations look.'

18 Computer Models

With that, he took the Treasurer's record of the trials and studiously added up for five minutes. When he had finished, he showed the Treasurer the following table:

Range	Number of cards drawn in the range
1-10	35
11-20	24
21-30	26
31-40	42
41-50	33

Table 2.4: Illustrating the chance variation in the number of cards the Treasurer drew in each of the stated ranges of numbers

'Good Heavens!', the Treasurer exclaimed. 'Why, there must be - let me see - yes, 75 per cent more cards drawn in the 31-40 range than in the 11-20 range. Can that have happened by chance?'

'Practically anything can happen by chance', observed the Programmer. 'I couldn't tell you offhand what the odds are on a variation of that size occurring by chance, but it doesn't look all that unlikely. Of course, there is also the possibility that there was some bias in your method of getting random numbers - the way you shuffled the deck, or some cards tending to stick together, or something like that. We have no easy way of telling. Anyway, now I've looked at the figures, my hunch is that your particular set of trials may have led to a rather pessimistic result. If you want more reliable figures, I reckon you should aim to get about 10 instances of outcomes under $3000; judging from the present results, that would mean about 1000 trials.'

'A thousand trials!' The Treasurer's voice was incredulity mixed with horror. 'Do you realize it took me three hours to do 80?'

'Oh, I'll get my computer to do it if you like. It's quite a straightforward problem - shouldn't take me more than a few minutes or so to write a program. While we're about it, why don't we correct the other things I mentioned? You never know, when your committee members see the results, they may be interested in outcomes other than those related to the original problem - it would be a pity if you didn't have reasonably accurate answers.

'First, let's go back to your original rainfall figures and construct histograms of the receipts that *would* have occurred in the past, by looking up the actual rainfall on your rainfall-against-receipts graph. We can build receipt histograms with a scale of, say, $1000 - that should be fine enough.'

Receipts	Gala frequency	Barbecue frequency	Receipts	Gala frequency	Receipts	Gala frequency
0	1	1	11 000	2	22 000	0
1 000	2	2	12 000	3	23 000	0
2 000	1	3	13 000	4	24 000	0
3 000	3	6	14 000	3	25 000	1
4 000	1	11	15 000	1	26 000	0
5 000	1	11	16 000	4	27 000	0
6 000	2	6	17 000	3	28 000	3
7 000	0	8	18 000	0		
8 000	2	2	19 000	3		
9 000	4		20 000	4		
10 000	2		21 000	0		

Table 2.5: The rainfall-against-receipts graph and rainfall histograms consolidated into a simpler table of receipt frequencies

After ten minutes work, they had constructed the consolidated figures shown in Table 2.5.

'Now let me draw a flowchart to describe the procedure we want the computer to follow', said the Programmer, and sketched out Fig. 2.7.

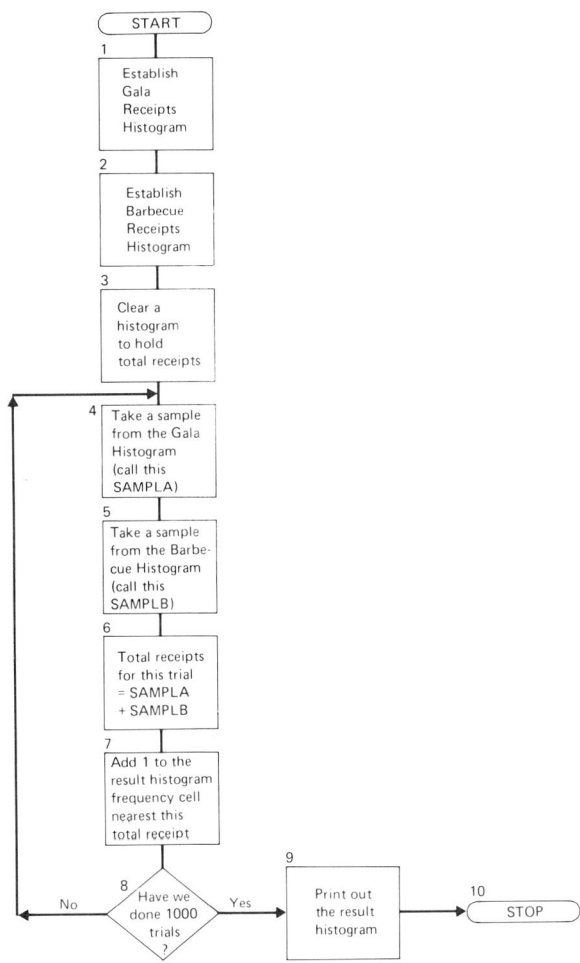

Fig. 2.7: Flowchart of the computer program to model the distribution of total receipts from the two events.

'Now I can write the program' continued the Programmer. 'It will be pretty easy to write in FORTRAN and it will also give us the mean total receipts of the whole series of trials - you might find that information useful later on.'

Five minutes later, he showed the Treasurer his program to model the receipts from the events.

20 Computer Models

```
C PROGRAM TO SIMULATE GALA & BARBECUE RECEIPTS
C
      IMPLICIT INTEGER(A-Z)
C GALA RECEIPTS HISTOGRAM HAS 29 CELLS, THE FIRST VARIATE
C VALUE BEING $0, IN STEPS OF $1000
      DIMENSION GALA(34)
      CALL DHIST(GALA,29,0,1000)
      DATA (GALA(I), I=6,34)/
     * 1,2,1,3,1, 1,2,0,2,4, 2,2,3,4,3, 1,4,3,0,3, 4,0,0,0,0, 1,0,0,3/
C BARBECUE HISTOGRAM HAS 9 CELLS, THE FIRST VARIATE VALUE
C BEING $0, IN STEPS OF $1000
      DIMENSION BARBQ(14)
      CALL DHIST(BARBQ,9,0,1000)
      DATA (BARBQ(I),I=6,14)/
     * 1,2,3,6,11, 11,6,8,2/
C RESULTS HISTOGRAM HAS 37 CELLS,THE FIRST VARIATE VALUE BEING $0,
C IN STEPS OF $1000
      DIMENSION RESULT(42)
      CALL DHIST(RESULT,37,0,1000)
      CALL CLEAR(RESULT)
C A FIELD IS NEEDED TO COUNT THE TRIALS
      COUNT = 0
C TWO SEEDS WILL BE NEEDED FOR RANDOM NUMBER GENERATION
      SEEDA = 1999
      SEEDB = 1979
C SIMULATION STARTS HERE
  100 SAMPLA = SAMPLE(GALA,SEEDA)
      SAMPLB = SAMPLE(BARBQ,SEEDB)
      TOTAL = SAMPLA + SAMPLE
      CALL TALLY(RESULT,TOTAL)
C TEST FOR END OF TRIALS
      COUNT = COUNT + 1
      IF (COUNT .LT. 1000) GO TO 100
C PRINT OUT RESULTS
      CALL PRHIST(RESULT,10HFREQUENCY., 15HTOTAL RECEIPTS.)
      STOP
      END
```

'I don't understand a word of it', said the Treasurer.
'Oh, it's pretty simple really. All the statements with a C are not instructions - they are just my comments. The first instruction, IMPLICIT, tells my computer we want to work only in integers - whole numbers. The next eleven lines of instruction correspond to steps 1,2 and 3 on my flowchart. Then, from the instruction numbered '100', the program follows the steps 4-10 of the flowchart almost exactly.
'Anyway, you needn't worry about it - I'll go and run it on the computer and call on you tomorrow with the results.'
He's a bit smooth, opined the Treasurer to himself, but he seems to know what he's talking about.

* * *

The next day, the Programmer returned with his results.
'I'm afraid you're not going to think much of my efforts', he said, apologetically, producing Fig. 2.8, 'they hardly change your conclusions at all. I make the 90 per cent probability only slightly different from yours,

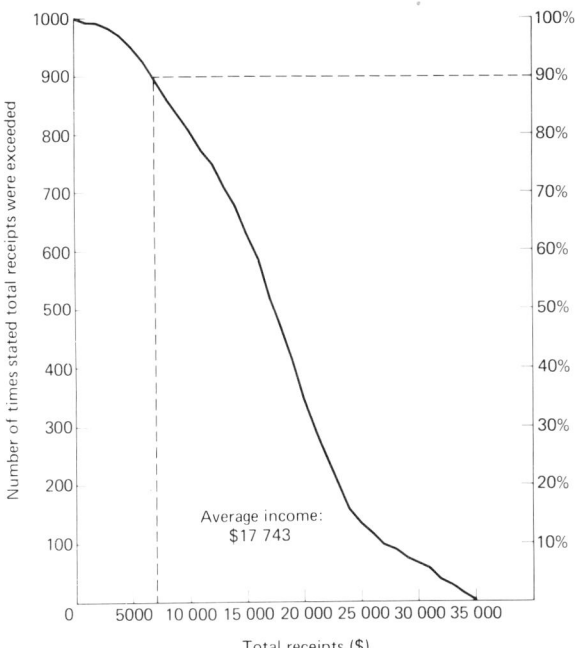

Fig. 2.8: *The Programmer's cumulative graph of receipts from the combined events during the 1000 trial years*

with receipts of about $6800. And it certainly seems the chance of getting $5000 less than that - $1800 - is less than one per cent. The only consolation I can offer you is that you can now have more confidence in your recommendation than you had before.'

'Your graph certainly looks a deal smoother than mine', the Treasurer conceded. 'When the Committee see the whole picture, I wouldn't be surprised if they wanted to revise their decision to take a less pessimistic view. And what's this average outcome - $17 743. That's very interesting. You know, it's just striking me that if I can persuade our bank manager that this is a good model, I might be able to get him to let us set our expenditure at - well, just a bit less than that for the sake of caution - say, $15 000 and to guarantee us overdraft facilities if we have a bad year. I take it that it *is* a good model?'

'Well, strictly speaking, you must qualify the results with a few 'ifs'. *If* the rainfall is the only influence on receipts, *if* your graph of rainfall against receipts is accurate and *if* rainfall follows the same pattern in the future as in the past, *then* you've got a pretty good picture of what will happen.'

'Fair enough', was the Treasurer's response. 'By the way, how long did it take your computer to do the thousand trials?'

The Programmer consulted his papers.

'Six seconds.'

22 Computer Models

Discussion

This imaginary case contains many features which aid an understanding of computer modelling. Before analysing these features, perhaps it is worthwhile pointing out how much the *context* in which the model was built influenced its development. The context here is typical of many business models:
the model was built to aid a decision;
the decision could not be delayed for a long time;
the parameters of the decision were arbitrarily chosen (i.e. subjectively);
the need, or desire, to validate the model was governed by the importance of the decision it was concerned with, as well as by the amount of time and money available for further validation.

Of course, you might have suspected that the stability of the population, habits and economy of Ruritanians was contrived to make our case study easier. It was, but even if these assumptions were relaxed a similar modelling technique might still have been used in practice. A model which described what might happen *if* the population etc. were stable might still have provided useful information. There are several possible avenues to follow if the preliminary assumptions are relaxed and it is worthwhile to outline these.

One might be to *dismiss* the other variables as unimportant. It may be that it is felt that the other variables are sufficiently stable not to affect the outcome by much and that the model is so coarse anyway that accounting for these other factors would not lead to a materially different conclusion. Of course, this is a subjective approach and might be criticised for lack of science but, nevertheless, it is one which often commends itself when a decision is urgently required.

If the modeller felt he could not confidently dismiss the other variables, an alternative would be to try to *establish the sensitivity* of the model to changes in the other variables. For example, the sensitivity of the model to random economic fluctuations could be tested by estimating best and worst effects of the economy, constructing an arbitrary distribution of economic effects between these two extremes and repeating the trials with, this time, the receipts modified by an economic effect sampled from the distribution of economic effects. Any difference between the outcomes of the two versions of the model now at hand must be caused by the difference in the assumptions.

This sensitivity analysis would still have subjective roots because of the arbitrary distribution of the new variable. In practice, trying out such possibilities, even though they are arbitrarily chosen, can give the modeller a good 'feel' for how his model responds to different assumptions and is likely to give good leads to choosing which variables should be followed up in more detail. This can be an important aspect of computer modelling and more will be said on this subject later.

Another approach would be to *extend* the model to take into account the additional variables. In the context of our case study, this could theoretically be achieved by building economic etc. effects into the model – assuming a basis can be found for predicting them. If the modeller were prepared to forecast trends but not to quantify them, a more subjective method would be simply to take a more optimistic or pessimistic decision than would otherwise be the case – this is in effect what the Treasurer did when he spoke of '$15 000 for the sake of caution'.

Developing the model

The case study also shows the development of a model through three stages – conception; construction and execution; criticism and correction. Quite what led the Treasurer to conceive his model we are not too sure; certainly, we do not think there is a simple set of rules which will guarantee that a model will be conceived. Perhaps the most useful aid to conception of a new model is experience of other models which will make the features of the new problem more salient.

Construction and execution

When it came to construction, the Treasurer chose a pencil-and-paper method. Was what he built a 'mathematical' model? Most people, we think, would say 'no', because we usually think of mathematical models as being formal and symbolic - for example, a set of simultaneous equations - but there are arguments either way. It is easier to classify the Treasurer's model as *stochastic*, which means 'by trial and error, letting chance have some play in the outcome', as distinct from a *deterministic* model which leads to only one outcome. An example of a deterministic mathematical model which may be familiar to many readers would be the economist's consumption function, $C = a + bY$, where C is total consumption, a is the so-called autonomous consumption, i.e. consumption irrespective of income, Y, and b is the marginal propensity to consume (describing the relationship between changes in income and changes in consumption). If figures are substituted for the symbols on the right-hand side, only one outcome is possible.

Other classifications of the Treasurer's model could be that it was *static*, as opposed to *dynamic,* and *discrete*, as opposed to *continuous*. A static model is one where time is not a variable which can influence outcomes - a later outcome or event is not influenced by an earlier outcome or event. Thus, in the Treasurer's model, Barbecue receipts were not affected by Gala receipts and receipts in a given trial year were not affected by receipts in earlier years. A dynamic model does contain these temporal influences (and often the purpose of a dynamic model is to find out how a variable changes over time - its 'time path').

A *discrete* model is characterized by the fact that its variables may go in 'jumps' from one value to another, whereas in a *continuous* model the variables can take any intermediate value. An example may help to make this clear. Figure 2.9(a) shows the Gala rainfall as a discrete graph (histogram), whereas Fig. 2.9(b) shows it as it might have appeared on a continuous graph describing relative frequency.

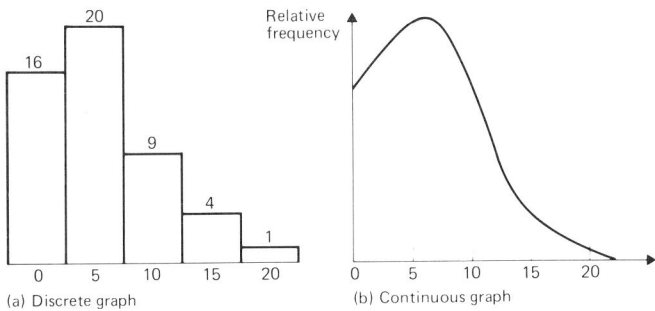

Fig. 2.9: *Illustrating the difference between discrete and continuous graphs*

24 Computer Models

Had the Treasurer found a way to take his samples from the graph on the right of Fig. 2.9, he would have been using a continuous model. It might be thought that a continuous model is always more precise, but in practice a discrete model can be built with finer and finer units (in this example, smaller and smaller cell intervals) to achieve any desired level of precision. The practical advantages of discrete models are that they are often easier to conceive (especially for non-mathematicians) and that many situations have some discrete factor which it would be wrong to model as a continuous one. The disadvantage of discrete models is that they may not lend themselves to ordinary mathematical manipulation and simplification.

Thus we have it that the Treasurer built a discrete, static, stochastic model which he worked by pencil and paper. What sort of model did the Programmer build? Of course, it was a discrete, static, stochastic model which he worked by computer. Basically, what the Programmer did was to take the *procedure* which the Treasurer was following and translate this into a *program* for the computer to follow. Moral: the term 'computer model' tells you only how a model was worked, it tells you nothing about its structure. Computer models may be stochastic or deterministic, static or dynamic, discrete or continuous. As it happens, stochastic models, dynamic models and discrete models are often difficult, or at least time-consuming, to work by hand and it is with models that have one or more of these attributes that the use of a computer is most advantageous.

Criticism and correction

We saw the criticism-and-correction phase entered when the Programmer came onto the scene. This phase may be re-entered several times until confidence in the model is established.

Criticism generally takes the form of testing the plausibility of the results and the structure of the model. Of course, if the Treasurer had been an experienced model-builder he would probably have avoided his mistakes at the outset, but this does allow us to draw a distinction between validation of the *model*, in the sense of proving its basic structure and assumptions, and validation of the *program*, in the sense of proving that the program does adhere to the desired structure and assumptions. It is to be hoped that the Programmer, when he had developed the program, took steps to satisfy himself that it was correct.

Validation of models and programs is by no means easy, especially in the case of stochastic models where no-one can say what the 'right' answer is. The general method is to try and show that the results are plausible and consistent and that the constituent parts of the model - e.g. the method used to generate numbers at random - are unlikely to bias the results.

The reader may have noticed that we did not question the original parameters for the Sports and Social Club decision, plucked out of the air by the Committee at their meeting. This raises quite a separate issue, viz. did the Committee's parameters properly describe its preferred outcomes? An admirable introduction to this type of topic may be found in Jones, L., *Decision Analysis*, published by the Open University Press (1975). For our purpose, we took it that the Committee was paying the piper and had the right to call the tune. Should the Treasurer decide to raise the question of these parameters again, though, we suspect that he now has much greater insight into the problem than he had originally.

Discussion questions

1. The quality of the California grape harvest depends mainly on the amount of rain that falls in the early part of the season, and the amount of sunshine in the later part. Can the viticulturists be helped to quantify their expectations of the quality of next year's harvest?

2. John Smith catches the 8.10 bus to the station, where he catches the 8.30 train to work. He never misses the bus, which is scheduled to arrive at the station just before the train is scheduled to leave. The bus is sometimes early in arriving at the station, sometimes late. The train generally leaves on time, but is also quite often late in leaving. What method could be used to find out how often John Smith will miss the train?

    What if Smith had to catch a scheduled bus at the train's destination?

3. Glottenburg City lives in constant fear of a nuclear bomb attack. The city's early warning radar system will give four minutes warning of the impending disaster. Once the radar has identified the attack, the defence service plans to contact the city broadcasting service, which will immediately issue a public announcement. The number of people who reach the deep shelters will depend on how many people were tuned in to the broadcasting service and what proportion of those reach the shelters in time. The timing of the attack is unpredictable.

    The city authorities have decided that they want to be 90 per cent sure that there will be sufficient provisions in the shelters in the event of attack. Is there any way of establishing the amount of provisions needed and, if so, what data would be required?

4. We define a semi-archaic word as one which has persisted in a vocabulary in one special sense or phrase, but which otherwise has been replaced by another more common word. Examples of semi-archaic words in our vocabulary are *cloven*, as in 'cloven hoof'; *scotch* (verb), as in 'he scotched the rumour'; *dudgeon*, as in 'in high dudgeon'. Our semi-archaic words are not necessarily the same as yours, because we might have different customary vocabularies (for example, if *scotch* were an everyday alternative to *stop* in your vocabulary, it would not qualify; or if you did not know *dudgeon*, meaning *indignation*, then this would not qualify). We have identified about twenty semi-archaic words in our vocabulary.

    People to whom we have explained this have readily grasped our concept and they quickly recognise further instances when we supply more examples. However, we notice that even very intelligent and articulate people have difficulty in giving us examples of their own. Our hypothesis is that most people have no recall method already established to retrieve examples of semi-archaic words, nor can they find any very successful strategy for searching memory for them. All our examples have been accumulated by recognizing them in our reading.

    If we knew the average frequency of occurrence of each of your semi-archaic words in the type of literature you read, and we knew the distribution of the probable number of words you read in a day, how could we model the length of time it would take you to accumulate twenty semi-archaic words?

    If the mode of the distribution of times so modelled were the same as the time it actually took you, would this be a confirmation of our hypothesis?

3 Designing a Computer Model

Event-based discrete simulation

Perhaps the most widely used computer models are those which seek to solve what operational researchers call 'queueing problems'. These models are usually discrete, dynamic *and* stochastic - small wonder that the computer is the favoured tool for working them. Indeed, this type of model is so popular that many computer languages have been specially designed to make building them easier; but it is perfectly feasible to build even these complex models in a general-purpose computer language such as FORTRAN, a task made easier if the modeller has a set of ready-made subroutines available to help with often-needed requirements (see Appendix C).

This type of model will appear rather specialized to some readers, but we believe it to be full of features which are of general application. There are few situations, we feel, which will completely defy analysis by a modeller who has grasped the concepts and possibilities of queueing models. (We look at a very different kind of model, based on a network of data relationships, in Chapter 6 and we survey the field of models generally in Chapter 5.) For this reason, we have chosen a queueing model to develop the ideas of model design. Computer scientists often refer to this type of model as 'event-based discrete simulation', hence the acronym EDSIM given to the subroutines described in Appendix C.

We believe the best way of developing these concepts is by example, but before doing that it might be helpful to introduce some of the terms and ideas which are common to this type of model.

Queue. The term 'queue' can have its ordinary meaning, such as a queue for a bus or a queue at the social security counter; however 'queue' is used in a general sense whenever some person or thing is waiting for 'service' and cannot get service immediately. Thus, the returning fishing fleet waiting to enter a narrow harbour mouth one at a time may not make a formal in-line queue, but they are 'queued' in this technical sense, waiting for service by the harbour mouth. The police department may be called to the assistance of victims of crimes; if the police are fully occupied attending to other crimes, each new victim is 'queued', waiting for service by the police, until an officer can be released to give him attention. The victims may all be at different locations and they may not be attended to on a first-come first-served basis (the police presumably assigning greater priority to some victims according to the apparent urgency of their predicament), but the term queue is applied even in a case such as this. The essential feature of a queue is that a person or thing is waiting for a service which is temporarily being denied.

Service channel. The service channel is the person or thing providing the service which is being queued for. The service channel corresponding to the preceeding examples are respectively the buses, the social security clerk, the harbour mouth, the police officers. A service channel is a limited

Designing a Computer Model

resource which, if it cannot immediately respond to all the demands for service made on it, creates a bottleneck with an ensuing queue.

Single-channel, single-queue model. The simplest case of a queuing model is one where there is one service channel and one queue. If there is only one social security clerk to attend to unemployed persons arriving for their benefits, we have a single-channel, single-queue case.

Clearly, if people arrive to collect benefits at a faster rate than they can be attended to by the clerk, a queue must form. The rate at which people arrive is usually described in terms of the *inter-arrival time*, i.e. the time that elapses between arrival of successive cases requiring service. The smaller the inter-arrival time, the faster the rate of arrival. The rate at which the clerk deals with his customers is described by the *service time*, i.e. the time that elapses between a customer's arrival at the head of the queue and leaving it as a serviced case. Thus, the previous proposition can be restated: if the service time exceeds the inter-arrival time, a queue must form.

What happens if the service time is exactly equal to the inter-arrival time? If the unemployed persons arrive at exactly two-minute intervals and it takes the clerk exactly two minutes to deal with each case, and the clerk is not busy when the first person arrives, it is obvious that no queue will form. Under this scheme of things, the clerk will know that if he remains at his station until two minutes after the doors close, he will have dealt with all the arrivals.

Of course, in the real world it is not possible to arrange things so neatly. Even if the service time and inter-arrival time *averaged* exactly two minutes, there are bound to be variations about the average. To see the effects of these variations, consider first three customers who arrive at 9.00, 9.02 and 9.04 and who take respectively one minute, three minutes and two minutes to serve. The first customer will have been served by 9.01 and the social security clerk must stand idle for one minute until the second customer arrives. When the third customer arrives, he will have to queue for one minute until the clerk finishes with the second customer. The fact that the service time is *distributed* about a mean of two minutes has led to a potential in the system for idleness of the service channel and queueing of the customers. In general, the greater the variations in the service time – the wider the distribution – the longer will be the periods of idleness at some points of time and the longer the queue at other points of time.

Suppose now the three customers each take exactly two minutes to serve, but they arrive at 9.00, 9.03 and 9.04. Again the clerk stands idle for one minute waiting for the second customer, and again the third customer has to queue for one minute. The distribution of inter-arrival times about the mean of two minutes has led to idleness and queueing and, as you might expect, this effect will be greater the wider the distribution.

The effect can be greater still when there are variations in both the service time and the inter-arrival time. Let us put the two previous cases together, i.e. customers arrive at 9.00, 9.03 and 9.04 and take one minute, three minutes and two minutes to serve. This time, the clerk is idle for two minutes and the third customer has to wait two minutes. We hope you can see that, even if the average service time is *less* than the average inter-arrival time, there is still a potential to build up a queue if the distributions about the mean are wide enough.

(If you followed what the Treasurer did in Chapter 2, you may suspect that the single-channel, single-queue system we have just described could be modelled by simulating a trial day in which the inter-arrival time between each customer was determined by a random sample drawn from a known distribution of inter-arrival times, while the service time for each customer was determined by a random sample drawn from a known distribution of service times. How long each customer had to wait during this trial could be established and, by repeating the trial often enough, reliable figures for average waiting time and for the distribution of customers' waiting times could be determined. If that was your suspicion, may we reward you straight away by telling you that you were right.)

Single-channel, multi-queue model. This situation arises when the channel is serving two or more queues. The queues may have different characteristics, e.g. different distributions of inter-arrival time, and if this type of model is to be built it will be necessary to find the rule which determines which queue is going to be drawn from next when the channel becomes free. This rule could be that the queues are serviced in rotation, one from each, or perhaps that the lucky queue is chosen at random, or perhaps some more complicated rule, e.g. the longest queue is always serviced first.

Suppose the returning fishing fleet is trying to go through the narrow harbour mouth, which can accommodate one vessel at a time, at the same time as the outgoing fleet is trying to get through the same harbour mouth. There are two queues, the incoming fleet and the outgoing fleet, being serviced by a single channel, the harbour mouth. (The service time in this example would be the time it takes a vessel to pass through the harbour mouth, leaving it clear for another vessel.)

Multi-channel, single-queue model. Suppose there are a large number of machines which are in the habit of breaking down, with two engineers available to repair them. The machines broken down at any one time create a single queue awaiting service, while the two engineers represent two service channels from which the machines can receive attention. (The inter-arrival time in this example is the time between breakdowns.)

Multi-channel, multi-queue model. Consider a bank with six teller windows at which six queues of customers may form. The six tellers represent six channels from which customers can receive service, each dealing with its own queue. The channels in this example are generally independent, i.e. what is happening at one teller station does not usually affect what happens at another teller station.

A more complicated multi-channel, multi-queue system would be a typical traffic intersection controlled by lights, as illustrated in Fig. 3.1, where the rule of the road is to drive on the right, vehicles forming a single-file queue at the lights, no left turns allowed.

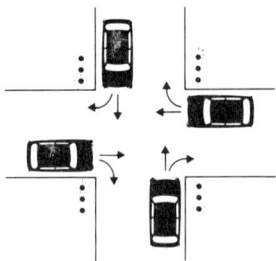

Fig. 3.1: This traffic intersection is a multi-channel multi-queue system

It is easy to see that there are four queues in this case, but what are the channels? It is tempting to conclude that the vehicles are 'serviced' by the lights - and there is more than a grain of truth in this. An interpretation

Designing a Computer Model 29

which could be preferred is that the roadways themselves are the channels and the service time is the time it takes a vehicle to get from its starting position to a point clear of the intersection. On this interpretation, the traffic lights have the effect of cutting off the service in the northbound and southbound channels while the east-west service is operating, and vice versa. The service channels are no longer independent of one another.

Steps in building a queueing model

1. Identify the question you are seeking to answer.
2. Identify the queues, the entities (people or things) that join the queues, and the inter-arrival times of the entities.
3. Identify the channels and service times.
4. Identify the states that the channels and entities can be in at any one time. Most commonly, queueing entities can be in one of three states:
    i) waiting in a queue,
    ii) being served,
    iii) not waiting in a queue nor being served.
   Most commonly, channel entities can be in one of two states:
    i) busy, providing the service,
    ii) not busy, i.e. idle or free.
5. Identify the rules for transition from one state to another.
6. Construct the model.
7. Validate the model.
8. Conduct experiments with the model.

The following example (based on fictitious data) illustrates the first six of these steps. Steps seven and eight are considered in Chapter 4.

Example - airport planning

Erewhon, the country adjacent to Ruritania, has an airport with only one runway.

The operations at the airport are illustrated in Fig. 3.2. If the runway is busy with an aircraft taking off, or with an aircraft landing (including one making its final approach to landing), an incoming aircraft is made to circle a few miles away from the airport. If another aircraft arrives, it too is made to circle, one thousand feet above the other, and so on, making a stack of waiting aircraft. When the runway becomes free, the aircraft at the bottom of the stack may be invited to make its final approach and land; the other aircraft are directed to descend one thousand feet.

Departing aircraft taxi from the terminal building to a hold point just off the runway. At the hold point, the pilot asks the control tower for permission to take off. This permission will normally be granted if there are no other aircraft on the runway nor on final approach.

Departing and arriving aircraft are normally dealt with on a 'first-come first-served' basis, but the traffic controllers have an additional rule that, if an aircraft has been waiting in the stack for 15 minutes or more, the arriving aircraft are given priority. This rule is designed to eliminate the possibility of an aircraft in the stack running out of fuel when conditions are congested (all aircraft are required to arrive with an absolute minimum of 40 minutes flying time left).

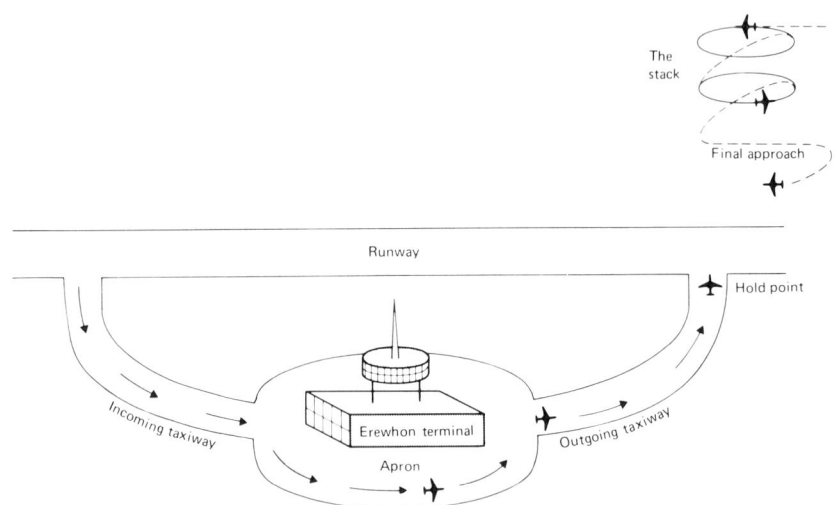

Fig. 3.2: Erewhon airport. Incoming aircraft circle in the stack if the runway is busy. Outgoing aircraft queue at the hold point.

Step 1: the question for which an answer is sought

The airport planning authorities are trying to work out how long it will be before the existing facilities require expansion. They are prepared to make forecasts of the rate of increase of air traffic; what they want to know is what percentage increase in air traffic will just cause the existing facilities to become inolerably congested.

'Intolerable congestion' might be a matter of opinion, but the airport authorities are prepared to make a more precise definition. They would regard the congestion as intolerable if any arriving aircraft had to wait more than 30 minutes in the stack or if any departing aircraft had to wait more than 40 minutes at the hold point.

Step 2: the queues, queueing entities and inter-arrival times

It is clear that the stack of arrivals and the queue of departures at the hold point are two queues of interest. The queueing entities in both cases are, of course, aircraft.

There are other queueing possibilities in the system. For example, if resources for disembarkation and unloading of cargo at the terminal apron are limited, it is imaginable that aircraft advancing along the incoming taxiway might have to queue for these facilities. If incoming aircraft compete with outgoing aircraft for these facilities, it is imaginable that incoming aircraft might cause delays to the departure of aircraft along the outgoing taxiway. Let us assume there is no such interaction, i.e. the rate of departure of aircraft is not influenced by the rate of arrival, and resolve to tell the planners that our model contains the assumption that the apron facilities will not become congested. On this assumption, we need not consider any queue forming in the incoming taxiway. From the point of view

of runway congestion, it would seem reasonable to consider just the two
queues, in the stack and at the hold point. Our next problem is to find the
inter-arrival times at these two queues.

Figures 3.3 and 3.4 show the average number of landings and departures at
Erewhon airport at different periods throughout a day in the busy season.

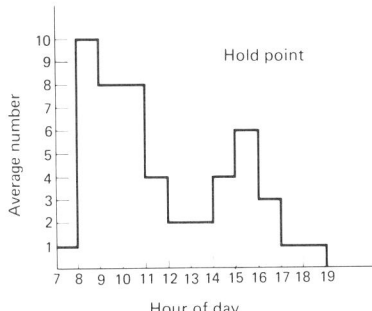

Fig. 3.3:   The average number of arrivals (total 50) at the
            hold point in each hour of the working day

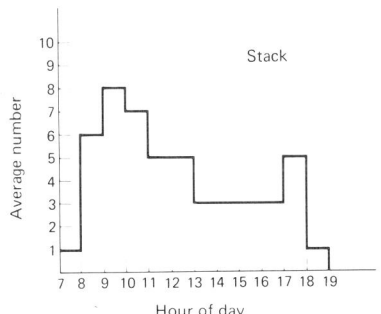

Fig. 3.4:   The average number of arrivals (total 50) at the
            stack in each hour of the working day

These data allow us to estimate the mean inter-arrival times at different
times of day. For example, mean inter-arrival time at the hold point
between 8 and 9 o'clock would be 60/10 = 6 minutes, while mean inter-arrival
time at the stack would be 60/6 = 10 minutes. We know these are only
approximations, because the grouping of the data into one-hour periods was
arbitrary, i.e. nothing significant happens in the real world at the
boundary of one hour and another. Let us accept these estimates as accurate
for our present purpose and return later to consider whether or not we need
to refine this assumption.

Considering first the arrivals at the stack, it must be assumed that most
aircraft (i.e. those on scheduled flights) have a scheduled time of arrival.
The actual time of arrival of an aircraft will differ from that scheduled
because of such variables as delays at the airport of origination, the wind
and weather encountered on the way, the aircraft's payload. These variables
are so complex that we may choose to conclude that, from the point of view
of our model, the actual arrival time of an aircraft is quite unpredictable.

This leads us to hypothesize that the aircraft arrive at *random* points of time with a mean inter-arrival time which varies according to the hour of day.

The interval that elapses between randomly chosen points of time is described by a negative exponential distribution (see Appendix A for an explanation of this point) which is of the type shown in Fig. 3.5.

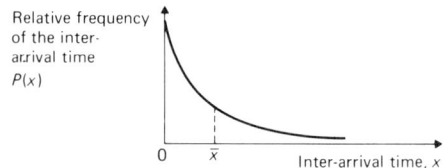

Fig. 3.5: *The interval between arrivals at random points of time is described by this negative exponential distribution. The mean inter-arrival time is shown as $\bar{x}$.*

This distribution indicates that there is a possibility of two aircraft arriving close together (inter-arrival time near to zero). This does not quite suit our model, however, for it so happens that in the airways which the aircraft follow to arrive at Erewhon airport, steps are taken to ensure that two aircraft do *not* arrive at the same place at the same time, for obvious reasons. These rules of flight separation mean that aircraft are always separated by at least 2 minutes flying time.

This suggests that if we have an inter-arrival time which has a mean of, say, 12 minutes we should model this as an inter-arrival time of 2 minutes *plus* a sample of a negative exponential distribution that has a mean of 10 minutes. We will defer discussion of the validity of this assumption to the next chapter.

A similar line of argument applies to the arrival of aircraft at the holding point. Although most aircraft have scheduled times of departure, their times of arrival at the holding point are not predictable, because of departure delays, varying times for movements on the apron and varying taxying speeds. Again, the ground traffic-control system ensures a certain separation of aircraft by giving permission to taxi only when the apron is clear of other taxying aircraft. Let us assume that this process leads to a minimum separation of 1 minute. This suggests that if the inter-arrival time at the holding point has a mean of, say, 6 minutes, we could model this as an inter-arrival time of 1 minute *plus* a sample of a negative exponential distribution which has a mean of 5 minutes. This may not be a watertight hypothesis and we should take steps to find out if it is very far from reality. We defer discussion of this point to the next chapter.

We now have a basis for describing inter-arrival times. Inter-arrival time at the stack is 2 minutes plus a sample from a negative exponential distribution with a mean of 2 minutes less than that which can be estimated from Fig. 3.4, according to the hour of day. Inter-arrival time at the hold point is 1 minute plus a sample from a negative exponential distribution which has a mean of 1 minute less than that which can be estimated from Fig. 3.3, according to the hour of day.

Step 3: the channel and service time

We hope it is now apparent that we are dealing with a two-queue single-channel case where the service channel is the runway.

Designing a Computer Model 33

The service time for departing aircraft at the head of the hold queue is the time taken from granting permission to take off until the aircraft clears the end of the runway. In order to find the distribution of these service times, we shall have to go down to the airport with our stop-watches but, before doing that, we can still form a hypothesis of the type of distribution we might expect.

It is clear that some portion of the take-off time is taken up with taxying from the hold point to the beginning of the runway. We imagine larger aircraft take rather longer to do this than smaller aircraft, but it is difficult to believe that there will be very much difference between aircraft in this respect. The rest of the time will be taken up with accelerating down the runway at full power and climbing out. Again, some aircraft will do this faster than others, but it is unlikely that there will be a really large difference between different types. Altogether, we might expect take-off times to be fairly narrowly distributed about the mean, as in Fig. 3.6.

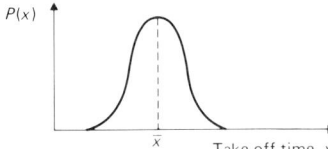

Fig. 3.6: The distribution of take-off times is expected to be similar to a 'normal' distribution.

You will recognize that this is rather like the bell-shaped normal curve. It is not *quite* like a normal curve, because you will notice that our curve cuts the horizontal axis, e.g. we are saying that there is some absolute minimum time for take-off which can never be beaten. This seems proper, because the normal curve would suggest that some probability should be attached (however remote) to an aircraft taking off in zero time - this does not quite square with our conception of the facts! Nevertheless, there does not appear to be much difference between a normal curve and ours, and the probabilities at the extremes are so remote anyway that they are unlikely to make any difference for our purpose. This leads us to hypothesize that a normal distribution will be an adequate model of take-off times.

Exercise of our stopwatch produced the distribution of actual take-off times at Erewhon airport shown in Fig. 3.7.

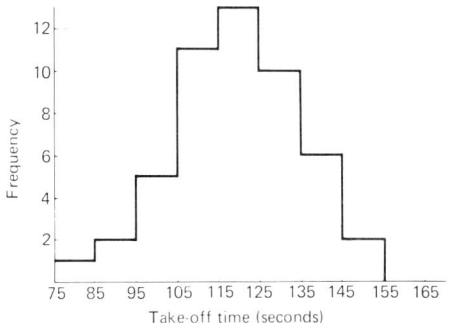

Fig. 3.7: The distribution of fifty observations of take-off times at Erewhon airport.

It will be seen there is a strong modal value around 2 minutes and the calculated mean approximates to two minutes. Of the fifty observations, about two thirds seem to lie in the range 1 minute 45 seconds to 2 minutes 15 seconds so, if we are to follow our previous hypothesis, we must conclude that take-off times are approximately described by a normal distribution with a mean of 2 minutes and a standard deviation of 15 seconds. This has been an estimate, and we should satisfy ourselves that it is reasonably accurate - this will be done in the next chapter.

A very similar set of arguments govern the service time the runway gives to landing aircraft. Approach and landing speeds vary, but are closely grouped about the mean. To save repeating a similar argument, we shall assert that the distribution of service times for landing aircraft is a normal distribution with a mean of 3 minutes and a standard deviation of 30 seconds.

Step 4: the states of the entities

The departing aircraft can be in the states:
i)   waiting at the holding point,
ii) getting service from the channel, i.e. taking off,
iii) not waiting at the holding point nor taking off.

It is possible to analyse other states of the departing aircraft (and, in passing, we should mention that the concept *states* we are using here is also commonly discribed by terms such as *attribute* or *set*). The third state, for example, includes taxying on the outgoing runway, waiting to load passengers at the terminal, in the air after taking off. Experience of analysing this type of problem has led us to conclude that these states are irrelevant to the particular question we are trying to answer but, if you should decide to include them in the model, no harm will be done.

The landing aircraft can be in the states:
i)   in the stack, waiting for permission to land;
ii) getting service from the channel, i.e. making approach and landing;
iii) not in the stack, nor approaching and landing.

Again a peculiar definition of the third state, which embraces such states as in the airway prior to arrival at the stack, on the incoming taxiway.

The runway can be in the states:
i) busy, i.e. occupied, dealing with a landing or take-off;
ii) free, i.e. not busy, not occupied etc..

At this stage, we would like to introduce the concept of a *null* state to describe the last state in the above three cases. This is just a convenient shorthand to describe the state of the entities when they are not in the states of most interest for our model, i.e. when they are outside the system with which we are concerned. For example, it will be useful, in the model, to have the aircraft start off in this null state before they go into arriving or departing states.

Step 5: the rules for state transitions

The objective of this step is to find out under what circumstances an entity may make a transition from one state to another. A convenient aid to making this analysis is to draw up a *state-transition matrix*. This is a table with all the states of the entity listed both across the top and down the side. The states at the side represent 'from' states while those along the top are the 'into' states. The analyst considers each box in the table and asks himself whether it is possible for an entity to go *from* the state at the side of the box *into* the state above the box, entering a √ if he deems it possible. Figure 3.8 shows the state-transition matrix for departing aircraft.

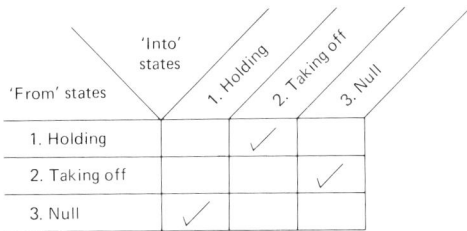

Fig. 3.8: *State-transition matrix for departing aircraft analyses the possible state transitions*

It is a simple matter to translate this information into a state-transition diagram, Fig. 3.9.

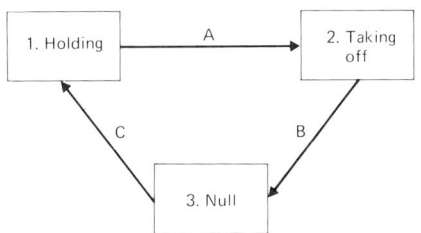

Fig. 3.9: *The state-transition diagram corresponding to Fig. 3.8*

This state-transition diagram gives us a picture of how a departing aircraft moves through our model. We must try to formulate precise rules which describe the *conditions* under which the three state transitions, corresponding to the arrows in Fig. 3.9, are made.

A. *Holding-to-taking-off transition*
You may recall from the description of airport operations on page 29 that departing and arriving aircraft are dealt with on a first-come first-served basis. We can express this as the condition:
A1: the aircraft at the head of the stack (if any) arrived after the aircraft at the head of the holding queue.

Although this is a *necessary* condition for an aircraft to be allowed to take off, it is not *sufficient*, because an aircraft in the stack might have been there 15 minutes or more, in which case it will have priority, i.e. aircraft waiting at the hold point will not be allowed to take off. We express this as the second condition:
A2: the aircraft at the head of the stack (if any) has been waiting less than 15 minutes.

Finally, there may be another aircraft already taking off or landing. We must have a third condition:
A3: the runway is not busy.

We can now express the rule for the holding-to-taking-off transition. If condition A1 is true *and* condition A2 is true *and* condition A3 is true, *then* the aircraft at the head of the holding queue will go into the taking-off state.

36 Computer Models

B. Taking-off-to-null transition

The condition for this transition is that the aircraft taking-off must have been in that state for some time. The period of time concerned is not known exactly, i.e. it is stochastically determined by a random sample from the distribution of take-off times, so we can express the condition for this transition:

B1: the aircraft has been in the taking-off state for a time equal to a sample from a normal distribution with a mean 2 minutes and standard deviation 15 seconds.

C. Null-to-holding transition

The condition for this transition is that the inter-arrival time (since the last aircraft entered the holding state or since the beginning of the hour in the case of the first arrival of an hour) has expired. This period of time is again stochastic and the condition for this transition becomes:

C1: a period of time has elapsed since the last aircraft entered the holding state (or since the beginning of the hour, in the case of the first departure of the hour) equal to one minute *plus* a sample from a negative exponential distribution with a mean one minute less than the mean inter-arrival time corresponding to the time of day (see Fig. 3.3).

At this point you may like to try for yourself constructing a state-transition matrix, state-transition diagram and rules for state transitions for arriving aircraft. Our analysis follows immediately.

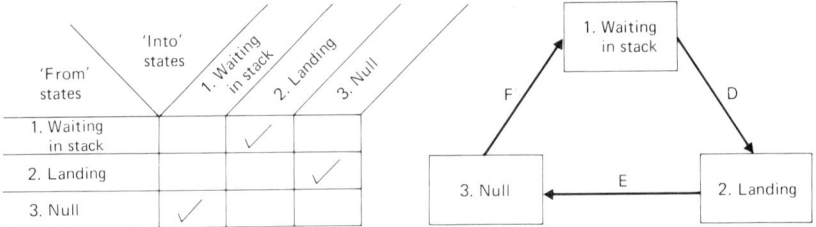

Fig. 3.10: The state-transition matrix and diagram for arriving aircraft

In considering the state-transition matrix, you might have thought of more possibilities than we did. For example, you might have said that an arriving aircraft could go straight from the null state to landing, without queueing in the stack, if there were no other aircraft waiting to land or take off and the runway was free. You would not be wrong to see things that way and - more important - a model built on those assumptions would work perfectly properly. We cheated a bit in our description because we could see, from our experience, that an aircraft arriving under those conditions would spend *zero* time waiting if we made it join the stack before landing; this will not affect the distribution of waiting times which, after all, is the only thing we are interested in. The advantage of analysing this way is that we end up with fewer transitions to consider and thus a simpler model to build.

You might have considered other possibilities, e.g. a waiting-in-stack-to-null transition caused by the aircraft being hijacked by terrorists from Ruritania. The purpose of drawing a state-transition matrix is, indeed, to try to force consideration of possibilities which otherwise might not be apparent. We have chosen to reject the less frequently occurring possibilities at this stage, so that we can get a model of the most normal situation working; we return to consider the less likely cases in the next chapter.

The rules for the state transitions are given below.

D. Waiting-in-stack-to-landing transition
D1: the aircraft at the head of the holding queue (if any) arrived after the aircraft at the head of the stack queue.
D2: the aircraft at the head of the stack queue has been waiting 15 minutes or more.
D3: the runway is not busy.
   An aircraft goes from the head of the stack queue to landing *if* condition D3 is true *and* either condition D1 or condition D2 is true.

E. Landing-to-null transition
E1: the aircraft has been in the landing state for a time equal to a sample from a normal distribution with a mean of 3 minutes and a standard deviation of 30 seconds.

F. Null-to-waiting-in-stack transition
F1: a period of time has elapsed since the last aircraft entered the waiting-in-stack state (or since the beginning of the hour in the case of the first arrival of the hour) equal to 2 minutes *plus* a sample from a negative exponential distribution with a mean 2 minutes less than the mean inter-arrival time relevant to the time of day (see Fig. 3.4).

We now have only to analyse the service channel.

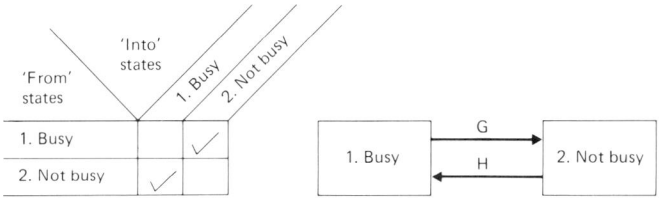

Fig. 3.11: The state-transition matrix and diagram for the runway

G. Busy-to-null transition
G1: an aircraft has left the 'in service' state (i.e. take-off or landing).

H. Null-to-busy transition
H1: an aircraft has entered the 'in service' state.

If you have exceptional insight into this model - or previous experience - there may be a worry gnawing at the back of your mind. If you turn back to conditions A3 and D3 you will see that both are defined in terms of states of the runway, yet the runway transition conditions, G1 and H1, are defined exclusively in terms of states of the aircraft, which have already been defined. This is because there is an exact correspondence between the busy state of the runway and an aircraft being in the 'in-service' (taking-off or landing) state. We could rewrite conditions A3 and D3 as 'no aircraft is in the 'in-service' state.' This condition is exactly the same as the condition 'the runway is not busy.' If we use the revised definitions of A3 and D3, we no longer need explicitly consider the state of the runway; the runway state is implied by the states of the aircraft. On this basis, we could remove the runway altogether from our model as it is redundant, duplicating something which can be deduced from other features of the model.

This position is quite often reached with models of this type, but not always - the queueing model in Chapter 7 is an example of a case where it is essential to include the channel as an entity in the model. We think it a good practice always to analyse the channel transitions, as we have here, and there is an argument for explicitly modelling the channel if it helps the modeller preserve his clarity of purpose. We propose to leave the runway in our model on these grounds, and also as an illustration of the fact that redundancy in a model may be no fault - if it is still logically sound, the model can properly achieve its purpose.

Step 6: construct the model

We have enumerated the constituent parts of our model. What we need to do now is put them together and specify the *procedure* that must be followed in order to make the model work and produce results. This is not as hard as might at first appear: it is just a matter of specifying in logical fashion the procedures that the entities follow in the real situation.

It is worthwhile to stand back for a minute and review the large aspects of the model. Our purpose is to find the distribution of waiting times of aircraft at the holding point and at the stack. Later on, we will want to increase the number of arrivals and departures so that we can see at what point the runway is intolerably congested but, for the time being, let us concentrate on modelling the present situation so that we can build up confidence in our model.

A question we should ask ourselves is, 'How long do we want the model to run for?' As a rule of thumb, we could say that if we were to collect from the model a thousand or so samples of waiting times at the hold point and at the stack, we could have a lot of confidence that our results were not being biased by chance outcomes. To get these thousand samples, we will have to process a thousand arrivals and a thousand departures through the model. Since there are about fifty arrivals and fifty departures each day, this suggests we should run our model for twenty trial days.

We can now describe the overall logic of our model as a flowchart of procedures as shown in Fig. 3.12.

Boxes 1, 5 and 6 in Fig. 3.12 are the ones that make the procedures repeat for twenty days. Boxes 2, 3 and 4 are the procedures which are to be followed on any one day. Box 7, of course, describes what we want to happen when the simulation is over.

We have put in box 2 to illustrate the fact that we must make sure the *initial conditions* are right at the beginning of the day, which in the case of this model means that no aircraft is already landing or taking off or waiting at the stack or holding point. We put in box 3 because there is a special procedure to follow to get the first arrivals. Normally, during the day, inter-arrival times are measured from the time of the last arrival (or from the end of the last hour if an hourly boundary is traversed). In the case of the very first arrivals, however, it is measured from the beginning of the day, so box 3 is establishing an initial condition.

Box 4 is a summary of a great deal of detail, on which we can now concentrate. Generally, the approach to analysing this type of model is to consider the state transitions of the entities as they are processed through the system. The order in which these activities are tackled must conform to the sequence that happens in the real world, *except* that the best place to start is with the transitions that occur when the entities leave the channel, i.e. when they finish receiving service from the channel (in our case this means we should start with the transitions B, taking-off-to-null, and E, landing-to-null). This may seem surprising, since it looks as though we are putting the cart before the horse - most people would start to analyse the problem from the point of arrival of the entity requiring service. There is,

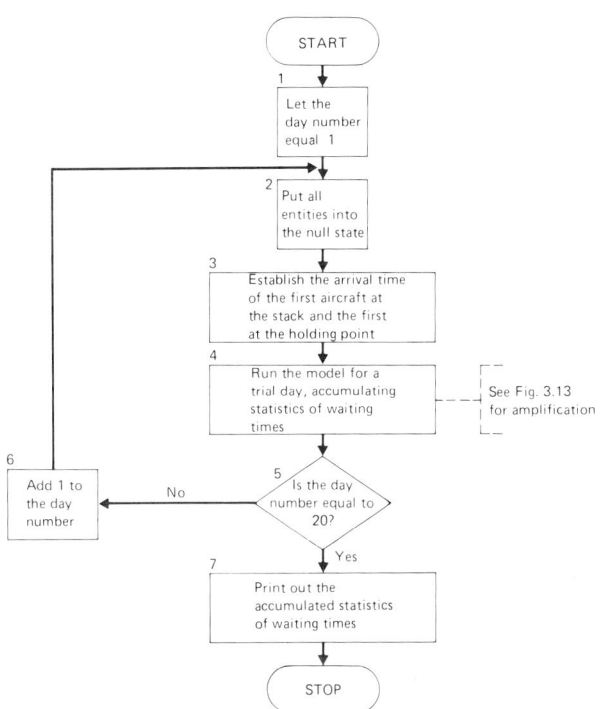

Fig. 3.12: Flowchart of the overall procedures to model 20 trial days

however, a good reason for starting with transitions that free the channel, but this will not become fully apparent until we deal with the practical details of how the model will work. (In the meantime, we can tell you that failure to start the analysis from the point at which entities leave the channel is likely to lead to a logical error when there is a simultaneous transition of the channel into the free state and an entity into the waiting-for-service state, e.g. an aircraft completing its take-off at exactly the same instant of time as another arrives at the holding point.)

If we accept that we are to start off with activities that free the channel, the statement in box 4 of Fig. 3.12 may now be amplified as in Fig. 3.13.

There remains one more step - to decide the smallest unit of time to which the model will work. This problem can be overcome by finding the smallest time interval mentioned - this is the 15 second standard deviation of condition B1. If we choose a ¼ minute unit of time, this would mean that samples from the distribution concerned would have to be taken to the nearest ¼ minute - a rather coarse scale under the circumstances, so we need a finer unit. One second is convenient and small enough - it does not matter if the time unit is smaller than necessary.

40 Computer Models

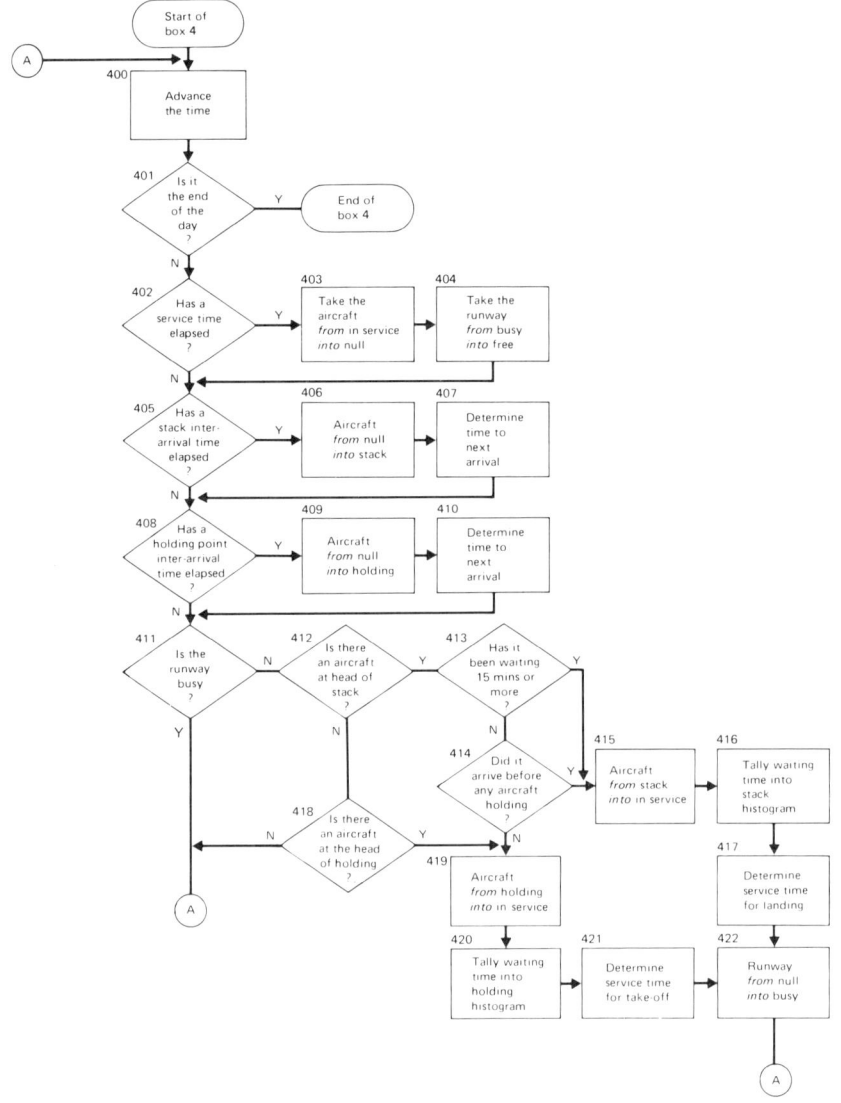

Fig. 3.13: Flowchart of the procedures that will model each trial day
(the flowchart is entered with the inter-arrival times of
the first aircraft to stack and hold already established)

The model is now logically constructed and can be translated almost
directly into a computer program which will follow the stated procedures.
You may recall that we said earlier that the only difference between a
computer model and other models is the way they are worked, so it must be
possible to work this model by hand. To do this even for one whole day would
be a substantial undertaking, let alone for twenty days. It will be helpful,
though, if we describe how this model can be worked by hand using the same
methods as would be employed on a computer, but we shall be able to do this
for only a handful of arrivals and departures.

To work the model by hand, we need to set up a scratch pad with a number of
tables and boxes to which we shall assign names, as shown in Fig. 3.14.

Designing a Computer Model 41

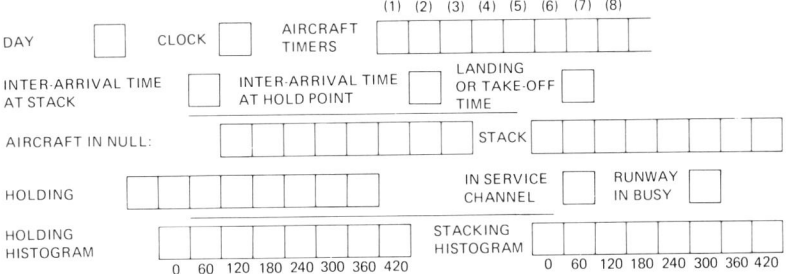

Fig. 3.14: *The scratch pad needed for a manual simulation*

The DAY box records the current day number. The boxes on the same line and the subsequent one are time cells which will record times of interest, in seconds. The first one of these, CLOCK, will show the current time of day, measured in seconds. The AIRCRAFT TIMERS will seem to go a bit haywire at first, but they are basically time cells associated with each aircraft which we shall use later on to find out how long each aircraft has been waiting in a queue - AIRCRAFT TIMER (1) meaning the time cell for aircraft 1, and so on. The other three time cells are used to keep a note of the inter-arrival times and service times. The next two lines of boxes are used to keep a note of which aircraft are in which state at any one time and which runway is in the busy state. We have only one runway, so this box will contain a 1 if the runway is busy and nothing if the runway is free.

We are now ready to establish the initial conditions by following boxes 1 to 3 of Fig. 3.12. DAY must be set to 1. We put all the aircraft into the null state. There isn't a null box for the runway, but we will know that if nothing is recorded in the 'busy' box then the runway is in null. We take a sample from the required distribution to find the first inter-arrival time at the holding point (this could be done with cards as the Treasurer did, or with dice, roulette wheels or tables of random numbers) - let us say this proves to be 1½ minutes, i.e. 90 seconds. We take another sample in the same way to find the inter-arrival time at the stack - let us say this is 2¼ minutes, i.e. 135 seconds. Now you must imagine that we are making all our entries in pencil, so that we can erase them and insert new entries if necessary. Our scratch pad with the initial conditions entered will appear as in Fig. 3.15, and it is time to turn to box 400 of Fig. 3.13.

Now, we *could* make the clock advance one second and see if anything is due to happen - but you can see that this would be a pointless exercise, because it is clear that no event of significance will occur until 90 seconds have elapsed. We might as well advance the clock straight away. It is because we can take this short cut that this type of model is called 'event-based' -

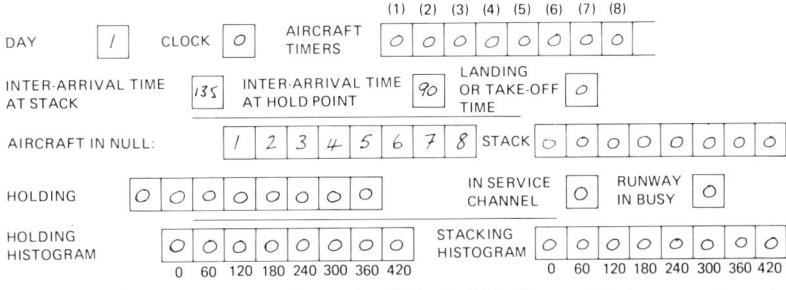

Fig. 3.15: *Scratch pad with initial conditions entered.*

42 Computer Models

we simply advance the clock to the next significant event. In fact, the general rule for advancing the time is as follows:
i) look at all the time cells (apart from the clock) and find the one with the lowest positive value - this is the 'time to the next event';
ii) *add* the 'time to the next event' to the clock and *subtract* it from all other time cells.

This procedure means that the clock shows the elapsed time of the simulation (in seconds) while the other positive time cells show how long there is to go to the events. After executing box 401, our scratch pad appears as shown in Fig. 3.16.

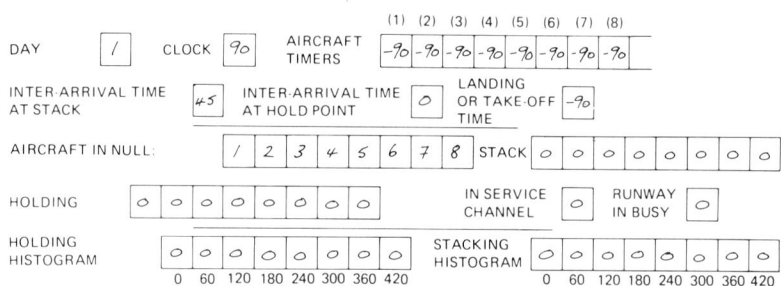

Fig. 3.16: Scratch pad at expiry of the holding-point inter-arrival time

We may now continue down Fig. 3.13. The tests labelled 401, 402 and 405 are false, but the test at 408 is true, as is clear from the zero in our holding-point inter-arrival time cell. Thus we must execute boxes 409 and 410. One additional rule is necessary: every time we put an aircraft into a queue, we must set its timer to zero - this is to allow us to find out how long it spends waiting. Assuming the next sample from the distribution of inter-arrival times at the holding point is drawn as 60 seconds, our scratch pad is as shown in Fig. 3.17.

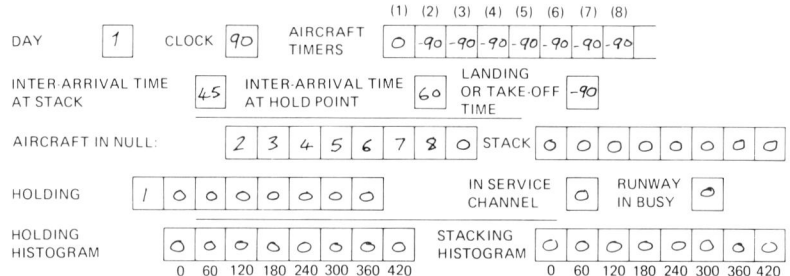

Fig. 3.17: Scratch pad after aircraft 1 enters the holding state

We now progress to test 411, which is false - the runway is not busy. There is no aircraft in the stack, so test 412 is false. Test 418 is true, so we must execute boxes 419, 420, 421 and 422. Assuming the take-off time generated is 140 seconds, the scratch pad now appears as in Fig 3.18.

When the aircraft was moved from holding to in-service, its timer - AIRCRAFT TIMER (1) - showed how long it had been waiting. On this occasion, it had been waiting zero time, so the corresponding variate value of the holding histogram was incremented by 1, showing that one aircraft had passed through

Designing a Computer Model   43

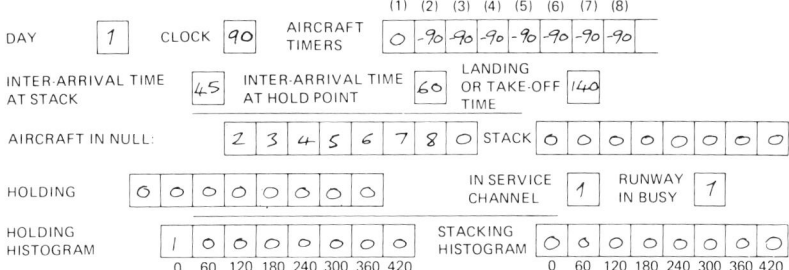

Fig. 3.18: Scratch pad as aircraft 1 starts its take-off

the holding point and had had to wait zero time.
Now we return to 400 to pass through the process again. Assuming the next inter-arrival time at the stack is 75 seconds, you may care to verify for yourself that Fig. 3.19 shows the position by the time the return to box 400 is made on this second occasion.

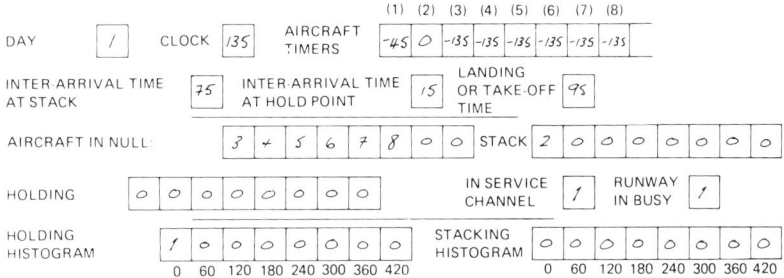

Fig. 3.19: Scratch pad after the next pass through the procedures. Aircraft 2 is queued in the stack waiting for aircraft 1 to clear the runway.

This time, test 405 was true, so aircraft 2 was placed in the stack and its time cell was set to zero. The aircraft could not land, because the runway was busy. Otherwise, things remained the same, except of course that the stack inter-arrival time cell has been set to 75 seconds while the other time cells show the advance in time of 45 seconds.
We return to box 400 for another pass through the procedures; let us suppose a holding-point inter-arrival time of 100 seconds is generated. The position when we return to box 400 is as shown in Fig. 3.20.

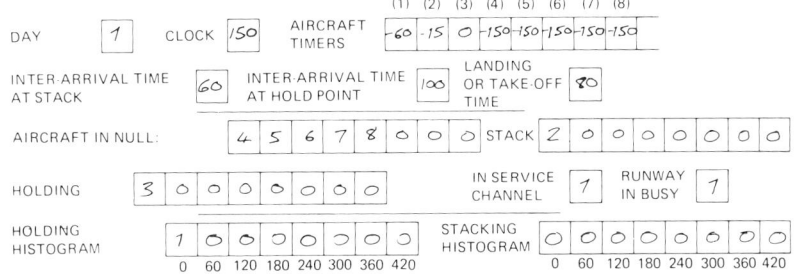

Fig. 3.20: Aircraft 3 has arrived at the hold point and must queue

44 Computer Models

This time, test 408 was true, so aircraft 3 went into holding and its time cell was set to zero. At this point, you may like to notice that the stacking aircraft's time cell (2) is more negative than the holding aircraft's time cell (3). This shows that the stacking aircraft arrived *before* the holding aircraft. We can use this fact to decide which will have priority when the runway becomes free. If a stacked aircraft's time cell reaches -900 or less, this will show us it has been waiting 15 minutes or more.

The next pass advances the clock 60 seconds. On completion of the procedures, assuming a stack inter-arrival time of 150 seconds was generated, the position shown in Fig. 3.21 is reached.

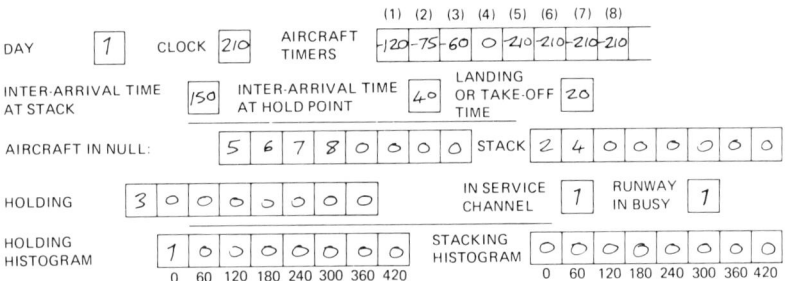

Fig. 3.21: Aircraft 4 has arrived and must stack

Another aircraft has joined the stack, its time cell being set to zero. The next pass advances the clock by 20 seconds; aircraft 2 can come in to land - let us say its landing time is 180 seconds. The position when we return to box 400 is as shown in Fig. 3.22.

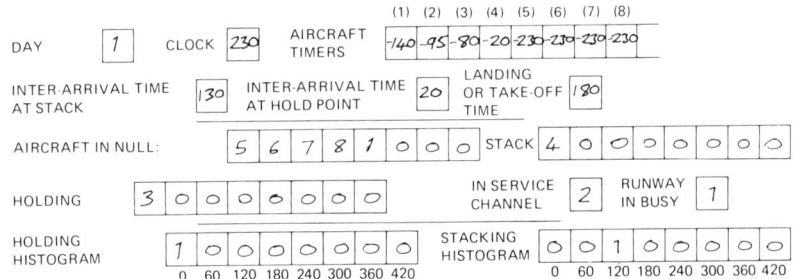

Fig. 3.22: Aircraft 1 completes its take-off. Aircraft 2 comes in to land and its stack waiting time is recorded.

The passage of aircraft 1 into the null state left the runway free after box 404; but this meant that aircraft 2 could come into land at box 415, making the runway busy again at box 422. When aircraft 2 came in to land, its time cell showed it had been waiting 95 seconds; thus, by box 416, the histogram of stacking times now shows that 1 aircraft has passed through the stack and that its waiting time was in the band 90-150 seconds.

We hope at this stage that it is quite clear how even this discrete, stochastic, dynamic model can be worked by hand. It took us rather a long time to describe the steps in detail but, with a pencil and a good eraser, progress can be made quite rapidly. It would be a good exercise for you to progress the model until another two aircraft have taken off and landed. For

the sake of this exercise, you might as well get the stochastic times from
your head. If you make up inter-arrival times about equal to take-off times
or landing times, you will be sure to get queues building up. If you wish to
run the model for a longer time, building up large queues, you will need to
start off with more aircraft in the null state than we did, otherwise you
might run out of aircraft.

We can now see why we should start off with state transitions that free the
channel. If we write the procedures the most natural way:
1. If the inter-arrival time has elapsed, an aircraft in the null state
   enters the holding queue.
2. If the runway is free, an aircraft holding enters the in-service state.
   The runway enters the busy state.
3. If the take-off time has elapsed, the aircraft in service enters the null
   state. The runway enters the free state.

Consider what these procedures dictate if aircraft 2 arrives at the same
instant of time as aircraft 1 completes its take-off. Aircraft 1 has already
been processed through steps 1 and 2 (making the runway busy) and is now due
to be processed through step 3. But we must consider that the procedures are
executed at any one instant of time in the order in which they are written,
so what will happen is:
step 1: aircraft 2 arrives at the holding point;
step 2: the runway is busy, so aircraft 2 is denied entry;
step 3: the runway is made free.

The runway is still busy at step 2, because step 3 has not yet been
executed. This is not what we wish to happen in this simultaneous case. We
could get over this by running through the procedures twice for each instant
of time; on the other hand, suppose we had written the procedures:
1. If the take-off time has elapsed, the aircraft in service enters the null
   state. The runway becomes free.
2. If the inter-arrival time has elapsed, an aircraft in the null state
   enters the holding queue.
3. If the runway is free, an aircraft holding enters the in-service state.
   The runway becomes busy.

Again aircraft 1 has been processed through steps 2 and 3 at an earlier
time. When we consider the simultaneous completion of take-off of aircraft 1
and arrival of aircraft 2, we see that the procedure followed at that instant
is:
step 1: aircraft 1 enters the null state; the runway becomes free;
step 2: aircraft 2 enters the holding state;
step 3: the runway is free, so aircraft 2 enters the in-service state; the
        runway becomes busy.

This is what we wanted to happen.

When this model is operated on a computer, the method used is practically
identical to the pencil-and-eraser method. The programmer first of all
reserves areas of the computer's memory which will act as the 'scratch pad'.
A name is declared for each of the cells concerned and this name can be
referred to in the procedures. Then the program is written to instruct the
machine to follow the procedures of the flowchart. The computer can be
instructed to get automatically a sample from a distribution - how this is
done is described in the next chapter. For those of you who are programmers,
the listing of the FORTRAN program for this simulation is given at the end of
this chapter and should present no difficulty when taken in conjunction with
the description of the EDSIM subroutines in Appendix C. The non-programmer
may also like to glance at this program - even though much of the detail may
be meaningless, we think the correspondence between the computer program and
the hand procedures will come across.

46 Computer Models

Before we dare conduct any experiments with the model, we must at least satisfy ourselves that it works properly for the present situation.

Listing of the computer program

```
C-        *
C-        * EREWHON AIRPORT
C-        *
C- ALL CELLS ARE TO BE INTEGERS; USUAL TYPE RULES OF FORTRAN ARE
C- OVER-RIDDEN BY THE NEXT STATEMENT (NOT AVAILABLE ON SOME COMPILERS).
      IMPLICIT INTEGER (A-Z)
C- EDSIM SUBROUTINES REQUIRE INITIALISED COMMON AREA EDSIMZ, AND EDSIM
C- LOGICAL FUNCTIONS/VARIABLES NEED TO BE DECLARED.
      LOGICAL DONE,IN
      COMMON /EDSIMZ/ DONE,DUMMY(105)
      CALL EDINIT(6)
C-        *
C-        * DECLARATIONS FOR THE MODEL
C-        *
C- A CLASS OF AIRCRAFT, PLANES, WITH ENTITIES CALLED PLANE.
C- 100 ENTITIES SHOULD BE AMPLE TO AVOID RUNNING OUT OF AIRCRAFT.
      CALL DCLASS(PLANES,PLANE,100)
C- THE STATES OF THE AIRCRAFT ARE CALLED SETS IN EDSIM. WE MUST DECLARE
C- ENOUGH CELLS IN EACH SET TO HOLD THE MAXIMUM NUMBER OF AIRCRAFT THAT
C- COULD POSSIBLY BE IN THAT STATE; PLUS 2 EXTRA CELLS PER SET FOR USE
C- BY SUBROUTINES.
      DIMENSION NULL(102),STACK(102),HOLD(102),INSERV(3)
      CALL DSET(NULL,102)
      CALL DSET(STACK,102)
      CALL DSET(HOLD,102)
      CALL DSET(INSERV,3)
C- THE CLASS OF RUNWAYS CONTAINS ONLY 1 ENTITY AND NEEDS ONLY 1 STATE
      CALL DCLASS(RWAYS,RUNWAY,1)
      DIMENSION BUSY(3)
      CALL DSET(BUSY,3)
C- THE TIME CELLS ARE DECLARED IN COMMON - FIRST, THE CLOCK
      COMMON ICLOCK
C- THEN CELLS FOR EACH AIRCRAFT, INTER-ARRIVAL TIMES AT STACK AND
C- HOLDING-POINT, SERVICE TIME FOR TAKE-OFF AND LANDING
      COMMON TPLANE(100),TSTACK,THOLD,TSERV
C- AN EXTRA TIME CELL IS NEEDED TO KEEP TRACK OF THE HOUR OF DAY
      COMMON THOUR
C- THE END OF THE TIME CELLS IS MARKED BY A COUNT OF THE NUMBER OF TIME
C- CELLS USED.
      COMMON ITIMCT
      ITIMCT = 106
C- THE TIME CELLS MUST BE REDEFINED INTO A SINGLE ARRAY FOR USE BY THE
C- TIME ADVANCE SUBROUTINE, AND CHECKED BY ITIMOK.
      DIMENSION ITIMES(106)
      EQUIVALENCE (ITIMES(1),ICLOCK)
      CALL ITIMOK(ITIMES,ITIMCT)
C- WE NEED 2 HISTOGRAMS FOR THE WAITING TIMES AT STACK AND HOLDING-POINT.
C- EDSIM HISTOGRAMS ARE DECLARED WITH 5 MORE CELLS THAN THERE ARE
C- VARIATE VALUES. LET US DECLARE HISTOGRAMS WITH 50 CELLS AT 60 SECOND
C- INTERVALS, THE FIRST CELL HAVING VARIATE VALUE ZERO.
```

```
      DIMENSION HSTACK(55),HHOLD(55)
      CALL DHIST(HSTACK,50,0,60)
      CALL DHIST(HHOLD,50,0,60)
C- WE MUST MAKE SURE THAT THE FRQUENCY COUNTS HAVE ZERO INITIAL VALUE.
      CALL CLEAR(HSTACK)
      CALL CLEAR(HHOLD)
C- WE ALSO NEED TABLES OF THE MEAN INTER-ARRIVAL TIMES AT THE STACK AND
C- HOLDING-POINT, INDEXED BY THE HOUR OF DAY. THE TABLES WILL BE READ IN
C- FROM CARDS SO WE CAN LATER RUN THE PROGRAM WITH SMALLER INTER-ARRIVAL
C- TIMES TO SIMULATE INCREASED NUMBERS OF ARRIVALS AND DEPARTURES.
C- ALL TIMES ARE IN SECONDS.
      DIMENSION MSTACK(12), MHOLD(12)
      READ (5,1000) (MSTACK(HOUR),HOUR=1,12)
      READ (5,1000) (MHOLD(HOUR),HOUR=1,12)
 1000 FORMAT(12I5)
      WRITE(6,1001)
 1001 FORMAT(1H ,14X,6HMSTACK,5X,5HMHOLD)
      DO 1002 HOUR=1,12
 1002 WRITE(6,1003) HOUR,MSTACK(HOUR),MHOLD(HOUR)
 1003 FORMAT(1H ,3I10)
C- STARTING VALUES ARE DECLARED FOR RANDOM NUMBER GENERATOR SEEDS.
      SEEDA = 1999
      SEEDB = 1979
      SEEDC = 1949
      SEEDD = 1889
C-       *
C-       * PROCEDURES OF THE MODEL
C-       *
C- STATEMENT NUMBERS CORRESPOND TO FLOWCHART BOX NUMBERS, FIG. 3.12,3.13
    1 DAY = 1
    2 CALL LOAD(PLANE,100,NULL)
      CALL ZERO(STACK)
      CALL ZERO(HOLD)
      CALL ZERO(INSERV)
      CALL ZERO(BUSY)
      CALL TIMCLR(ITIMES,ITIMCT)
    3 HOUR = 1
      TSTACK = 120+NEGEXP(MSTACK(HOUR)-120,SEEDA)
      THOLD = 60+NEGEXP(MHOLD(HOUR)-60,SEEDB)
C- THE FIRST HOUR ELAPSES AFTER 3600 SECONDS
      THOUR = 3600
C-       *
C-       * PROCEDURES FOR THE DAY
C-       *
  400 CALL TIMADV(ITIMES,ITIMCT)
C-
C- THE FIRST ACTIVITY UPDATES THE HOUR OF THE DAY EACH 3600 SECONDS.
C- IF AN HOUR HAS ELAPSED, THE TIMES TO THE FIRST ARRIVALS IN THE NEW
C- HOUR ARE DETERMINED.
      IF (THOUR .NE. 0) GO TO 402
      HOUR = HOUR + 1
C- TEST FOR END OF DAY
  401 IF (HOUR .GT. 12) GO TO 5
      THOUR = 3600
      TSTACK = 120+NEGEXP(MSTACK(HOUR)-120,SEEDA)
      THOLD = 60+NEGEXP(MHOLD(HOUR)-60,SEEDB)
```

```
C-
C- END OF SERVICE
   402 IF (TSERV .NE. 0) GO TO 405
   403 FS = FIRST(INSERV)
       CALL FROM(PLANE,FS,INSERV)
       CALL INTO(PLANE,FS,NULL)
   404 CALL FROM(RUNWAY,1,BUSY)
C-
C- ARRIVAL AT THE STACK
   405 IF (TSTACK .NE. 0) GO TO 408
   406 FN = FIRST(NULL)
       CALL FROM(PLANE,FN,NULL)
       CALL INTO(PLANE,FN,STACK)
       TPLANE(FN) = 0
   407 TSTACK = 120+NEGEXP(MSTACK(HOUR)-120,SEEDA)
C-
C- ARRIVAL AT THE HOLDING-POINT
   408 IF (THOLD .NE. 0) GO TO 411
   409 FN = FIRST(NULL)
       CALL FROM(PLANE,FN,NULL)
       CALL INTO(PLANE,FN,HOLD)
       TPLANE(FN) = 0
   410 THOLD = 60+NEGEXP(MHOLD(HOUR)-60,SEEDB)
C-
C- COMMENCE LANDING
   411 IF (IN(RUNWAY,1,BUSY)) GO TO 400
   412 FS = FIRST(STACK)
       IF (FS .EQ. 0) GO TO 418
   413 IF (TPLANE(FS) .LT. -900) GO TO 415
   414 FH = FIRST(HOLD)
       IF (FH .NE. 0 .AND. TPLANE(FH) .LT. TPLANE(FS)) GO TO 419
   415 CALL FROM(PLANE,FS,STACK)
       CALL INTO(PLANE,FS,INSERV)
   416 CALL TALLY(HSTACK,-TPLANE(FS))
   417 TSERV = NORMAL(180,30,SEEDC)
       GO TO 422
C-
C- COMMENCE TAKE-OFF
   418 FH = FIRST(HOLD)
       IF (FH .EQ. 0) GO TO 400
   419 CALL FROM(PLANE,FH,HOLD)
       CALL INTO(PLANE,FH,INSERV)
   420 CALL TALLY(HHOLD,-TPLANE(FH))
   421 TSERV = NORMAL(120,15,SEEDD)
   422 CALL INTO(RUNWAY,1,BUSY)
       GO TO 400
C-
C- TEST FOR END OF SIMULATION
     5 IF (DAY .EQ. 20) GO TO 7
     6 DAY = DAY + 1
       GO TO 2
     7 CALL PRHIST(HSTACK,10HFREQUENCY.,23HWAITING TIMES IN STACK.)
       CALL PRHIST(HHOLD,10HFREQUENCY.,28HWAITING TIMES AT HOLD POINT.)
       STOP
       END
```

Discussion questions

1. A bank has six teller windows which are open for business all day except when the tellers go to lunch. Customers queue at each window for service, which means that a later-arriving customer quite often gets served ahead of the others if he happens to be lucky in his choice of queue (much to the annoyance of other customers).
   The bank is considering converting to the 'queue-and-call' system in which customers form a single queue, the customer at the head of the queue being called to a free window by a teller. However, the bank wishes to do this only if it will give a substantial reduction in the number of long waits suffered by customers. How could the effect of the proposed system be established?
2. Consider a busy traffic intersection you are familiar with. Would a roundabout there improve traffic flow? (Or consider a roundabout, mutatis mutandis).
3. A new town is to be built below a reservoir, which will supply the town with water. How could you establish what capacity the reservoir should have?
   The maximum rate of discharge of water from the sluices is less than the maximum rate of inflow from the supplying river system. It will be most undesirable to have the reservoir overflow. At what point should the sluices be opened?
4. Suppose you played the game of 'Monopoly' with one of two strategies:
   (a) buying a property at every opportunity, until your cash is exhausted,
   (b) buying three properties in different sets at the first opportunity and preserving your cash to buy other properties in those sets at the first opportunity.
   If you were to play in a group of four, two of the others always using strategy (a) and one always using strategy (b), how could you determine what your best strategy would be (assuming there was no trading of properties)?
   If we assume that two players who each hold the single missing property of the other's set will agree to trade on the basis of exchanging the properties and making a cash adjustment equivalent to the difference in face values, would this affect your choice of strategy?
   Suppose you could formulate a hypothesis about the actual strategies of people you play with regularly. How could you test this hypothesis?
5. Consider the informal communication channels of any of the groups of which you are a member. What happens when one member of the group recieves a piece of gossip which will be of great interest to all the members? Could you predict how long it would be before all members of the group knew the news?
6. At what point does a computer model become a game?

4 Experiments with Computer Models

The results of running the model of the existing traffic at Erewhon airport, described in the last chapter, were as shown in Figs. 4.1 and 4.2.

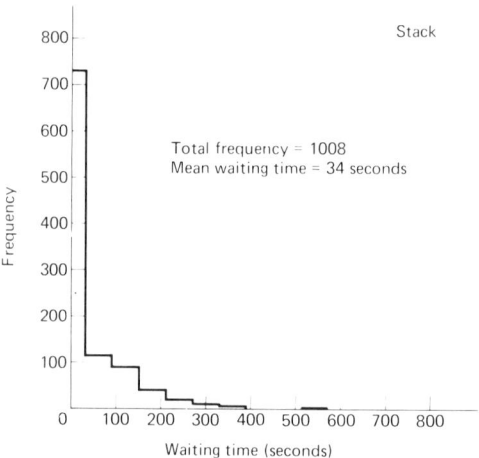

Fig. 4.1: Results of running the program with the present traffic: distribution of waiting times at the stack

It may occur to you that the next step is to establish that the results of our model correspond to the real situation. What will it prove if they do? One thing it *won't* prove is that our model is right. The only thing such a correspondence can prove is that our model *could* be right. If we fail to find any correspondence between the outcomes of the model and those of the real world, we can be sure the model was wrong in at least one important particular. On the other hand, correspondence between the model and reality might be fortuitous, or caused by some compensating errors, and the model might go seriously wrong when used with some new parameters to try to predict the future.

Although testing the results of the model is an essential step in validation, it is more important to establish that the *structure* of this model corresponds to reality, or at least does not deviate from reality in a particular that is important for the purpose in hand. With some types of model, e.g. corporate business models based on established rules of accounting procedure, this task is comparatively easy because all the rules are known (i.e. all the rules of such a corporate model can be established because they have been *defined* by accountants) - in such a case, validation boils down to establishing that each rule is being correctly followed. But

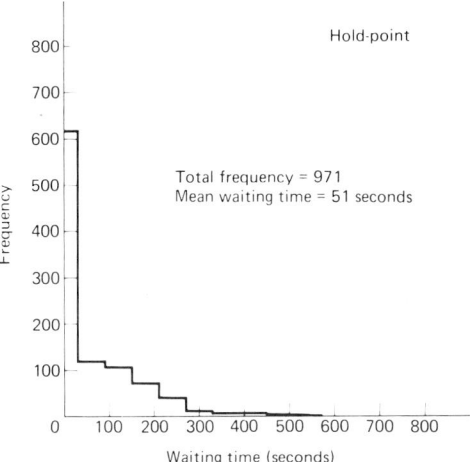

Fig. 4.2: Results of running the program with the existing traffic: distribution of waiting times at the holding point

what about Erewhon airport - can we be sure we have all the rules right?

The short answer is that we cannot. What happens at Erewhon airport is an *open* system - it is open to influences from the environment which are more or less unpredictable. It is not a bit like the *closed* accounting system, where all the rules are established by definition. The most we will be able to do is satisfy ourselves that the Erewhon airport model is plausible and that its structure corresponds to reality in all the significant features we have been able to conjecture. If, by mistake, we have left out some feature which, although it does not cause our model of the present situation to go wrong, will cause our predictions of the future to be inaccurate - well, that is a cross we shall have to bear. In other words, when we predict the future we shall have to say '*if* our model is right, *then* so-and-so' and we shall have to temper our confidence in the model's predictions with our confidence in its realism.

This discussion leads us to propose the following steps in the validation of our model.

1. Establish that the distributions from which we drew samples in the model are consistent with what we observe in the real world.
2. Establish that the procedures we defined for the model correspond to what we observe as the most important procedures in the real world.
3. Establish that the procedures in the computer program we wrote correspond to the procedures we defined on the basis of our observations.
4. Establish that the results of the program are consistent with the results we observe in the real world.
5. Establish that changes in the assumptions of the model, e.g. fewer aircraft arriving or departing, cause changes to the results in the direction indicated by common sense, i.e. fewer long waits.
6. Establish the sensitivity of the model to those features in the real world which we did not originally consider important enough to warrant inclusion.

You will appreciate that steps 1 and 4 require detailed observations of inter-arrival times, service times and waiting times at Erewhon airport. We

52 Computer Models

previously dismissed observation of the service times (i.e. the times taken in taking off or landing) as 'exercise of our stop-watch'. The implication that this is a straightforward and facile business was quite wrong (our excuse is that we did not want to digress from the matters then being developed); in fact, it is our experience that it is in the act of 'exercising the stop-watch' - making detailed observations - that modellers often make their mistakes.

Making observations

Perhaps the reason why mistakes are often made is that inadequate preparation and thought is given to the matter beforehand, i.e. no detailed plan of exactly what is required, and how it is going to be achieved, is made before going into the field. At worst, poor planning may lead to errors in the model; at best, it may mean return trips to the field to get things right. Since making the observations is time-consuming and, often, a very expensive part of model-building, return trips to the field are something to be avoided if possible.

This is why we have left discussion of observation to this late stage. Obviously observation played a part in the construction of our model in Chapter 3, and you might be thinking that we should have covered the subject there - but the point we wish to emphasize is that an adequate plan for making detailed observations cannot generally be worked out until the structure of the model has also been defined in some detail. If you jump in too quickly with your stop-watch, you may end up with a set of useless figures which do not correspond exactly to your model.

For example, suppose we had gone down to Erewhon airport to measure take-off times by standing at the edge of the runway and starting our stop-watch at the moment a holding aircraft started to roll, stopping it when we judged the aircraft to be clear of the runway. Would that have corresponded to our model? Broadly, yes - but in detail, no. The time we are interested in is the time during which the runway is made 'busy' by a take-off, denying service to other aircraft wishing to take off or land. From the point of view of our model, this is a question not so much of the activity of an aircraft (is it rolling or not?) as of the rules which the traffic controller follows (has he given permission to take off?). The traffic controller will not deliberately give permission to a second aircraft to take off or land if he has already granted permission to a first, even if the first is still stationary at the hold point, perhaps delayed making final checks. The runway is busy in this precise sense from the moment the controller grants permission to take off until *he* judges that the aircraft is clear and that he can assign the runway to another activity. Far from taking our stop-watch to the edge of the runway, this analysis is telling us we should take it to the control tower and obtain the co-operation of the traffic controller in observing what *he* does. This conclusion brings new problems, for the knowledge that he is observed may affect the controller's normal behaviour (for better or worse) and bias the observations - we should be prepared at least to discard our initial observations and use only those made after the controller has settled down to our presence.

Applying a similar analysis to the other features of interest, we can draw up a schedule of the things we wish to observe:
1. Take-off time. From: granting of permission to take off. To: controller declaring take-off complete.
2. Landing time. From: granting of permission to land. To: controller declaring landing complete.

3. Inter-arrival time at the hold point. From: aircraft arriving at hold point requesting permission to take off. To: next aircraft requesting permission to take off.
4. Inter-arrival time at stack. From: aircraft announcing arrival at stack and requesting permission to land. To: next aircraft requesting permission to land.
5. Waiting time at holding point. From: request for permission to take off. To: granting of permission to take off.
6. Waiting time in stack. From: request for permission to land. To: granting of permission to land.

These definitions of what we want to observe represent a tight logical structure of clearly observable events. Now we can plan our trip to the field.

Can we go single-handed? How are we going to keep a record of the events and log the times? If we need more than one observer, how will we assign the work? Questions like these need to be worked out *before* arriving in the field.

In the case of Erewhon airport, it *might* be possible to manage with one observer - after all, the traffic controller has to manage on his own. But he does not have to write down all the times and we do not have anything like as much experience of the procedures as he has. We have six different events to keep track of and, during a busy period, we are quite likely to get confused and make mistakes in the heat of the moment. If we had two observers, we could arrange a roughly equal division of work if one timed landing aircraft right through the system while the other timed departing aircraft. How exactly would we log observations on this basis?

Taking incoming aircraft as an example, we could rule off a sheet of paper into rows and columns as in Fig. 4.3:

Aircraft number	(a) Arrival at Stack	(b) Given permission to land	(c) Landing complete
1			
2			
3			
4			
5			
6			
7			

Fig. 4.3: A log for recording observations

The procedure the observer would follow is:
1. Aircraft requests permission to land - enter time (hour, minute, second - maximum of six digits - takes about six seconds to write) in the topmost blank box of column (a).
2. Aircraft given permission to land - enter time in topmost blank box of column (b).
3. Controller declares landing complete, or gives permission to land or take off when there is an entry in column (b) but no entry in column (c) of the same row - enter time in topmost blank box of column (c).

Successive inter-arrival times could later be established by deducting 1(a) from 2(a), 2(a) from 3(a), and so on. Waiting times are given by deducting (a) from (b) in a given row. Landing times are given by deducting (b) from (c) in a given row. The sheet could be mounted on a clip-board for ease of writing - there are proprietary clip-boards available complete with brackets for one or more stop-watches, leaving an extra hand free. If you know anyone who works in the fields of time-and-motion study, work study, method study or organisation and methods, he will probably be able to put you in touch with a source, as well as giving good advice on designing procedures for observation in these sorts of circumstances.

The method we have sketched out looks plausible enough and a very similar method could be used for departing aircraft. Will it work in practice? If we can help it, we do not want to arrive at the control tower only to find there is some 'bug' in our procedure which we had not expected. One way of combating this problem would be to make mock observations, one person calling out 'request to land', 'request to take off', 'permission to land' etc. in a realistic sequence while the observer follows the designed procedures and logs the times. Not only is this likely to demonstrate flaws in the observation procedure, it also has the advantage of training the observer, so he is less likely to suffer any initial confusion in the field. In some cases it is practicable to go into the field for a short period to make test observations whose only purpose is to get the bugs out of the observation procedure.

Another important question is 'when should we go, and how many observations should we make?' There is no general answer to the first part of the question, while the general answer to the second part - 'as many as you can' - is not very helpful. In practice the number of observations that can be made is usually limited by the time and money available for making them (or, in the case of events in the past, by what has been recorded). In our particular case, we can at least surmise that less than five observations of any time of interest will be useless and less than twenty or so will be somewhat suspect. If we can spend a whole day at the airport and collect about fifty observations, we shall be reasonably well off.

But wait - in the case of inter-arrival times, we have modelled these as samples from different distributions according to the time of day. If we wish to test our hypothesis for each distribution, we should aim to accumulate twenty or more observations in each hour of the day. In the case of the inactive hours, that might mean going to the airport on twenty different days.

Assuming we do not find this feasible, we shall have to compromise. Bearing in mind that we are interested only in congestion, we can surmise that the major causes of congestion are the arrivals and departures at the busiest time of day - what happens in the rest of the day probably makes little difference by comparison. Further, if we cannot find a feature which distinguishes the type of activity in one hour from that in another, it would seem fair to assume that, if the assumption behind our hypothetical distribution proves satisfactory for one hour, it is likely to be satisfactory for the others. So, if we are obliged to abandon testing our hypothesis for each hour, we may feel reasonably happy if we test only the busiest hours. From the airport statistics of the average number of departures and arrivals in each hour (see Figs. 3.3 and 3.4), it would seem that if we make observations between 8 a.m. and 11 a.m. on five different days, we will collect enough statistics for the busiest hours.

Which five days? Clearly they should be days in the busy season. If one day's activity is much like any other's, it will not matter which particular days we choose. If we have reason to suppose that a particular day of the week is regularly busier than the others, we should choose that day in five different weeks. No doubt the traffic controllers can advise us if such a regular weekly cycle occurs.

When we go to the airport, we must be on our guard against any freak circumstances which will make our observations atypical. If we arrive to find the airport in the hands of Ruritanian terrorists, all incoming flights diverted and no departures allowed, we might as well pack up and go home again. It is just our bad luck if something like this happens; we shall just have to return another day.

Lastly, but not least by a very long chalk, the observer should be on guard against the social implications of going into the real world with a stop-watch and clip-board. If he suddenly turns up to observe people at work, he may find himself the unwitting perpetrator of an industrial dispute! Apart from getting authority for the observation, he should take steps to alleviate any fears or misapprehensions that might arise in the minds of the people observed. Assuming the observer does not have an offensive or frightening personality, this is probably best achieved in the sort of case we have been talking about by a verbal presentation to the people concerned of the purpose of the observations, what statistics will be collected and to whom they will be made available if they are not going to remain the observer's secret.

Goodness-of-fit tests - input distributions

We want to establish how well the theoretical distributions we used in our program match the samples we have observed. The problem is sometimes expressed as 'could the observed samples have come from the theoretical distribution?', but this is not strictly the question. There is always some chance in a case like ours, albeit remote, that random samples from the theoretical distribution could give rise to the observed samples, even if the parent distribution in the real world were quite different from our theoretical one. Strictly speaking, the most we can hope to prove is a rather negative thing - that our observed samples are *unlikely* to have come from the theoretical distribution. If we succeed in proving this, we should discard our hypothesis about the theoretical distribution and look for an alternative hypothesis. If we cannot find an alternative, we are obliged to revise our model so that samples are drawn from the *observed* distribution, on the grounds that this is the best evidence we have. (This is what the Treasurer did in Chapter 2 - he did not make any hypothesis about how rainfall could be expected to occur, he just took his samples from the distribution of observations made by the weather bureau.)

Figure 4.4(a) shows a theoretical distribution expressed as a frequency histogram. Since it is a theoretical distribution, no vertical scale is marked; we are asserting that the frequencies shown are the relative frequencies we would expect if we made an infinite number of observations. The question we would like you to consider, subjectively, is this: suppose Figs 4.4(b), (c), (d) and (e) are histograms of 50 observations made in the real world - which of these do you consider are *unlikely* to have Fig. 4.4(a) as a parent distribution?

We think most people fairly quickly react that (c) and (d) are unlikely to have come from (a). Histogram (e) is a bit more equivocal. It is rather similar to (a) except right at the beginning. If we had just a few more observations in cell 0 of (e), we would have something very like (a); on the other hand, if we took many more samples from the distribution which gave rise to (e) and it still preserved the shape shown, we would be inclined to think that (e) did not derive from (a). If we cannot take any more samples, we have to try to judge the likelihood that 50 random samples drawn from (a) could *by chance* have produced the result recorded in (e) - we cannot say much more at this stage.

We think it is fairly clear that it is very difficult to reject histogram (b) as unlikely to have come from (a) - it is the same general shape apart from a slight kink at the right-hand end. These small differences are just

56 Computer Models

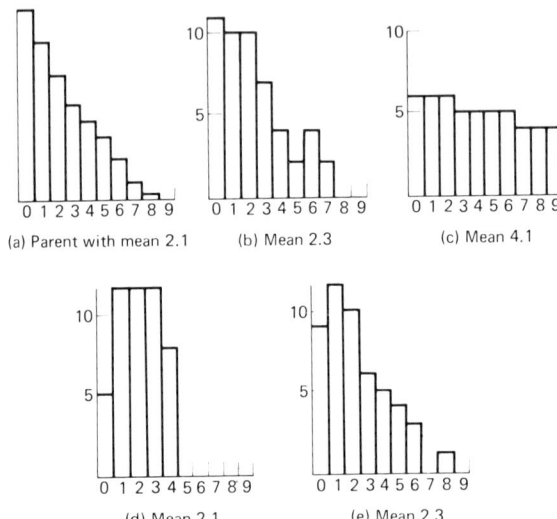

Fig. 4.4: Which of the observed distributions are unlikely to have distribution (a) as their parent?

the sort of thing we would expect from chance observations.
What led us to reject (c) and (d) so quickly? Well, (d) is clearly the wrong shape: the frequencies recorded in each cell are outrageously different from those we would expect from samples drawn at random from (a). Histogram (c) is not quite so outrageously different - in fact, it does have some similarities with (a), i.e. frequencies diminish from left to right - but there are far too many observations of large values, with the result that the mean of (c) is twice that of (a). Gross distortions such as these are fairly obvious to the eye, but how do we judge the more subtle case, such as (e)?

A statistical test, called the 'chi-square' test (pronounced *kye-square*, often written χ^2), comes to our aid. There is nothing magic about this test; all it does is what we have just done by visual inspection of the histograms, i.e. it measures the difference between the observed frequencies in the cells and the frequencies we would expect if the observations were samples from the theoretical distribution. The beauty of this test, from our point of view, is that it is very easily applied to distributions which have been expressed in terms of histograms, which is just the type of data we have.

Perhaps the best way to explain how the chi-square test is applied is by demonstration: let us apply it to something useful for our case study, e.g. to test whether our observed inter-arrival times at the stack during the busy hour 9 a.m. to 10 a.m. are inconsistent with the theoretical distribution we used in our model, 120 seconds (2 minutes) *plus* a negative exponential distribution with a mean of 330 seconds.

The observed results were as shown in Fig. 4.5. Our problem now is to find what frequencies could be expected from our theoretical distribution. If we were mathematicians, we could do this by integrating the negative exponential function between the limits of each cell (that is, finding the area under the theoretical curve, corresponding to the cell width). We are not mathematicians, so we will find a non-mathematical way by using our computer. We have already mentioned that we can get the machine to generate a sample from a negative exponential distribution. Assuming this function has been checked to work properly, why don't we just get it to generate a large number of samples from

Experiments with Computer Models 57

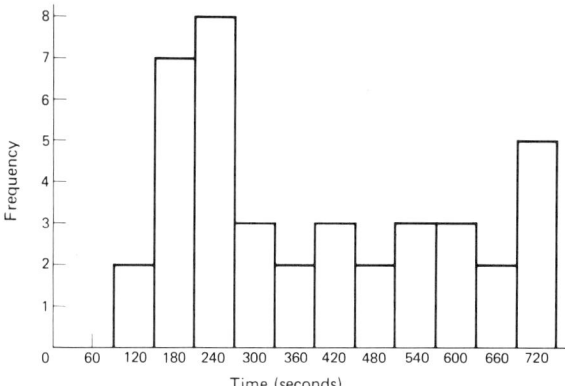

Fig. 4.5: *Observed inter-arrival times at the stack, 9-10 a.m.*
(total number of observations = 40)

our theoretical distribution and tally them? If we generate a large enough
number of samples - say, 1000 - the difference between what we generate and
what in theory should have been generated will be so small that we can ignore
it. The program to do the work is a tiny one:

```
      INTEGER SEED, TRIAL, HNGEXP(18)
      CALL DHIST(HNGEXP,13,0,60)
      SEED = 1999
      DO 10 ICOUNT = 1,1000
         TRIAL = 120 + NEGEXP(330,SEED)
   10    CALL TALLY(HNGEXP,TRIAL)
      CALL PRHIST(HNGEXP,10HFREQUENCY.,8HSECONDS.)
      STOP
      END
```

The results of this program are given in Fig. 4.6.

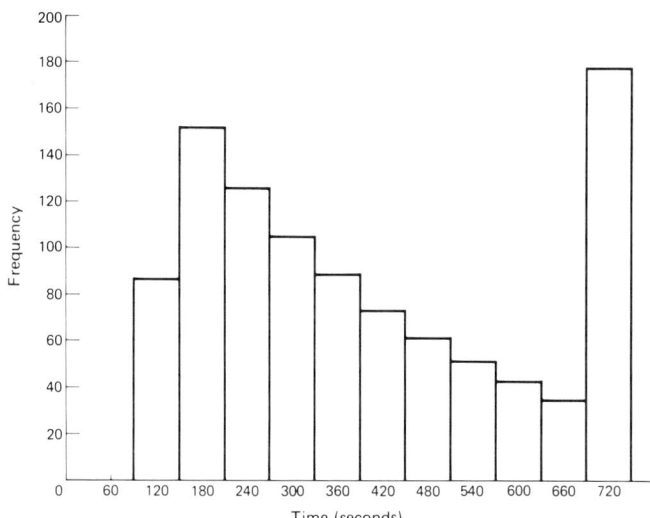

Fig. 4.6: *Computer-produced approximation to the theoretical distribution*
assumed for stack inter-arrival times 9-10 a.m. (total number of
'observations' = 1000; the last cell holds all times over 690 s)

58 Computer Models

The first step is to scale down the histogram of the theoretical frequencies so that the total number of 'observations' in it is the same as the number of genuine observations, i.e. 40. This is done by multiplying each cell in Fig. 4.6 by 40/100; the result is the histogram of frequencies we would expect if the observed frequencies exactly matched the theoretical distribution. Calling these expected frequencies E and the observed frequencies O, we have two sets of figures:

Cell	E	O
90-149	3.48	2
150-209	6.08	7
210-269	5.04	8
270-329	4.20	3
330-389	3.56	2
390-449	2.92	3
450-509	2.44	2
510-569	2.04	3
570-629	1.72	3
630-689	1.40	2
690 and over	7.12	5

The chi-square test is not suitable for small numbers and, as a general rule, we should not deal with any cells where the expected frequency is 5 or less. It will be seen we are breaking this rule in all but three of the cells. We can overcome this by regrouping our figures into wider cells where necessary, giving us only six cells with figures as follows:

Cell	E	O
90-209	9.56	9
210-269	5.04	8
270-389	7.76	5
390-509	5.36	5
510-689	5.16	8
690 and over	7.12	5

It does not matter that our cells now accumulate different breadths of values.

We can calculate the value of chi-square, which you will recall is just a measure of the difference between expected and observed cell contents, as the sum of $(E-O)^2/E$ for each cell, as follows:

Cell	E	O	E-O	$(E-O)^2$	$(E-O)^2/E$
90-209	9.56	9	0.56	0.31	0.03
210-269	5.04	8	-2.96	8.76	1.74
270-389	7.76	5	2.76	7.62	0.98
390-509	5.36	5	0.36	0.13	0.02
510-689	5.16	8	-2.84	8.07	1.56
690 and over	7.12	5	2.12	4.49	0.63
	40	40		chi-square =	4.96

The bigger the value of chi-square, the more the difference between the two distributions. Apart from this, though, chi-square may strike you as a rather meaningless number. Before we can understand whether the value we have calculated for chi-square represents a *significant* difference in the distributions, we must appreciate the statistical concept of *degrees of freedom*.

It may have struck you that when we merged the cells with small frequencies, to make wider cells, we reduced the information we had about the shape of the distributions. It will perhaps not surprise you that we have to pay a penalty for this. In the statistician's jargon, we have reduced the degrees of freedom and we will not be able to make statements about differences in the distributions with the same confidence as we might have done if we had more degrees of freedom. A degree of freedom in this context is the number of cells into which observations may go when we know the total number of observations.

An extreme example will help us to explore this concept. Suppose we were to regroup our expected frequencies into only *one* cell (with a count of 40 in it) - we would have lost *all* the information about the shape of the distribution. This case could be said to have no degrees of freedom, because there is no freedom about which cell observations can be counted into.

Suppose instead we regrouped the frequencies into two cells, one taking values in the range 90-269, the other 270 or more. The histograms would appear as shown in Fig. 4.7.

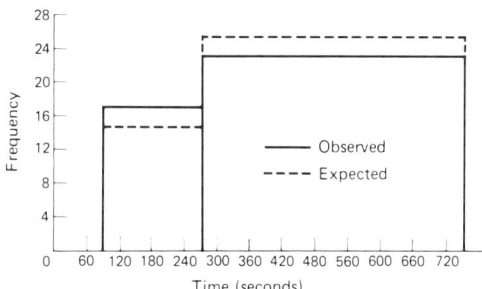

Fig. 4.7: The expected and observed stack inter-arrival times as two-cell histograms would give only one degree of freedom

This time, the statistician would say we have one degree of freedom - when we know the contents of one cell, the content of the other one is predetermined because we know the total number of observations. We have a little bit more information about the shape of the two distributions, but not much: the two distributions could still be very dissimilar, despite the similarity of their histograms on this basis. Consider Fig. 4.8, which shows two histograms which are outrageously different but which, if revised as histograms of two cells 0-3 and 3-6, would lead to identical frequencies in the cells (and a chi-square value of zero).

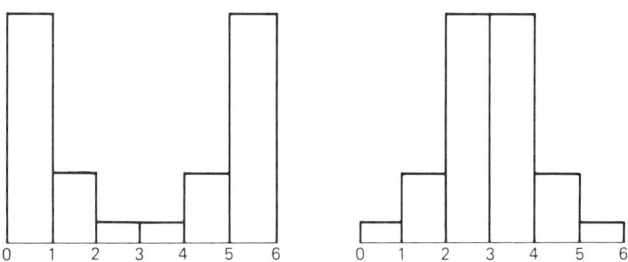

Fig. 4.8: These two distributions are obviously dissimilar but would look identical in histograms with two cells 0-3 and 3-6

60 Computer Models

With only one degree of freedom, chi-square does not tell us very much. On the other hand, if we partitioned the distribution of Fig. 4.8 into three cells of 0-2, 2-4 and 4-6, radically different histograms would result and chi-square would take a very large value. This time we would have two degrees of freedom - when the contents of two cells are known, we can deduce the contents of the third if we know the total number of observations. The point of these examples is that the significance of the value of chi-square is dictated by the number of degrees of freedom. The number of degrees of freedom in cases like ours is one less than the number of cells used for the chi-square calculation. Figure 4.9 shows graphically the relationships between the value of chi-square, the number of degrees of freedom and the probabilities that a given chi-square value could have arisen by chance variations in the observations.

Returning from this long detour to our problem, the chi-square of the observed inter-arrival times against those predicted by our theoretical distribution was 4.96 and, since we calculated this value with six cells, we have five degrees of freedom. We can now look up on our graph (Fig. 4.9) the point represented by a chi-square of 4.96 and five degrees of freedom. We see this lies well within the two curves marked '10% level' and '90% level'. This means we can breath a sigh of relief - if the observed times did come from our theoretical distribution, then the differences between the expected and observed frequencies are easily accounted for by chance variations. Note that this is not the same as saying that our theoretical distribution is the right one - there are many theoretical distributions that could have given rise to the same value of chi-square - what it means is that we have no reason to exclude our theoretical distribution and we can expect it to perform satisfactorily in our model.

It would be a different kettle of fish if the chi-square value we calculated had been much larger, say 15. Looking up a chi-square of 15 on the graph (still with five degrees of freedom) we see it lies about on the line marked '1% level'. This means there would be only 1 chance in 100 that our observed frequencies could have come from the theoretical distribution. This would be very hard to swallow and we ought to think again about our original hypothesis. If we couldn't find another one, we would be obliged to sample directly from the histogram of observations.

If the chi-square value had been a little less, say 11, it would lie about on the line marked '5% level'. This would also be fairly suspicious and our hypothesis would be in doubt. If we were not prepared to reject it, we should at least make some more observations and repeat the test.

A chi-square lying on the '10% level' line would mean there would be 1 chance in 10 that our observed frequencies could have come from the theoretical distribution. It is at this level that we do not have quite enough evidence to warrant rejection of the hypothesis. We have put this line in as a sort of warning, just to ring a small note of alarm; if the chi-square lies between the 10% and 5% levels and we wish to accept the hypothesis, we are doing so at some risk and we ought to consider whether or not this risk is acceptable, bearing in mind the purpose of the model.

Similar considerations apply to the lines marked '90% level', '95% level', etc. These lines are marking the points at which the observed frequencies are matching the expected frequencies *too well*, i.e. the chi-square test has not found the chance variations one would expect. To make this idea clear, suppose you tossed ten coins - you would expect half to come up heads and half tails, so you would not be all that surprised if that was the result you got. But suppose you repeated the experiment twenty times and each time you got exactly five heads and five tails: that would be almost too good to be true - although you expect half heads and half tails, you do not expect your

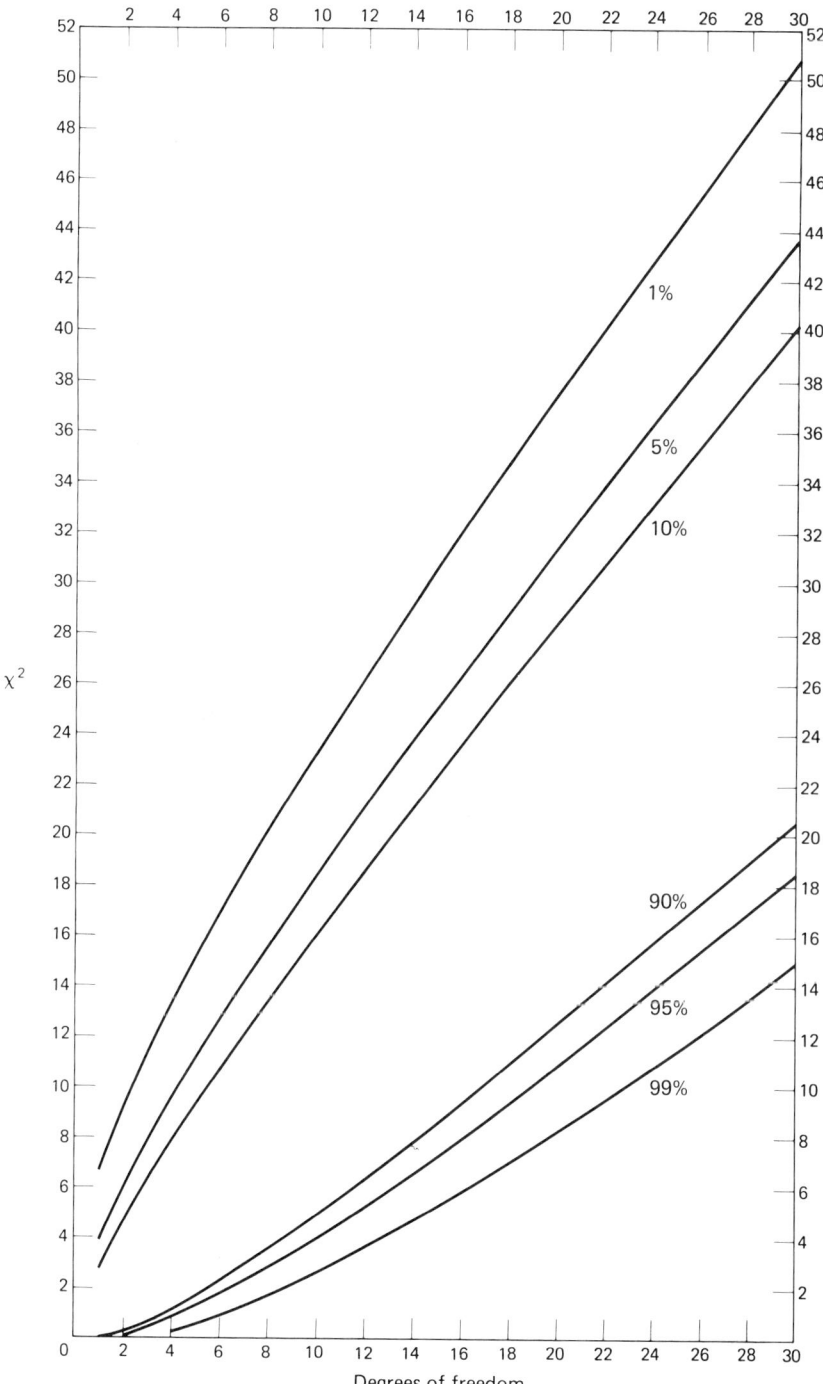

Fig. 4.9: Showing the probabilities that chi-square values with the stated degrees of freedom could have arisen by chance variations in the observations made

expectations to come up every time! In other words, these lines are telling you that, because they are too close to the expected values, something other than chance has probably played a hand in your observations. Perhaps the observer has accidentally or deliberately biased his observations to fit the theoretical distribution.

You may like to try doing a chi-square test for yourself. Here are the figures for the observed landing times and the (unscaled) figures for a normal distribution with mean 180 seconds and standard deviation 30 seconds.

Cells	Theoretical (1000 observations)	Observed (50 observations)
60-89 s	1	0
90-119	22	1
120-149	136	8
150-179	341	21
180-209	341	15
210-239	136	3
240-269	22	2
270 and over	1	0

We make the chi-square value 2.4 with three degrees of freedom, suggesting that we can regard the theoretical distribution as adequate for our model.

Testing the hold point inter-arrival times and take-off times follows the same method. Let us continue on the basis that these tests have been made and we have no reason to be suspicious of our theoretical distributions.

You may be wondering why we bothered to hypothesise the theoretical distribution in the first place - i.e. if we can get the computer to sample directly from a histogram of observations, why don't we just do that and skip all this testing? After all, the Treasurer got away with it in Chapter 2.

There are two reasons for wanting a theoretical distribution - one good, one bad. The good reason is that the observations are just a sample of their parent distribution and, by the heads-and-tails argument earlier, it is likely that they do not exactly match the parent. Sampling from the observed distribution amounts to the assumption that the parent distribution is exactly the same, yet the laws of chance tell us that it is very unlikely that a set of observations of the type we have been talking about will exactly match their parent distribution. So the one thing we can be fairly sure of is that an assumption that the parent is the same as the observed distribution will be wrong. We have no way of knowing in which direction it will be wrong (although we can say that the more observations we make, the closer they are likely to come to the parent distribution). For this reason, unless we have a very large number of observations (e.g. 1000), we prefer to try to find reasons why events occur as they do and formulate a hypothesis about the nature of the parent distribution. If we can find good reasons, we may have more confidence in our theoretical distribution than in an assumed distribution based on the observations - if you like, we believe we are 'correcting' the observations for the chance variations in them. If we cannot postulate the reason why things occur as they do, we have no way of knowing what corrections to apply, so we are forced in that case to use the uncorrected observations. The moral is that we sample from the observations as a last resort and, if we are obliged to do it, then we collect as many observations as we can.

The bad reason for wanting a theoretical distribution is that the computer can take samples from it by a mathematical method that is very fast. To take a sample from an observed distribution is much slower, perhaps increasing the computer time needed by a factor of 2 to 10. This doesn't matter much, perhaps, with models where running times are a few seconds, but with models

Experiments with Computer Models 63

involving extensive trials where running times are measured in minutes or even hours it can be an overriding practical consideration.

Testing the logic of the model

In effect we started to test the logic of the model at the end of the last chapter, when we were illustrating how the model could be worked by hand. The basic idea is to trace through the defined procedures to make sure at each point that the model behaves in the way we think the real world behaves or, at any rate, does not depart from it in a way that is likely to affect our purpose. The modeller has to try to conjecture all the possible circumstances and combinations of circumstances and make sure by inspection of his procedures that such cases are handled in the desired way. In practice, it is impossible to inspect every such case, so we try to imagine cases which we believe will test the structure of the model we have built at crucial points. Thus, we might run through the procedures for the following cases:

an aircraft arrives and lands when no aircraft is waiting to take off;
an aircraft departs and takes off when no aircraft is waiting to land;
an aircraft arrives at the hold point while another is landing;
an aircraft arrives at the hold point while another is taking off;
an aircraft arrives at the stack while another is taking off;
an aircraft arrives at the stack while another is landing;
aircraft simultaneously arrive at the stack and the hold point;
a take-off is completed simultaneously with an arrival at the stack;
a landing is completed simultaneously with an arrival at the stack;
a take-off is completed simultaneously with an arrival at the hold point;
a landing is completed simultaneously with an arrival at the hold point;
an aircraft arrives at the hold point at the exact moment the aircraft at the head of the stack has been waiting 15 minutes.

One thing we noticed when doing this for our model is that, if two aircraft simultaneously ask for permission to land and take off, the landing aircraft will always take priority. This means that our stack waiting times might be slightly optimistically biased, while our holding times might have a slight pessimistic bias. If we run our model again with exactly the same assumptions except for reversal of these activities, so that an aircraft waiting to take off gets priority in this simultaneous case, we will be able to judge from the difference in results whether or not this bias has much effect. (We have, and it hasn't).

During this mental inspection of the consituent parts of the model, we will probably have further ideas for events which might occur, based on our understanding of the real-world situation, but which are perhaps too unlikely obviously to demand inclusion in the model. What if a plane crashes during landing or take-off, blocking the runway? What if a landing aircraft 'overshoots' (i.e. the pilot aborts his landing at the last moment, having to circle and make another attempt)? What if an aircraft at the holding point develops an engine fault and has to return? We make a note of all such exceptional cases, so that we may consider them later.

A particular point to look for in this inspection is the *initial conditions*. In our case, the initial conditions look all right - all the aircraft start off in the null state at the beginning of the day, which seems to be proper since no activity is in progress until the airport opens.

Suppose, though, we were just modelling the activity during the hours 10 a.m. to 11 a.m. - our initial conditions would be quite wrong. At

64 Computer Models

10 a.m. there might be aircraft all over the place, waiting at the stack or taking-off or landing. It could bias our results if we started this version of the model with all the aircraft neatly stacked away in the null state. If we know what the initial conditions should be, we should set them up before simulation of the activities begins. If we do not know what the initial conditions should be, we should try to arrange a plausible initial condition. One method would be to run the revised model to simulate, say, an hour and a half instead of one hour, but introduce a new procedure which at the end of the first half hour discards the results accumulated up to that point (i.e. makes zero the frequency cells of the histograms of waiting times). The results we would accumulate from that point on would represent a one-hour period, as required, with initial conditions which were established by the first half hour. The idea behind doing this is to get rid of most of any bias that might have been introduced by the original assumptions.

Checking the computer program

A visual check of the statements in the program is essential, but not adequate (as every programmer knows) because programmers make mistakes when mentally following through the logic of their programs. The problem seems to be a psychological one: because the programmer knows what he wants to happen, he somehow manages to read his desires into the program even when a blatant error is staring him in the face. For example, psychologists have noticed that many people glancing at the following poster:

```
PARIS IN THE
THE SPRING
```

will read it as 'PARIS IN THE SPRING' as their expectations have led them into error.

The computer, of course, will follow the procedures ruthlessly, mistakes and all. We can use this fact to get the computer to tell us what it is doing, step by step, by putting in some extra instructions which will print out times, entities in each set, and counts in histograms at important points. This computer-produced output, which aims to produce the same sort of information as we used to run the model by hand at the end of chapter 3, can then be checked through to make sure that the program is acting in the desired way. We will not usually be able to check all this output, but we should aim to keep checking until we are satisfied that each aspect of the program has been used and works correctly.

Sometimes it is possible to get so bogged down in detail that one forgets the big things. It can pay to stand back from the program and look at its output in a purely common-sense way. Is the output roughly what we expected? When we ran our first attempt to model Erewhon airport we found that we ended up with 140 entries in the waiting-in-stack histogram and 666 in the waiting-at-holding-point histogram. Common sense told us that if we had about 50 arrivals and 50 departures per day, and if we modelled 20 days, we ought to have about 1000 entries in each. We pretty soon found a blatant error which was causing the queer result. (Yes, we are human. If you liked that one, how about this: on our first run of the model in Chapter 7 we managed to put 53 people into operating theatres and take 64 out. Hey presto !)

We have mentioned before that a major difficulty in testing stochastic models is that the 'right answer' is not known. The approach to overcoming this problem is to ensure that the constituent stochastic parts are working as expected. The most fundamental of these parts is the random-number generator, which is used for taking samples from distributions.

It is possible to make a device which will generate random numbers, i.e. numbers which are quite unpredictable in the sense that no rule can be found which will tell what the next number in the series will be. Such a device is not much use to us, because we want to be able to retain control over our model. For example, you may recall (page 63) that we wanted to investigate possible bias in our model by repeating the trials under identical conditions except for the reversal of the sequence of two activities. Only if we were certain that the same random numbers were used for sampling in the two versions of the model could we definitely ascribe any difference in results to the change in procedure. If we used truly random numbers, we would expect some difference in result anyway, through chance variations in the numbers generated, and we would have no quick way of separating out this chance difference from the difference (if any) caused by the change in the model.

So what we want are *repeatable* sequences of numbers, in large quantities, which otherwise have the same characteristics as random numbers. Most computer manufacturers supply a software function called a pseudo-random-number generator, which is designed to do this job. You might think that, because the computer manufacturer will have tested this function, you could accept it as adequate for your models. If that were the case, we would leave the subject here and move on to pastures new - but life isn't that simple.

Once, testing a pseudo-random-number generator supplied by a particular computer manufacturer, we decided it would be interesting to plot points on a graphic display (like a television screen), using successive pseudo-random numbers from the generator to determine the co-ordinates of successive points plotted. If the numbers were truly random, we would expect points to appear on the screen in no particular pattern or place and (since each plotted point remains visible) that the screen would reasonable evenly 'silt up' with points. What actually happened was this: the points appeared in no discernable pattern at first, but the places where they appeared could be joined by straight lines. At the end of the experiment, all we had was seven slanting lines on the screen. Furthermore, after a few seconds from the start of the experiment (during which time some thousands of points had been plotted) it became obvious, watching the flickering points of light on the screen, that a regular flicker pattern had emerged, which meant that the pseudo-random-number generator had deteriorated into producing a small cycle of the same numbers over and over again.

It is not our intention to go into the theory of pseudo-random-number generation, but the following example will show the general idea. Suppose we want to generate pseudo-random integers in the range 0 to 9. We start by supplying an arbitrary number (called the *seed*) and multiply this by a constant, say 13. So

$$17 \times 13 = 221 \rightarrow 2$$

We will always take the second digit from the right in the result as our 'random' number, so this first attempt has produced a 2. We now use the first result as the seed for our next attempt, dropping everything except the right two digits, and so on, producing a stream of pseudo-random numbers as follows:

Seed	x	Constant	=	Result	→	Pseudo-random number
17		13		221		2
21				273		7
73				949		4
49				637		3

66 Computer Models

Seed	x Constant =	Result	→	Pseudo-random number
37		481		8
81		1053		5
53		689		8
89		1157		5
57		741		4
41		533		3
33		429		2
29		377		7
77		1001		0
01		13		1
13		169		6
69		897		9
97		1261		6
61		793		9
93		1209		0
09		117		1

This method doesn't look too bad at first sight. If you care to check, you will find that each number has been generated twice - and we certainly want a generator which will produce equal frequencies of each number in the long run. But, in fact, it is a very bad method, because it has deteriorated very quickly (we chose it so we could illustrate this concept). If you consider the next seed due to be used, 17, you will see it is the same as the first seed. In other words, this generator deteriorates after 20 numbers - it will go on producing the same sequence of numbers over and over again. If you care to try it for yourself with an initial seed of 5, you will see it deteriorates even more quickly. It would be very dangerous to use this generator in our model: if this sequence happened to produce a particular outcome then using it over and over again would distort the frequency of occurrence of that outcome.

A lot of work has been done to find ways of postponing this deterioration, through the use of more sophisticated constant multipliers, addition of constants, shifting of digits and so on (some of the mathematical problems arising from this search are very taxing and even expert mathematicians have fallen into error in analysing them). As our example shows, deterioration can also be postponed by a good choice of initial seed. Large prime numbers seem to be good choices generally, but deterioration will set in ultimately and, for this reason, it is unwise to rely upon any particular seed to produce a stream of more than, say, two or three thousand numbers from a supplied pseudo-random generator. Furthermore, as our experiment with the graphic display demonstrates, there *is* a relationship between successive pseudo-random numbers in a stream, and this relationship might upset the model. We would have had a better result from our experiment if we had plotted points by drawing vertical co-ordinates from one stream and horizontal co-ordinates from another stream; the moral is to ensure that each sampling activity in a model is provided with its own stream of random numbers (see, for example, our program on page 47 where the samples from theoretical distributions are drawn using different seeds, each of which was initially set to a high prime number).

Testing pseudo-random-number generators is not easy. An obvious method is to make a chi-square test by writing a small program to produce say, 500 pseudo-random numbers from the generator in the range 1 to 100 and tally them in a histogram of, say, 10 cells of equal width. The observed frequencies for the chi-square test are the results so accumulated; the expected frequencies for a random distribution are equal observations in each cell, i.e. 50 in each. This experiment should be repeated for each seed which is to be used in programs, so the modeller can build up a list of trustworthy seeds. (There is a reason why we suggest producing only 500 numbers for the chi-square test, and not some much larger number. For a given seed, you can usually be sure that the first few numbers generated will be used in a program; probably the first few hundred, but rarely a much larger number. If the generator starts off with some bias but eventually comes good then, if we take a very large stream for the chi-square test, the original bias will be swamped and will not show up. Since we will probably be using only the early part of the stream, it is that part which should be tested - it is no consolation that the later numbers in the stream will tend to correct the bias if we are not in fact going to use them.)

Unfortunately, chi-square will not tell us about any *pattern* in the numbers which could cause bias. Patterns are very difficult to detect, especially when they have a long cycle. The method we outlined earlier using a graphic display is probably as good as any for long cycles, since the human visual apparatus seems to be rather good at detecting such patterns. On the other hand, not everybody has this type of equipment at their disposal; but alternative methods of pattern analysis are an extremely long business and in practice are usually limited to testing for short cycles only. e.g. by a chi-square test on the distribution produced by every second number in the stream, every third number, every fourth, and so on.

The uncertainty surrounding pseudo-random-number generators leads us to make the following recommendations.

1. Use only tested seeds.
2. Use a different seed for each sampling function. (This is desirable anyway from the point of view of experimental design: if functions share the same seed, then experimentally changing the order of execution of the activities may mean an implicit change in the stream of samples used by a function, confounding the experiment.)
3. Try to avoid taking more than a thousand numbers or so from a given stream (alternatively, conduct tests of the continued 'randomness' of longer streams).
4. Repeat each experiment using different seeds. The results of the experiments can be added together; so, if you wanted to conduct 2000 trials of a situation, you could have more confidence in the summed results of four experiments of 500 trials, using different seeds for each experiment, than in one experiment of 2000 trials. (This assumes you have no bias caused by initial conditions.)

One final note of caution. Testing the pseudo-random-number generator only lets you have more confidence that it was not a source of bias in your model. The best pseudo-random-number generator in the world cannot make a poor model good.

Goodness-of-fit tests - results

Our problem in testing the results, the distributions of stack and hold point waiting times (Figs 4.1 and 4.2), is not quite the same as in testing our assumptions, where we were comparing sample observations with our theoretical distribution. With the results, we have what amounts to two sets of observations - one set which was really observed at the airport and another set which was 'observed' by the model. What we seek to find is: is it unlikely that these two sets of observations share the same parent distribution?

We can use the same notion as we used earlier, where we had a set of observations from the real world and another set of 'observations' taken from the theoretical distribution. Because we had a large number (1000) of observations from the theoretical distribution, we said we would take this as a sufficiently good approximation to the expected observations to enable us to apply the chi-square test. Since we have about 1000 observations in the results of our model we can do something similar, namely, we can say that our results are likely to be a good approximation to the theoretical distribution of results from the model, i.e. if we ran it for an infinite number of trials, and we can apply the test as before.

What if the number of observations from our model had been much less than 1000 and we no longer felt we could regard them as a sufficiently good approximation to the theoretical distribution? This type of problem is referred to by statisticians as 'two-sample' testing.

We can make a quite good judgement, without breaking new ground, by a 'two-sample chi-square test'. The rationale behind this test is as follows. The two sets of observations are added together to make a best approximation to the hypothetical parent distribution. This parent is then scaled down in the usual way so that it has the same number of observations as the total in each sample, giving the expected frequencies, E_1 and E_2, corresponding to the two samples. Let us call one sample O_1 and the other O_2. We now calculate chi-squares for both O_1 and O_2 in the usual way and *add* them together to give a total chi-square which is now a measure of the combined variances in the samples from the hypothetical parent distribution.

To illustrate the procedure, let us apply it to the waiting times at the stack.

Cell	Airport observations O_1	Model observations O_2	Total observations $O_1 + O_2$	Airport expected E_1	Model expected E_2
0-29	36	732	768	36.30	731.70
30-89	9	117	126	5.95	120.05
90-149	4	84	88	4.16	83.84
150-209	0	37	37	1.75	35.25
210-269	1	23	24	1.13	22.87
270-329	0	9	9	0.42	8.58
330-389	0	5	5	0.24	4.76
390-449	0	0	0	0.00	0.00
450-509	0	0	0	0.00	0.00
510-569	0	1	1	0.05	0.95
570 and over	0	0	0	0.00	0.00
Totals	50	1008	1058	50.00	1008.00

After merging cells with small E, we can carry out calculations as follows:

Cell	O_1	O_2	E_1	E_2	$(O_1-E_1)^2/E_1$	$(O_2-E_2)^2/E_2$	Total χ^2
0-29	36	732	36.30	731.70	0.00	0.00	0.00
30-89	9	117	5.95	120.05	1.56	0.08	1.64
90 and over	5	159	7.75	156.25	0.98	0.05	1.03
							2.67

Bearing in mind that the contents of E_1 and E_2 are calculated from the contents of O_1 and O_2 (or, if you prefer, the contents of O_2 - the extra set of observations - are dictated by the contents of O_1, E_1 and E_2), we have no more degrees of freedom than we had in the one-sample case. Practically the same value of chi-square would be obtained in the one-sample approximation, which illustrates that our previous simplified approach was, indeed, adequate when one of the sets of observations is large. Using the graph of chi-square significance is the same in the two-sample case as in the one-sample case.

Crude experiments

Crude, arbitrary experiments should be conducted to ensure that the model behaves broadly in the way expected. Only a small number of trials need be included in each of these experiments, using just one set of seeds, since the objective is just to identify gross errors of logic.

For our model, the crude experiments we conducted (keeping all other parameters the same) and our expectations were:

reduce mean inter-arrival times at stack - more long waits in both queues
reduce mean inter-arrival times at hold point -   ditto
increase service times for take-off -   ditto
increase service times for landing -   ditto
more aircraft entities defined - no change.

(The last is designed to check that the model does not 'run out' of aircraft - see page 45.)

Sensitivity testing

By this stage, we can have a lot of confidence that the computer model conforms to our original conception of the normal happenings at Erewhon airport. We can be sure that the rarer happenings which we left out do not make an everyday, dramatic difference, because if they did it is very unlikely that the results of our model would have survived the comparison with what was observed. On the other hand, we know that the rarer happenings would influence the results - so what are we going to do: put them in or leave them out?

There are many other happenings we could analyse, ranging from an earthquake wrecking the runway to take-over by those Ruritanian terrorists. Assuming events like those are rare ones at Erewhon airport, we can virtually reject them out of hand. Apart from the rarity of their occurrence, the sort of situation where there is a national emergency is not what we are trying to model - if such an emergency arose, presumably flights would be diverted or cancelled or aircraft would have to take their chances along with the rest of mankind.

On the other hand, there are some happenings which might approach 'everydayness' and it is right that we should consider the effects of these. We can try to analyse them - in doing so, we might find that there are some events which tend to cancel out one another in their effect. For example, if an outgoing flight is cancelled because of technical trouble, that will tend to reduce congestion, while if a landing aircraft 'overshoots', that will tend to increase congestion. Bearing in mind our purpose, it will matter rather less if we ignore the possibility of cancellation than if we ignore the possibility of overshooting.

What we are getting at is that there are some possibilities which we think could be important, while there are others which we do not think will affect our purpose. The important happenings are not necessarily the most frequent ones (although they often are) so much as they are the ones which have the greatest impact on the results we are interested in. If we could establish whether or not the most important unmodelled happenings have a *material* effect, then we would know how to proceed. If they have an effect which we consider material, we must investigate further. If they have an effect which we consider immaterial, we can reject them along with all the other less important happenings.

Let us consider overshooting as one of the most important happenings. (Another important one might be a crash on the runway - a rarer event, we assume, but important because it ties up the service channel for a long time, causing congestion.) We have not collected statistics on how often an aircraft overshoots, nor have we observed what happens when it does. How, then, can we model this happening or establish whether or not we need to model it?

As a first step, let us take a pessimistic guess at the frequency of overshoots. We know we did not see one in our observations, so we can rule out really frequent possibilities like one aircraft in two overshooting. We observed fifty landings without overshoot occurring, so if the frequency were one in ten we would have expected to see five overshoots. That does not seem very likely either; let us take a stab and guess that overshoots occur in fewer than one landing in twenty. What happens when an overshoot occurs? Does the traffic controller assign the runway to another aircraft while the overshooting plane circles? Perhaps he does, but let us make the pessimistic assumption that he does not. How long does the overshooting plane take to circle and repeat the landing? We do not know, but from the general tenor of landing times a reasonable guess might be an extra five minutes.

Now we are getting somewhere. We have enough guesses to be able to model overshoots on a reasonably pessimistic basis. After we have assigned the landing time to an aircraft in our model, we could get a random number in the range 1 to 20 and, if it were a particular number which we decided upon arbitrarily, say 10, we could add five minutes to the landing time. (The amendment to the FORTRAN program on page 48 would be to insert the line

```
     IF (RANDOM(20,SEEDE) .EQ. 10) TSERV = TSERV + 300
```

immediately after the line 417 TSERV = NORMAL(180,30,SEEDC) - the 300, of course, being five minutes in seconds.) This amounts to saying that there is a one-in-twenty chance that an aircraft will tie up the runway for an extra five minutes because it is overshooting.

We run the model on this basis, and compare it with the results of our first model (using the same seeds, so we are sure that all the difference in result is caused by our changed assumptions). If the results are not materially different, we can reasonably decide we do not need to model overshoots. If they are materially different, we should go back to the field and collect information about overshoots so we can model them more precisely. If we are unable to do this, at least we have some idea of the effect that overshoots could have on the model, on pessimistic assumptions, and we can interpret the results of experiments in the light of this knowledge.

What we have just done is a sensitivity analysis, i.e. we have established the sensitivity of the model to a change in the assumptions. This can be a most valuable feature of computer modelling because the modeller, as it were from his armchair, can conduct crude sensitivity analyses to give him leads into those aspects of his model which are likely to be worthwhile examining in more detail.

Conducting experiments with the model

Assuming we have established confidence in our model, we can now use it to

predict the future. Sometimes, if the structure of the model is to be
changed, e.g. if we wish to introduce a second runway at Erewhon to see by
how much it could reduce waiting times, we must re-test the logic of the
model and re-check the program to establish that the new version of the model
conforms with what we would expect to observe. However, our particular
problem requires only a minor change, namely, to handle an increased number
of arrivals and departures.

Suppose there were a twenty per cent increase in traffic - that would mean
ten more departures and arrivals per day. We have not been told how we might
expect these extra arrivals and departures to be distributed. We might
assume they would be uniformly distributed throughout the day, but that seems
optimistic - more likely, they would show the same preference for particular
hours of day that our present arrivals and departures show. So it seems
proper to model the increased traffic by an equivalent percentage decrease in
inter-arrival times, i.e. if the new traffic is 120 per cent of the old,
120/100, then the new inter-arrival times will be 100/120 of the old.

We could try out the model on this basis, i.e inter-arrival times diminished
to 100/120 of their original value. If we found that no aircraft is yet
waiting 30 minutes in the stack, or 40 minutes at the hold point, we could
have another try in the light of the results - say, setting inter-arrival
times to 100/140 of their original value. In this inelegant but practical
way we can home-in on the percentage increase that causes intolerable
congestion (clearly we do not carry this process too far; attempts to find a
fraction of a per cent increase would be an illusion of accuracy and in any
case inconsistent with the sort of approximation the airport planners
presumably want).

We ran the program with inter-arrival times which were reduced to correspond
to various percentage traffic increases. The program was run once for each
given percentage increase, so we had the results of a twenty-day trial for
each such increase, and we made a note of the maximum time an aircraft had to
wait in the hold queue. The results are shown in Fig. 4.10.

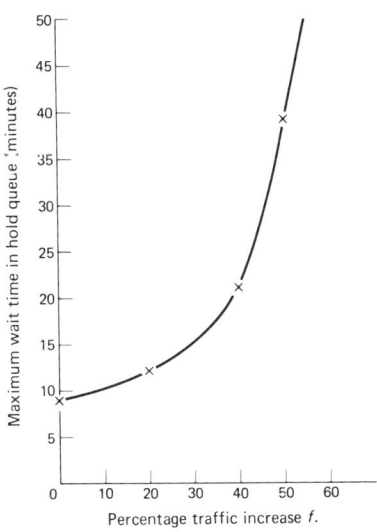

Fig. 4.10: The maximum time (in minutes) that an aircraft had to wait
in the hold queue for the percentage traffic increase shown

72 Computer Models

If the traffic is increased by 50 per cent, our model predicts that the mean waiting time for an aircraft at the hold point is about four minutes but, on average every twenty days or so, one aircraft would be waiting for about 40 minutes.

Discussion questions

1. Should the 'overshoots' sensitivity analysis be repeated on the 50-per-cent-increase version of the model?
2. Precisely how should the findings be phrased when they are presented to the airport planning authorities?
3. The procedure we suggested for collection of service times had two different bases for the observations: one where the controller was asked to explicitly declare the termination of the service when no other aircraft was waiting, and the other where the termination of service was revealed by the action of the controller in assigning the runway to another aircraft.

   Should we have discarded one of these types of observation? Could we determine the sensitivity of our model to the type of observation? What if the controller's judgement of completion of service was in fact affected by the amount of congestion he saw, i.e. by the queue lengths?
4. If the model's predictions were in error, i.e. an intolerable congestion occurred with a lower percentage increase in traffic than that forecast, would this be due to chance, or to an error in the methods or assumptions of the model?
5. What validation problems do you foresee for the models suggested by the discussion questions at the end of Chapters 2 and 3?
6. Is a model that cannot be validated worth building?

5 The Variety of Computer Models

We implied earlier that our definition of social science would include in it the words 'human behaviour'. Yet the two examples we have explored so far - the Ruritanian Sports and Social Club and Erewhon airport - may have struck you as having more to do with meteorology or aircraft and runways.

Our examples were chosen deliberately because those types of model are less contentious than many with a high human content. We wanted to be able to illustrate the principles applied to reasonably complex and detailed examples without being side-tracked into issues which, while no doubt fascinating or urgent to a social science discipline, might distract us from our immediate purpose. Nevertheless, the models we offered do have an implicit human content even though the explicit purpose may have appeared non-human (i.e. the explicit purposes were to forecast receipts from the events or congestion on the runway). Both examples modelled a system which included a human part. In the case of the Ruritanian Sports and Social Club, the human behaviour included was that of the potential Gala- and Barbecue-goers when faced with a more or less rainy day. The theory embodied in the model was that in the aggregate they would spend their money in the quantity described by the receipts-against-rainfall graph (Fig. 2.2). In the case of Erewhon airport, the human behaviour implicitly modelled was the traffic controller's observation, decision-taking and communication, coupled with the individual responses of the pilots of incoming and outgoing aircraft.

We have already introduced a number of terms which can be used to classify models according to the techniques used in their construction - discrete, stochastic, dynamic, etc. In explaining the variety of computer models that have been built for a social science purpose, however, we have found another classification useful:

i) impersonal models, i.e. models of systems which do not include a human element;
ii) one-person models, i.e. models of systems which comprise or include only one person or part of a person;
iii) many-person models, i.e. models of systems which comprise or include more than one person, each of whom is treated as a separate entity in the model;
iv) aggregated models, i.e. models of systems which comprise or include people whose behaviour is considered only in the aggregate.

A given model may have more than one of these characteristics, e.g. an individual person's response to the aggregate behaviour of others. In that event it may be convenient to classify it according to the sub-system which is the primary concern or main interest of the model.

Impersonal models

We include a classification of impersonal models both for the sake of completeness and because even a genuine social science model may have an impersonal part. This is the case with the Treasurer's model in Chapter 2, which included a simple prediction of the weather.

Furthermore, there are impersonal models (for example, models of water resources) which are of traditional interest to social scientists, perhaps because they form part of a larger system which is of interest as a social science problem. A few models of this type have been included in the bibliography at the end of this chapter.

One-person models

Descriptive models of individuals may try to show 'how people work' or to predict the responses a person may make to given stimuli.

An example is the Lindsay-Norman model of human memory which hypothetically explains the logical structure in which information is stored in the brain. This model is of special interest from a computing point of view, since it is probably strongly influenced by the development of modern computers and the practical methods adopted by computer scientists for storing and retrieving information. Although the Lindsay-Norman model is quite easy to understand in principle in a pencil-and-paper version, the working of the model with a large amount of inter-related information is not so easy to do by hand. A description of our own implementation of the Lindsay-Norman model on a computer is given in Chapter 6.

As a second example we choose Sorel Reisman's model of how his wife plays dominoes[1]. The version of the game used was the one where each of two players draws 7 of the 28 tiles and matches his tiles in turn to one or other end of the chain of tiles until one player, the winner, has played all his tiles. Should a player have no match for an exposed end of the chain, he draws from the bank until he finds a match, which he must then play.

The computer model followed three strategies of play, selected by Reisman from a set of strategies gleaned from various players' comments during play.

1. As a general rule, the computer played the tile from which the longest chain could be made from amongst its own tiles.
2. If the opponent has to draw from the bank, he reveals that he is lacking tiles that match either end of the chain. This information may be used to make a blocking play.
3. Guesses may be made, e.g. if the opponent played the left end, maybe it was because he couldn't play the right, so the computer will try to block on the left.

Reisman played five games against the computer model and then played his wife using the same draws and making the same plays from his side. The plays his wife chose were the same as the computer's in 46 out of 50 turns. Questioning his wife about the four different plays revealed that in each case she considered two plays equally useful (and she was asked to play the same tile as the computer had previously chosen, so that the experiment could continue). Playing the same games against two other players produced 35 and 39 identical choices respectively.

Reisman refrains from drawing much conclusion about these results other than that they are 'interesting'. The author has plainly gone for simplicity in his description and in so doing has left some questions unanswered for the critical reader - this is a continuing dilemma for authors who describe simulations which contain a lot of detail. It is an interesting discussion point to consider alternative experimental strategies which might influence confidence in the model's accuracy; for example, if the author's same five games were ' played' against an opposing play which was a random selection from the legal tiles, this experiment being repeated many times, it would be possible to determine the probability that a model using chance plays would produce the correspondence of 46 out of 50 turns. Naturally such an experiment would be a large undertaking by hand, but since all the rules of play in the experiment can be stated and the author's own plays are predetermined, the experiment could be conducted entirely by a further computer model.

Research which illustrates different aspects of the use of a computer is that of John H. Greist and others[2] in predicting suicide attempts of persons who have thoughts of suicide. Readers will probably be familiar with the 'programmed text' type of educational book or training manual where the student goes from frame to frame in a sequence dictated by his answers to test questions at the end of each frame. The process of presenting the next frame of information and questions, collecting the answer and determining the continuation frame can be straightforwardly done by computer through a visual-display terminal, either as an educational aid or as an interviewing aid. Greist uses the technique to have the computer 'interview' patients with thoughts of suicide and systematically to collect data on up to 8 levels of 35 factors (symptoms) which influence a human therapist's opinion of the likelihood of a suicide attempt within three months.

The computer program uses this data to make an estimate of the likelihood of a suicide attempt within three months by making use of Bayes' theorem. In principle this says that if you know the likelihood of a suicide attempt for patients in the aggregate, p(attempt), and you know the likelihood that a patient who does make an attempt will have a given symptom, p(symptom given attempt), then the likelihood that a patient with a given symptom will make an attempt is given by:

$$p(\text{attempt given symptom}) = \frac{p(\text{symptom given attempt}) \times p(\text{attempt})}{p(\text{symptom})}$$

The program held a table of probabilities, supplied by clinicians working in the field, of p(attempt), p(symptom given attempt), etc. (The need to estimate the probability of a symptom irrespective of a suicide attempt, p(symptom), was avoided by considering the ratio of probabilities

$$\frac{p(\text{attempt given symptom})}{p(\text{no attempt given symptom})} = \frac{p(\text{symptom given attempt} \times p(\text{attempt})}{p(\text{symptom given no attempt}) \times p(\text{no attempt})}$$

The table entries corresponding to the symptoms detected during the 'interviews' were retrieved by the program and were used to calculate the probability that a suicide attempt would take place given all the symptoms found.

The program was tested by using case histories of 20 past suicide-risk patients whose outcomes were known (10 attempts, 10 non-attempts) and whose profiles were also given to 21 clinicians for human assessment. The computer correctly predicted 7 attempts and 9 non-attempts. The clinicians managed correct predictions of 4 attempts and 9.4 non-attempts ('correctly predicting' in this context meaning assigning the highest probability to the actual outcome).

In classifying this model we would draw attention to three aspects. First of all there is the Bayesian model at the heart of the program which attempts to *describe* the behaviour of a patient with suicidal thoughts. Secondly there is the programmed interview. This is not an attempt to emulate an interview as conducted by an actual therapist; it is an attempt to find the best or most effective interview questions and method. The interview, then, is not a *descriptive* model, it is more of a *prescriptive* model which hypothetically seeks to show how an interview *ought* to be conducted. Finally, the overall diagnosis of the program does not attempt to describe the diagnosis of a physician; it attempts to prescribe the diagnosis that ought to be made.

Many-person models

We have already explained that the fictitious Erewhon airport model would come under this classification, as do a very large number of interesting and often complex models. The case study we give in Chapter 7, of the use of recovery beds by patients undergoing surgery in a hospital, is a classic example of a queuing model applied to a real case.

A rarer, and often more speculative, type of model tries to describe the responses or actions of interacting individuals whose behaviour is not constrained by custom, established rules or clear-cut choices. A case in point is R. Edward Overstreet's model of the 'prisoner's dilemma'.[3] The story of the prisoner's dilemma goes something like this. Two prisoners have been arrested on suspicion of committing an offence and are held in separate cells. If they both maintain their innocence, they will both be convicted of only a minor offence and go to jail for one year. If they both confess, they will both be convicted of a more serious offence but the sentence they get, three years, will take into account their co-operation. If only one confesses, he will receive a suspended sentence (be allowed to go free) for securing the conviction of the other on a serious charge, for which the latter will get five years in jail. The dilemma can be seen by considering the possible train of thought of one of the prisoners: 'If I maintain my innocence, and my accomplice does the same, I'll only get a one-year sentence. But if my accomplice maintains his innocence, I would get let off by confessing. But if he reasons the same way, he'll confess too and I'll get three years. So we'll be better off if we both claim innocence. But then if my accomplice deduces that I'll claim innocence, he'll confess and I'll get five years. So ...."

Overstreet proposed seven different models of behaviour under similar circumstances where the subjects had not just two choices of action but six or 21 choices (with outcomes equivalent to a range of possibilities between full confession and absolute denial in our example) and compared the output of his models with the choices actually made by a large number of pairs of individuals in an experimental situation. Each pair made a new choice in a sequence of trials so that eventually they were choosing on the basis of previous experience - after ten or twenty such repeats a participant's behaviour had usually adopted some regular pattern, e.g. always making the same choice.

One of Overstreet's models was a program which responded contingently according to the outcomes of the preceding trials. The preceding sequence could fall into one of 68 categories which were analysed on the basis of comments taken from some of the subjects in one of the experiments. A sequence could go in principle something like this: if on the first trial the first prisoner chose to maintain innocence (hoping that the second prisoner would co-operate with a similar choice) and the second prisoner chose to confess (thereby gaining a selfish advantage), then on the next trial the first prisoner would choose to confess in retaliation, and so on.

Two of the other models were included as a sort of check: the Naive model was a simple one which predicted that the next choice would be the same as the last one; the Chance model assumed that subjects made their choices completely at random.

When the abilities of the models to predict the actual behaviour were compared, the Contingent model and Naive model were clearly better in

performance than the Chance model. However, the performance of the
Contingent model was practically the same as that of the Naive model (as,
for that matter, was the performance of the best of the other models
tested), lending no support to the accuracy of the Contingent model - indeed,
refuting any hypothesis that the Contingent model would more successfully
predict the behaviour of the participants.

Because the same model was used to predict the behaviour of all the
participants, it could have been a perfect predictor only if all
participants had shown identical behaviour. As Overstreet points out, there
might have been more success had he tried to predict the relative frequency
with which a particular choice was made. Nevertheless, we found the model
a good example of a refutation and we also found comparing the experimental
techniques and underlying assumptions of Overstreet and Reisman (above)
informative and thought-provoking. The reader with access to a library is
urged to examine the original papers.

A probabilistic approach was taken by Robert B. Smith in his computer
simulation of President John F. Kennedy's decision-taking during the Cuban
missile crisis[4]. This crisis started on 16 October, 1962, when the United
States obtained photographic evidence that the Soviet Union was deploying
offensive weapons - missiles and bombers - in Cuba. The President called
together an Executive Committee and other consultants, numbering about two
dozen individuals (military commanders, State Department and Defense
Department officials, intelligence and other aides) who met regularly
throughout the crisis to formulate strategies. Several alternatives were
considered; hard-liners (absolutists, or Hawks) advocated a surprise bombing
attack to destroy the weapons on the ground, while others (pragmatists, or
Doves) favoured a Naval blockade to prevent further arms shipments, with a
threatened subsequent air strike and invasion should the Soviet Union fail
to withdraw. The President chose to blockade on 20 October and this was
implemented on 24 October. After four days of such confrontation, during
which period a world war seemed likely, the Soviet Union agreed to withdraw
its missiles (after they had been told that US missiles in Turkey would
probably be removed in a few months).

Each member of the Executive Committee and consultant is individually
modelled in Smith's program and is given an initial rating, based on
contemporary chroniclers' accounts, of his absolutist or pragmatic
dispositions. The disposition, taken with the stimulus of the pressure
of events (the influence of such pressure on each predisposition being
determined by sampling a distribution of pressures, the sampled distribution
making high pressure more likely as the simulated time elapses) is used
to determine the individual's view (Hawk or Dove) at a given time. If the
strength of the view does not exceed a certain threshold value, the
individual concerned counts as undecided.

In the model, each member of the Executive Committee will daily discuss
his intentions with a colleague, provided their strengths of view are on
average above this threshold. If they hold differing opinions, their
dispositions will be affected by the sampling process just described, but
any change of heart will be 'smoothed' by the subject's past history of
opinions. If they hold the same opinions, their dispositions will remain
the same. In this way the model can follow through the opinions of each
individual as the crisis develops - including, of course, the crucial
opinion of the President.

In three simulation runs of the thirteen crisis days, the President
favoured blockade throughout on two runs, while on the remaining run he
favoured blockade on eleven out of thirteen days (spending one day in an
undecided state and one day favouring bombing). Individuals who were in

real life consistent advocates of one course or the other showed similar choices in the model. Perhaps most impressively, the Secretary of State in the real crisis did not commit himself, arguing for one position and then the other, and in the simulation he spent a larger time than most in the undecided state (about thirty per cent of the time) while having a general leaning towards blockade (about fifty per cent of the time). In the real situation, the Secretary of the Treasury switched from advocating bombing to advocating blockade. In the model, he spent nearly half his time believing in bombing and a similar amount preferring blockade; he was rarely undecided.

We cannot do full justice to Smith's work in this précis - the original paper is well worth reading. It is interesting that Smith chose a probabilistic approach to modelling an event that occurred only once with named participants (cf. Overstreet's Contingent model, above). The fact that it assigns high probability to Kennedy's actual decision cannot alone be taken as much evidence of validity (it is some such evidence, since if one had to choose between the present model and another which assigned low probability to the actual outcome, the present model would stand out as the more likely to be correct). Since the modelled event can occur only once, there is no way of determining whether or not actual decisions would be distributed in the way predicted by the model. The confidence one has in this particular model must rest on Smith's detailed analyses and arguments for its constituent parts, while the underlying experimental method and theory of influence in decision-taking by political groups could be tested by the further versions Smith suggests which could model similar past Presidential decisions (the bombing of Hiroshima, Korean intervention, Vietnam war escalation or de-escalation) or, better still, future ones.

Aggregated models

The Ruritanian Sports and Social Club was a simple aggregated model of a fictitious economic situation. Many economic models take the form of expressions of aggregate demand, supply, employment etc. in a particular economy or economic sector. Commonly, practical models take the general equations suggested by an economic theory, quantify the coefficients of variables in the equations by fitting them to past data and use the model so particularized to forecast economic trends or to judge the sensitivity of the economy to different policies. Such models often include stochastic elements and usually have 'time-lags' on important variables, e.g. this month's consumption is a function of last month's income, or this year's agricultural production is a function of last year's prices. Such lags and the changes of the variables with time can be easily modelled on a computer by a program that goes in month-by-month or year-by-year steps. Of course, the practice of fitting equations to past data is an expedient, and the fact that the program succesfully 'predicts' past events does not do much to confirm the model's capability of predicting the future (in the last chapter, we described this as 'cooking the results'), though it may help to confirm that the program is free from programming error. Although it is often possible to criticize economic models for lack of validation, it is not so easy to offer practical alternatives because, like the Cuban missile crisis, economic circumstances do not precisely repeat themselves.

In Chapter 8 we describe William B. Stronge's implementation of a classical macroeconomic model. This model has the educaional objective of relating economic theory to practice, and no validation is offered.

Ilan Vertinsky's work on the effect of birth-control programmes in Costa Rica[5] is an interesting aggregate model encompassing several academic disciplines. The model works on an annual cycle, with two calculations for each simulated year. The first calculation seeks to estimate the proportion of fertile women, i.e. potential child-bearers, who will adopt a contraceptive device and the effect of such adoption on the birth rate. The second calculation uses the revised birth rate to update population statistics. (In principle, the population at the end of the year - ignoring migration - equals the population at the beginning of the year plus births less deaths, but, since the births of the following year will depend in part upon the number of women of child-bearing age, it is necessary to keep a more detailed account of the populations at different ages and at the year's end to transfer the survivors of one age to the next).

For the first calculation, the model considers women in two groups: those 'susceptible' to adoption of birth control (i.e. those who might seek to limit the size of their families in the coming year) and those 'not susceptible' because, for example, their existing family size is less than that considered desirable by their society. Only the birth rate of the 'susceptible' portion is adjusted by modelled successful birth-control adoption.

The probability of adoption of a birth-control method is modelled by a number of factors: the likelihood of institutional advice (in turn modelled by the fraction of deliveries attended to by health-care institutions, the average distance to the health-care centre and the cost of health-care as a fraction of income) and the availability and attractiveness of different techniques (e.g. inter-uterine device or oral contraceptive). Attractiveness of a technique is in turn taken to be a function of knowledge of the technique, cost, discomfort and side effects of use, religious taboos on the technique and a bandwagon factor relating adoption of a particular technique in the current year to the extent of use of that technique in the previous year.

The probability of success with the adopted technique is calculated as a function of a general effectiveness of the technique in the best hands, adjusted by its sensitivity to error, complexity of use and the degree of education of the adopters.

Quantification of the various parameters of the model was achieved through official population statistics, surveys, ranking of alternatives and professional judgements. Some parameters differ for each age group or technique and are held as tables in the program. Vertinsky did not use published data on adoption of different techniques in the years 1969-71 in estimating the starting parameters, so he could legitimately use the model's 'prediction' of those years as a validation test - the model's simulated adoptions of IUDs and oral contraceptives are within three per cent of the actual for each technique in each of those years. However, as Vertinsky points out, more validation is desirable. The potential of the model in exploring the effect of different policy variables, such as better service from health-care institutions or public campaigns to influence 'susceptibility', is considerable.

Further Reading

We hope the bibliography at the end of the chapter will give you leads to recent models constructed in the discipline of your interest. We believe that critical consideration of the models of others is very helpful to the incubation of one's own ideas. The principles of experimental design and many other aspects of modelling are cross-disciplinary and much is to be learned from models constructed in other disciplines - the journals

80 Computer Models

Simulation and *Simulation and Games* publish computer models without severe restriction of disciplines. A very good survey discussion and collection of papers is published in the massive work of Dutton and Starbuck, which also includes the most comprehensive pre-1970 bibliography; Guetzkow et al is another large and useful source (see bibliography for references).

Many speculative, unclear or unvalidated models have been published. Such papers can add to the discussion of possibilities, provided that they are not too glib, but the reader who wants *useful* models is cautioned to read with all his critical faculties switched on.

References

1. Reisman, S., 'Dominoes - a computer simulation of cognitive processes'. *Simulation and Games*, June 1972, 155-164.
2. Greist, J. H., et al, 'Suicide risk prediction'. *Life-threatening Behaviour*, 4(4), 212-223, 1974.
3. Overstreet, R. E., 'Simulation models of the prisoner's dilemma game'. In Dutton, J. M. & Starbuck, W. H., *Computer simulation of human behaviour*, Wiley, N.Y., 260-273, 1971.
4. Smith, R. B., 'Presidential decision-making during the Cuban missile crisis: a computer simulation'. *Simulation and Games*, June 1970, 173-201.
5. Vertinsky, I., et al, 'Family planning computer simulation: the Costa Rica population control model'. *Simulation and Games*, June 1972, 123-145.

Bibliography

Documents are included in the bibliography if they describe computer models or modelling, and if they were published in 1970 or later. Items for inclusion in the bibliography were evaluated by reference to the originals or, in the majority of cases, by means of abstracts contained in the following sources:

Anbar Management Services Abstracts
British Education Index
Computer and Control Abstracts
Computing Reviews
Economic Abstracts
Education Index (June 1975 onwards)
Ergonomic Abstracts
International Political Science Abstracts
Psychological Abstracts
Public Administration Information Services Bulletin (1973 onwards)
Sociological Abstracts.

The comprehensiveness and content of the bibliography depends largely on the efficiency of these services in indexing and on the quality of their abstracts. In some of the more popular areas, we have cited other bibliographies which provide a major source of information.

General

Bekey, G. A., (Ed.), Proc. Symposium on *Mathematical models of public systems*. Simulation Councils Inc., La Jolla, Calif., 1(1), 1971.
Brier, A. & Robinson, I., *Computers and the social sciences*. Hutchinson Educational, 1974.

Broermann, B.G., 'Computer simulation in place of analytic models for strategic planning'. In Goldberg 2, 129-147, 1973.
Collins, L. (Ed.), *The use of models in the social sciences*. Tavistock, London, 1976.
Computers and urban society. Proc. 6th. Annual Symposium, ACM, New York, 1971.
Dutton, J.M. & Starbuck, W.H., *Computer simulation of human behaviour*. Wiley, N.Y., 1970.
Emshoff, J.R. & Sisson, R.L., *Design and use of computer simulation models*. Macmillan, London, 1970.
Goldberg, W. (Ed.), *Proc. Conf. on computer simulation versus analytic solutions for business and economic models*. Vols 1 & 2, University of Gothenberg, 1973.
Guetzkow, H., Kotler, P. & Schultz, R.L., *Simulation in social and administrative science*. Prentice Hall, Englewood Cliffs, N.J., 1972.
Johnson, E.R., *Simulation and gaming in business and economics in the 1960's: a bibliography*. College of Business Admin., University of Iowa, 1969.
Maisel, H. & Grignoli, G., *Simulation of discrete stochastic systems*. SRA, Chicago, 1972.
Naylor, T.H. (Ed.), *Symposium on the design of computer simulation experiments*. Duke University Press, Durham, N.C., 1969.
Oren, T.I., 'A bibliography of bibliographies on modelling, simulation and gaming'. *Simulation* 23(3), 90-95, 1975.
Penney, G., *Computers in the social sciences: a study guide*. National Computing Centre, Manchester, England, 1973.
Reitman, J., *Computer simulation applications*. Wiley, N.Y., 1971.
Rivett, P., *Principles of model building - the construction of models for decision analysis*. Wiley, N.Y., 1973.

Behavioural sciences

Anderson, J.R., 'FRAN: a simulation model of free recall'. In Bower, G.H. (Ed), *The psychology of learning and motivation: V*, Academic Press, N.Y., 1972.
Becker, J.D., 'A model for the encoding of experimental information'. In Schank, R.C. & Colby, K.M., 396-434, 1973.
Bellman, R. & Smith, C.R., *Simulation in human systems: decision-making in psychotherapy*. Wiley, N.Y., 1973.
Brightman, H.J., 'Individual behaviour and the small work group: a simulation study'. *Diss. Abs. Int.*, 31(7-A), 3098-3099, 1971.
Cook, V.J. & Herniter, J.D., 'NOMMAD, or how consumers behave'. *Sloan Management Review* 12(3), 77-97, 1971.
Denisov, P.N., *Principles of constructing linguistic models*. Mouton, The Hague, 1974.
Emshoff, J.R., 'A computer simulation model of the prisoner's dilemma'. *Behavioural Science* 15(4), 304-317, 1970.
Finney, J.C. et al, 'Computer simulation of psychologists' decision-making'. In *Proc. ACM Annual Conf.*, ACM, N.Y., 899-902, 1972.
Frijda, N.H., 'Simulation of human long-term memory'. *Psychological Bulletin* 77(1), 1-31, 1972.
Gregg, L.W., 'Simulation models of learning and memory'. In Gregg, L.W. (Ed.), *Cognition in learning and memory*, Wiley, N.Y., 1972.
Gullahorn, J.T. & Gullahorn, J.E., 'Computer simulation of role conflict resolution'. In Dutton, J.M. & Starbuck, W.H., 350-363, 1970.
Hare, A.P. & Scheiblechner, H., 'Computer simulation of small group decisions; model three'. *Behavioural Science* 16(4), 399-403, 1971.

Hummel, T.J., Lichtenberg, J.W. & Shaffer, W.F., 'CLIENT 1: a computer program which simulates client behaviour in an initial interview'. *J. of Counseling Psychology* 22(2), 164-169, 1975.

Indow, T & Suzuki, S., 'Strategies in concept identification: stochastic model and computer simulation:1'. *Japanese Psychological Research* 14(4), 168-175, 1972.

Joyner, R.C., 'Computer simulation of individual concept learning in the three-person common target game'. *J. of Mathematical Psychology* 7(3), 478-514, 1970.

Kidder, S.J., 'Simulation games: practical references, potential use, selected bibliography'. *Centre for Social Organisation of Schools Report* 112, John Hopkins University, 1971.

King, J.H., 'First step toward a computer model of human behaviour'. *Theory and Decision* 2(2), 141-173, 1971.

Krolak, P.D. & Melton, J.D., 'A simulation model for the rent-or-buy decision'. *Simulation* 16(5), 217-226, 1971.

Loehlin, J.C., 'Individual behaviour simulations - personality'. In Guetzkow, H., 117-131.

McLeod, J., 'Behavioural science, system theory-and simulation'. *Behavioural Science* 19(1), 57-69, 1974.

Merritt, M.J., 'Simulation of human communications'. In Bekey 1(1), p.87.

Moser, U., Von Zeppelin, I. & Schneider, W., 'Computer simulation of a model of neurotic defence processes'. *Behavioural Science* 15(2), 194-202, 1970.

Newsted, P.R., 'Simulation as an aid to understanding cognitive processes'. *Simulation* 22(2), 85-88, 1974.

Olshavsky, R.W., 'Prediction of the meaningfulness level of nonsense syllables via computer simulation'. *Cognitive Psychology* 2(2), 206-211, 1971.

Perry, M. 'Computer simulation of consumer brand choice'. In Goldberg 2, 7-21.

Pierson, G.R., 'Computer assisted personality analysis (CAPA) and simulation (CAPS)'. *J. of Multivariate Experimental Personality & Clinical Psychology* 1(1), 31-37, Fall 1973.

Ross, W.L., *Functional determinants of leadership effectiveness: a computer simulation.* Diss. Abs. Int., 32(3-B), 1893, 1971.

Schank, R.C. & Colby, K.M. (Eds), *Computer models of thought and Language.* Freeman, San Francisco, 1973.

Schultz, R.L., 'The use of simulation for decision making'. *Behavioural Science* 19(5), 344-350, 1974.

Scott, D.A., *Computer simulation of pattern recognition using statistical decision funtions.* Diss. Abs. Int., 31(9-B), 5678, 1971.

Shoemaker, D.M. & Osburn, H.G., 'A simulation model of achievement testing'. *Educational and Psychological Measurement* 30(2), 267-272, 1970.

Simon, C.W., *Experiment simulation.* Government Reports Announcements (AD-754 215), 1972.

Simon, H.A. & Feigenbaum, E.A., 'An information-processing theory of some effects of similarity, familiarization, and meaningfulness in verbal learning'. In Guetzkow, H, 103-116.

Srinivas, K.M., *A computer simulation model of Newcomb's consistency theory: a case in theory development.* Diss. Abs. Int., 31(4-A), 1890, 1970.

Starbuck, W.H. & Dutton, J.M., 'Computer simulation as a tool for descriptive behavioural science'. In goldberg 1, 257-289.

Waters, C.W. & Bayroff, A.G., 'A comparison of computer-simulated conventional and branching tests'. *Educational and Psychological Measurement* 31(1), 125-136, 1971.

Winograd, T. 'A procedural model of language understanding'. In Schank, R.C. & Colby, K.M., 152-186, 1973.

Wright, A.D., *Schematic concept formation: an extension of previous models*. Diss. Abs. Int., 30(11-B), 5271-5272, 1970.

Demography

Lawrence, E.E. & Mundigo, A.I., 'REALPOP: a mathematical model for resource allocation in population programs - results from a test in the Dominican Republic'. *Studies in Family Planning* 6, 64-71, 1975.
MacCorquodale, D.W. & Pullum, T.W., 'A mathematical model for determining effects of family planning clinics'. *Studies in Family Planning* 5, 232-238, 1974.
Picardi, A.C., 'A demographic and economic growth model for Bolivia'. *Simulation* 20(4), 109-118, 1973.
Pollard, *Models of Human Population*. Cambridge University Press, Cambridge, 1974.
Vertinsky, I., 'Family planning computer simulation: the Costa Rica population control model'. *Simulation and Games* 3(2), 123-145, 1972.
Weinberg, D. & Weinberg, G.M., 'Using a computer in the field: Kinship information'. Soc. Sci. Inform. 11(6), 37-59, 1972.

Economics

Abkin, M.H. & Manetsch, T.J., 'A development planning-orientated simulation model of the agricultural economy of Southern Nigeria'. *IEEE Systems, Man and Cybernetics Group Annual Symposium Record*, IEEE, N.Y., 303-308, 1971.
Adamec, S. & Fundarek, M., 'A long-term econometric model for Czechoslovakia and economic policy simulation'. In Goldberg, 2, 1-13.
Adams, F.G. & Burmeister, E., 'Economic models'. *IEEE Trans. Syst. Man and Cybernetics SMC-3* (1), 19-27, 1973.
Bagrinovski, K.A., 'Decisions in a system of models for planning national economy'. *IFIP Congress* 5, 1067-1071, 1974.
Batt, C.D. & Fowkes, T.R., 'Management Science models in bank planning'. *Computer Weekly*, 244, 1971.
Bergeron, I. & Matuszewski, T., 'Un modele de simulation de la demande regionale pour les materiaux de construction'. *Econ. appliquee*, Paris 27(4), p641, 1974.
Blitzer, C.R., et al (Ed), *Economy-wide models and development planning*, O.U.P., Oxford, 1975.
Christ, C.F., 'Econometics and model building', 1967-1972. *Annals American Academy of Political and Social Science* 493, 153-162, 1972.
Corsi, Paelo & Stajanor, A., 'An interactive programming system to solve econometric non-linear models'. In Goldberg 2, 15-69.
Eckstein, O. & McLagan, D.L., 'National economic models help business to focus on the future'. *Computer decisions* 3(10), 12-17, 1971.
Foy, N.S., 'Unmasking the black art of financial modelling'. *Computer Management*, Jan. 1970, p12.
Frazer, P. et al, 'Computers in banking'. *Computer Weekly*, 22 Nov. 1973, p15.
Henry, S.G.B. & Desai, M., 'Fiscal policy simulations and stabilisation policy'. *Rev. of Economic stud.* 42(131), p347, 1975.
Hoehenwarter, W.P. & Reich, K.E., 'BANKMOD - an interactive decision aid for banks'. In *Proc. AFIPS 1971 Fall Joint Computer Conf.*, AFIPS Press, Montvale, N.J., 639-649.

McCracken, M.C. & Sonnen, C.A., 'A system for large econometric models - management, estimation and simulation'. In *Proceedings ACM Annual Conference*, ACM, N.Y., 964-973, 1972.
Naylor, T.H., *Computer simulation experiments with models of economic systems*, Wiley, N.Y., 1971.
Pissarides, C.A., 'A model of British macroeconomic policy 1955-1969'. *Manchester School of Economics and Social Studies* 40, 245-259, 1972.
Simon, J.L., Puig, C.M. & Anschoff, J., 'A duopoly simulation and richer theory'. *Review of Economic Studies* 123, p353, 1973.
Sujan, I., Kolek, J. & Gergelyi, K., 'Attempted comparison of Czechoslovak and Hungarian economies on the basis of a joint econometric model'. In Goldberg 2, 71-115.
Witt, B., *Economic models - a selective bibliography*. Council of Planning Librarians, 1973.
Wagner, J. & Pryer, L.J., 'Simulation and the budget: an integrated model'. *Sloan Management Review* 12(2), 45-48, 1971.

Education

Baisuck, A. & Wallace, W.A., 'A computer simulation approach to enrolment projection in higher education'. *Socio-economic Planning Sciences* 4, 365-381, 1970.
Boardman, G.B., 'Computer-based simulation model for the feedback and analysis of the administrative in-basket exercise'. *Educational Adm. Q.* 11, 55-71, 1975.
Bassel, H., 'College student and dropout problem: a qualitative dynamic simulation'. *Instructional Science* 3, 23-50, 1974.
Broadbent, F.W. & Meehan, R., 'A learning disability simulation for classroom teachers'. *Simulation and Games* 11(4), 489-500, 1971.
Gunnell, J.B., 'University faculty recruitment'. *Simulation and Games* 2(3), 349-375, 1971.
Heinlein, A.C., *Decision models in academic administration*. Kent State University Press, Ohio, 1974.
LoCascio, V.R., 'A computerized simulation model for colleges and universities'. *Manage Controls* 20(8), 195-200, 1973.
McKay, C.W. & Cutling, G.D., 'A model for long-range planning in higher education'. *Long Range Planning* 7, 58-60, 1974.
Mitchell, P.D., 'Computer simulation of a classroom: an educational game to study preinstructional decisions'. *Aspects of Educational Technology* 7, 199-210, 1973.
Pfeiffer, M.G. & Kuhl, J.M., 'An organisational model of college-level teaching performance'. *16th Annual Meeting of Human Factors Society*, Los Angeles, 346-356, 1972.
Roberts, N., 'A computer system simulation of student performance in the elementary classroom'. *Simulation and Games* 5(3), 265-290, 1974.
Taschdjian, E., 'A systems approach to higher education with special reference to the core curriculum'. *Policy Sciences* 3(2), 219-233, 1972.
Vergrugge, W.G., 'Implementation of NCHEMS and other planning and management systems: small college level'. *Ph. D. Thesis*, Purdue University, 1974.
Wildberger, A.M., 'Review of modelling and simulation in education and training'. *AEDS Journal* 7(3), 65-74, 1974.
Windeknecht, T.G. & D'Angelo, M., 'The stereotype approach to the modelling and simulation of an elementary school'. *IEEE Trans. Syst., Man and Cybern.* SMC-5(2), 216-225, 1975.

Ergonomics

Ayoub, M.A. & Pearson, R.G., 'Assessment of human work capacity in occupational systems'. *16th Annual Meeting of the Human Factors Society*, L.A., p177, 1972.
Bekey, G.A., *New techniques for the analysis of manual control systems. Final technical report. 15 June 1965 - 15 June 1971*. NASA Rep. No. CR-138515.
Bellezza, F.S., *Computer simulation of operant learning under interval, ratio and response rate schedules of reinforcement*. Diss Abs Int, 32(1-B),577,1971.
Bevis, F.W. & Towill, D.R., *Dynamic cost modelling for productivity increase in repetative tasks*. TRL Report No. T72-01216, 1971.
Booth, T.L. et al, *Man-machine systems for detection, recognition, transmission and perception of information. Vol II Final Report, Sept. 1969 - May 1971*. U.S. Government Research and Development Reports (AD-727 610), 1971.
Diehl, A.E., 'A computer simulation model to analyze occupational safety and health problems and countermeasures'. In *18th Annual Meeting of the Human Factors Society*, Huntsville, USA, 92-96, 1974.
Evans, R.L., Hunter, S. & Rolfe, J.M., *A bibliography of human factors research using flight simulators*. Royal Air Force Institute of Aviation Medicine, IAM Scientific Memorandum 119, 1974.
Gallenstein, J. & Huston, R.L., 'Analysis of swimming motions'. *Human Factors* 15(1), 91-98, 1973.
Graefe, U. & Nenonen, L.H., *Interactive computer models of industrial operations*. TRC Rep. No. T75-6687, 1975.
Hatch, R.S. et al, *Training line simulator (enhanced version)*. US AFHRL Technical Rep. No. 73-50(2), 1974.
Knox, E.G., 'Computer simulation of industrial hazards'. *British J. of Industrial Medecine* 30, 54-63, 1973.
Luczak, H., 'The use of simulations for testing individual mental working capacity'. *Ergonomics* 14(5), 651-660, 1971.
Peter, B., 'A hierarchical model of a helicopter pilot'. *Human Factors* 12(4), 361-374, 1970.
Shield, B.M. & Corlett, E.N., 'A simulation of factory noise'. *Production Engineer*, 54(9), 489-492, 1975.
Siegal, A.I., Wolf, J.J. & Lautman, M.R., *A model for predicting integrated man-machine system reliability: model logic and description*. Rep. No. AD-A009814/5GA, 1974.
Van Gigch, J.P., 'Applications of a model used in calculating the mental load of workers in industry'. *Can. Oper. Res. Soc. J.*, 8(3), 176-184, 1970.
Williges, B.H., Roscoe, S.N. & Williges, R.C., 'Synthetic flight training revisited'. *Human Factors* 15(6), 543-560, 1973.

Management

Agizy, M.N., 'Economic order and surplus quantities model'. *IBM J. of Research and Development,* 18(1), 72-75, 1974.
Allner, D. et al, 'Computer-aided corporate planning'. *Computer Management* Sept 1974, p18, Oct 1974, p33, Dec/Jan 1975, p28.
Amstutz, A.E., *Computer Simulation of competitive market responses*. MIT Press, Cambridge, Mass., 1970.
Assmus, G., 'NEWPROD: the design and implementation of a new product model'. *J. of Marketing* 39(1), p16, 1975.
Blasch, H.F. et al, 'Computer model for investment analysis'. *Management Controls,* Dec 1973, p273.
Boulden, J.B. & Buffa, E.S., 'Corporate models: on-line, real-time systems'. *Harvard Business Review* 48(4), 65-83, 1970.

86 Computer Models

Boulden, J.B., 'Computerised corporate planning'. *Long Range Planning* 3(4), 2-9, 1971.
Boulden, J.B., 'Corporate models as an aid to on-line decision making'. In *Computing economics: international computer state of the art report*, Infotech Information, Maidenhead, 315-328, 1973.
Bowersox, D.J., 'Planning physical distribution operations with dynamic simulation'. *J. of Marketing* 36, 17-25, 1972.
Bruggeman, J.J. & Salveson, T.E., 'TESTCAP: a management decision-making tool'. *1974 Winter Simulation Conference,* ACM, Edmont, N.Y., 1, 61-65.
Burrill, C.W. & Quinto, L., *Computer model of a growth company.* Gordon and Breach, N.Y., 1972.
Cantellow, D.G., Pitt, R.V. & Saw, R.J., 'Machine-shop problems: an operational research approach'. *Oper. Res. Quarterly* 24(4), p503, 1973.
Canter, E.E., & Cohen, K.J., 'Portfolio aspects of strategic planning'. *J. of Business Policy,* Summer 1972, p8.
Ceriello, V.R. & Frantzreb, R.B., 'A human resource planning model'. *Human Factors* 17(1), 35-41, 1975.
Chambers, A., 'Computers in management'. *Computer Weekly,* 12 Apr. 1973, p6; 26 Apr. 1973, p6; 3 May 1973, p6.
Clarke, T.E., 'Decision-making in technologically based organisations: a literature survey of present practice'. IEEE Trans. Eng. Manage. EM-21(1), 9-23, 1974.
Cook, T.M., Gitman, L.J. & Defelice, C., 'Simulation of a corporate cash budget: application and validation'. *1974 Winter Simulation Conference,* ACM, Edmont, N.Y. 1, 128-138.
Cort, S.G. & Dominguez, L.V., 'PLAN*IT: simulation applied in a marketing decision system'. *1974 Winter Simulation Conference,* ACM, Edmont, N.Y. 2, 633-639.
Davis, K.R., 'Market strategy via simulation'. *1974 Winter Simulation Conference,* ACM, Edmont, N.Y. 2, 621-630.
Demaire, J.D., 'Simulation applied to a manufacturing expansion problem area'. *1973 Winter Simulation Conference,* AFIPS Press, Montvale, N.J., 298-310.
Eiloart, T. & Searle, N, 'Business games off the shelf'. *Simulation* 20(2), 63-66, 1973.
Engwall, L., *Models of industrial structure.* Heath, Lexington, Mass., 1973.
Engwall, L., 'Simulation of structural changes'. In Goldberg 2, 1-16.
Faus, D.J., 'Financial models: a European survey'. *J. Gen. Mgt.* 1(3), 48-59, 1974.
Forrington, C.V.D., 'Realising the benefits of modelling'. *Computer Weekly,* 20/27 Dec 1973, p6.
Gershefski, G.W., 'Corporate models - the state of the art'. In Schreiber, 26-42.
Gilmour, P., 'Applied industrial computer simulation - a dynamic physical distribution model'. *Australian Computer Journal* 4(2), 58-64, 1972.
Gofton, K., 'British steel consults its oracle'. The executive's world page of *The Financial Times,* 16 Jan 1973.
Goldberg, W. et al (Eds.), *Management information systems.* Auerbach, N.Y., 1971.
Grinyer, P.H., 'Corporate financial simulation models for top management'. *Omega* 1(4), 465-482, 1973.
Hamilton, W.F., 'Corporate simulation models - a review and appraisal'. *1973 Winter Simulation Conference,* AFIPS Press, Montvale, N.J., 719-733.
Hammond, J.S., 'Computer models for planning'. *Harvard Business Review,* March/April 1974, p110.
Harris, R.D., & Maggard, M.J., *Computer models in operations management.* Harper & Row, N.Y., 1972.
Helferich, O.K. & Monczka, R.M., 'A dynamic simulation model for planning materials input systems'. *J. of Purchasing,* Aug 1972, p17.
Higgins, J.C. & Whitaker, D., 'Computer aids to corporate planning'. *Computer Bulletin* 16(9), 434-439, 1972.

Hughes, G.D. & Guerrero, J.L., 'Simultaneous concept testing'. *J. of Marketing*, Jan, 1971, p28.

Hull, J.C. & Wheeler, B.M., 'Computer aids to financial planning'. *Management Today*, Dec 1973, p37.

Kawal, D.E., 'A systems model of a construction firm'. Ph. D. Thesis, Iowa State University, USA, 1970.

Kotler, P. & Schultz, R.L., 'Marketing system simulations'. In Guetzkow, 481-549.

Krouse, C.G., 'A model for aggregate financial planning'. *Management Science* 18(4), 555-566, 1972.

Labys, W.C., 'Commodity modelling alternatives for policy simulation analysis'. In Goldberg 2, 19-44.

Lederer, L.S., 'SIMARI: techno-economic simulation of the process industries'. In Goldberg 2, 23-35.

Lewis, G.H., 'How ICL uses its company model'. *International Management*, Jan 1971

McCarthy, D.J. & Morrisey, C.A., 'Preparing corporate financial models'. *Financial Executive*, June 1972, p40.

Macintosh, N.B., 'An econometric model of Canada Packers Ltd'. *Infor* 10(3), 240-251, 1972.

Mallinson, A.H., 'A risk analysis approach to profits forecasts'. *Accounting and business research*, Spring 1973, p83.

Meyhak, H., 'Formalized long range planning in the firm with simulation models'. In Goldberg 2, 193-213.

Michael, G.C., 'A computer simulation model for forecasting catalog sales'. *J. of Marketing Research* 8, 224-229, 1971.

Morris, G.D., 'Models and computers in corporate planning'. *European Business*, Spring 1974, 60-69.

Naylor, T.H., 'Corporate simulation models'. *Simulation* 21(2), 61-64, 1973.

Naylor, T.H., 'Towards a theory of corporate simulation models'. In Goldberg 2, 149-177.

Naylor, T.H., 'Methodological considerations in simulating social and administrative systems'. In Guetzkow, 647-672.

Niedereichholz, J., 'Business simulation and management decisions'. *Management International Review* 1, p47, 1971.

Peters, D.H., 'The impact of financial control on financial performance'. In Goldberg 2, 19-55.

Poole, T.G., 'Simulation - simple steps to success'. *The Management Consultant*, March 1974, p5.

Portes, M.J., 'Marketing men and their models'. *European Business*, Autumn 1970, p53.

Puck, G., 'A market simulation for top management games'. In Goldberg 2, 13-24.

Root, H.P., 'Implementation of risk analysis models for the management of product innovations'. In Goldberg 2, 93-127.

Rupli, R.G., 'Credit control'. *Management Accounting*, Nov 1973, p16.

Ruthberg, C., 'Simulation as a tool for concern-wide financial and cash flow analysis'. In Goldberg 2, 63-79.

Schreiber, A.N. (Ed.), *Corporate simulation models*. Graduate School of Business Administration, University of Washington, Seattle, 1970.

Seaberg, R.A., 'An application of simulation models (in APL) to corporate planning processes'. *1973 Winter Simulation Conference*, AFIPS Press, Montvale, N.J., 604-621.

Smith, J.V.M., 'Computer for planning and control'. In Yearsley, R.B. & Graham, G.M.R., *Handbook of Computer Management*, Gower, Epping, 233-249, 1973.

Sord, B.H. et al, *Decision simulation of a manufacturing firm: a manual for company managers*. Bureau of Business Research, University of Texas, Austin, 1974.

Thabor, A. & Noblanc, P.Y., 'Marketing information and simulation systems for the tire producers'. In Goldberg 2, 117-148.

Thomas, G.R., 'Simulation study of a quick-service take-out restaurant'. *Simulation* 22(5), 139-144, 1974.
Tyran, M.R., 'A computerized decision-simulation model'. *Management Accounting* 52(9), 19-26, 1971.
Urban, G.L., 'Building models for decision makers'. *Interfaces* 4(3), 1-11, 1974.
Vinturella, J.B., 'Product distribution: the transhipment problem'. In *Proc. ACM 1972 Annual Conf.*, ACM, N.Y., 877-882.
Wagle, B. & Jenkins, P.M., 'Corporate planning models and computer systems'. *Computer Journal* 17(3), 194-200, 1974.
Wagner, J. & Pryor, L.J., 'Simulation and the budget: an integrated model'. *Sloan Management Review* 12, 45-58, 1971.
Westwood, D., 'Market planning: the impact of the new technology'. *European Research* 2(6), p232, 1974.
Wheelwright, S.C., 'What can we expect from computerised models?'. *European Business*, Aug 1972, p55.
Wheelwright, S.C., 'Management by model during inflation'. *Business Horizons* 18(3), p33, 1975.
Zabransky, F. & Duncan, G., 'A model for a computer-based interactive system of cash management'. In Goldberg, W. et al (Eds.), 359-380.
Zant, T.F., 'CMS/1 - a corporate modelling system'. *1973 Winter Simulation Conference*, AFIPS Press, Montvale, N.J., 814-827.

Planning

Baxter, R., Echenique, M. & Owers, J., (Eds.), *Urban development models*. LUBFS Conf. Proc. 3, Construction Press, 1975.
Batty, M., *Urban modelling: algorithms, calibrations, predictions*. CUP, Cambridge, 1976.
Bernstein, S., Mellon, W.G. & Handelman, S., 'Regional stabilisation: a model for policy decision'. *Policy Sciences* 4(3), 309-325, 1973.
Brookbanks, E. & Yule, A., 'Simulation comes to town'. *Computing* 17 Jan 1974, p10.
Dickson, G.W., Mauriel, J.J., & Anderson, J.C., 'Computer assisted planning models: a functional analysis'. In Schreiber, A.N., 43-70.
Grant, D.P. & Thompson, B., 'Simulating conflicts of interest over the location of public housing with the aid of a computer-aided space allocation technique'. In *Computers and Urban Society*, 80-93.
Harper, H.A.B., 'The uses of business and economic models in the field of property development to service the North Sea oil industry'. In Goldberg 2, 57-61.
Harris, B., 'Computer simulation of the metropolis'. *Proc. AFIPS 1972 Fall Joint Computer Conf.* 41(1), 415-421.
House, P., *The urban environmental system: modelling for research, policy-making and education*. Sage Publications, London, 1973.
Meise, J. & Wegener, M., 'Computers in city planning: the simulation of urban development'. *Management Informatics* 1(1), 31-37, 1972.
Nelson, P.M., *A computer model for determining the temporal distribution of noise from road traffic*. Transport and Road Research Lab., TRRL Rep. 611, 1973.
Perraton, & Baxter, R.(eds.), *Models, evaluations and information systems for planners*. LUBFS Conf. Proc. 1, Construction Press, 1974.
Ricks, R.B., *National housing models: application of econometric techniques to problems of housing research*. Lexington Books, Lexington, Mass., 1973.
Rowlands, R.O., *Model studies in acoustics*. TRL Report No. P-172909, Dec 1970.
Seader, D. & Grava, S., 'A demonstration of the use of computer-aided land-use modeling for regional service system design'. In *Computers and Urban Society* 110-127.

Sears, D.W., 'The New York State regional housing model'. *Simulation & Games* 11(2), 131-148, 1971.
Wilson, A.G., *Urban and regional models in geography and planning*. Wiley, N.Y., 1974.

Politics

Bloomfield, L.P. & Gearin, C.J., 'Games foreign policy experts play: the political exercises come of age'. *Orbis* 16(4), 1008-1031, 1973.
Borrow, D.B., 'Computers and a normative model of the policy process'. *Policy Sciences* 1(1), 123-134, 1970.
Chadwick, R.W., 'Theory development through simulation - a comparison and analysis of associations among variables in an international system and an inter-nation simulation'. *Int. Studies Quarterly* 5(2), 131-150, 1972.
Francis, W.L., 'Political process simulations'. In Guetzkow, H., 245-263.
Harvey, T.G., 'Computer simulation of peergroup influences on adolescent political behaviour: an explanatory study'. *Midwest J. Polit. Sci.* 16(4), 570-602, 1972.
Kornberg, A., et al, 'Socializing political party officials: a simulation experiment'. *Simulation and Games* 3(4), 379-406, 1972.
Laing, J.D. et al, 'Computer models of political coalitions'. *Political Science Annual* 4, 41-74, 1973.
Lee, J.S. & Kornberg, A., 'A computer simulation model of multiparty parliamentary recruitment'. *Simulation and Games* 4(1), 37-58, 1973.
Modelski, G., 'Simulations, 'realities' and international relations theory'. *Simulation and Games* 1(2), 111-134, 1970.
Porat, M.U., & Martin, W., 'World IV: a policy simulation model of national and regional systems'. *Stanford Journal of International Studies* 9, 71-166, 1974.
Ruloff, D., 'Digitale simulation internationaler Prozesse: Eskalation, De-Eskalation und Rüstungswettlauf'. *Ann. Suisse Sci. Polit.* 14, 69-83, 1974.
Schauland, H., 'Strategic vs. tactical analysis of survey research data: a micro approach'. In Goldberg 1, 41-58.
Shapiro, M.J., 'The House and the federal role: a computer simulation of roll-call voting'. In Guetzkow, H., 264-295.

Public administration

Berger, E., Boulay, H. & Zisk, B., 'Simulation and the city: a critical overview'. *Simulation and Games* 1(4), 411-428, 1970.
Blumberg, D.F., 'The city as a system'. *Simulation* 17(4), 155-167, 1971.
Blumstein, A., 'Management science to aid the manager: an example from the criminal justice system'. *Sloan Management Review* 15(1), 35-48, 1973.
Brewer, G.D., *Politicians, bureaucrats and the consultant: a critique of urban problem solving*. Basic Books, 1973.
Chmura, T.J. & Wallace, W.A., 'A test of a municipal budget simulation in a small city'. *Socio-econ. Planning Sciences* 9, 131-136, 1975.
Crecine, J.P., 'A computer simulation model of municipal budgeting'. In Guetzkow, 613-643.
Day, P. & Tampoe, M., 'Revenue and capital management model'. *Public Finance and Accountancy*, May 1974, p166.
Devor, R.E., Doheny, R.C. & Hogg, G.L., 'Quantitative models for the criminal justice system. I. A review with projected directions'. *Proc. 6th Hawaii Int. Conf. on Systems Sciences*, Suppl. II, North Hollywood, Cal, 108-112, 1973.
Fox, R.D., 'Teeside financial planning model'. *Public Finance and Accountancy*, Apr 1974, p115.

Gabrovski, K., 'Computers in planning in People's Republic of Bulgaria'. In *Systems for management and administration,* North Holland, 5, 1076-1079, 1974.
Gandy, R.J., *The computer simulation of a hospital ward.* M.Sc. Thesis, Manchester University, 1974.
Herrick, C.S., 'Simulation of a simple legislature'. *Simulation and Games* 2(4), 405-423, 1971.
Hogg, G.L., Strong, G.M. & Devor, R.E., 'Quantitative models for the criminal justice system. II. Stochastic network simulation models'. *Proc. 6th Hawaii Int. Conf. on System Sciences,* Suppl. II, North Hollywood, Cal., 113-116, 1973.
Jacobs, R.L., 'Sentencing by computer - one model and its implication: PartII: American implications of sentencing by computer'. *Rutgers J. of Computers and the Law* 4(2), 302-323, 1975.
Kim, Yun Haeng & Kim, Seong-in, 'Sentencing by computer - one model and its implication: Part I: A proposal to facilitate the uniform administration of justice in Korea through the use of a mathematical model'. *Rutgers J. of Computers and the Law* 4(2), 284-301, 1975.
McLaughlin, D., 'The use of simulation to study the implications of public policy - an economic example'. *Proc. Int. Conf. on Cybernetics and Society,* IEEE, N.Y., 574-578, 1972.
Markland, R.E., & Granstaff, P.J., 'Modelling demographic-employment interactions in an urban economy'. *Simulation* 24(1), 33-43, 1975.
Oliver, L.A., Burwell, B.H. & Brewer, J.W., 'Comparison of three methods for developing models of resource demand'. *Simulation* 24(1), 1-13, 1975.
Olson, S.H., Berlin, G.N. & Guiland, L.S., 'Computer modelling in a course on urban decision making'. *Simulation and Games* 4(4), 440-453, 1973.
Rath, G.J., 'Public system simulations'. In Guetzkow, H., 573-612.
Sain, M.K., Henry, E.W., & Uhran, J.J., 'An algebraic method for simulating legal systems'. *Simulation* 21(5), 150-158, 1973.
Scott, C.D., 'The New Haven expenditure model: a new approach'. In *Forecasting Local Government Spending,* Urban Institute, Washington, D.C., 3-10, 1972.
Schlenger, W.E., 'A systems approach to drug user services'. *Behavioural Science* 18(2), 137-147, 1973.
Swanson, C.V., & Waldmann, R.L., 'A simulation model of economic growth dynamics'. *J. of the American Inst. of Planners* 36, 314-322, 1970.
Weintraub, R., 'The full employment model: a critique'. *Kyklos* 25, 83-98, 1972.
Wong, A.K.C. & Au, T., 'A dynamic model for planning patient care in hospitals'. *IEEE Trans. Syst. Man. and Cyber.,* SMC-2(2), 226-231, 1972.
Woodham, J.B., 'The Teesside long range financial model'. *IBIICC 1st World Conf. on Informatics in Government,* Intergovernmental Bureau for Informatics, Rome, 2, 735-750, 1972.

Sociology

Bartholomew, D.J., 'Stochastic models for social processes: a review and bibliography'. *Sociological Review Monograph* 19, 129-139, 1973.
Burton, M.L., 'Recent computer applications in cultural anthropology'. *Computers and the Humanities* 7(6), 337-341, 1973.
Chenhall, R.G., *Computers in anthropology and archeology.* IBM Corp. Technical Publ. Dept., White Plains, N.Y., GE20-6384-0, 1971.
Coplin, W.D., 'Approaches to the social sciences through man-computer simulations'. *Simulation and Games* 1(4), 391-410, 1970.
Forrester, J.W., 'A national model for understanding social and economic change: Part 1'. *Simulation* 24(4), 125-128, 1975.
Gremy, J.P., 'The use of computer simulation techniques in sociology'. *International Social Science Journal* 23(2), 204-218, 1971.

Gullahorn, J.T., & Gullahorn, J.E., 'Social and cultural system simulations'. In Guetzkow, H., 144-190.
Hanneman, G.J., 'Simulating diffusion processes'. *Simulation and Games* 11(4), 387-404, 1971.
Harper, D., 'Computers in behavioural science: the computer simulation of sociological surveys', *Behavioural Science* 17(3), 471-480, 1972.
Inbar, M. & Stoll, C.S., *Social Science Simulations*. The Free Press, N.Y., 1970.
Morrill, R.L., 'The Negro ghetto problems and alternatives'. In Guetzkow, H., 391-411.
Sakoda, J.M., 'The checkerboard model of social interaction'. *J. of Mathematical Sociology* 1(1), 119-132, 1971.
Tepperman, L.J. & Tepperman, B., 'Dynasty formation in eight imaginary societies'. *Canadian Review of Sociology and Anthropology* 8, 121-141, 1971.
Werner, R., *A model and simulation of the awareness process within innovation diffusion: a synthesis of empirical research*. Unpublished Ph. D. Thesis, Syracuse University, USA, 1972.

Transport

Baise, V.K. & Rockwell, T.H., 'Evaluation of visual field requirements of vehicles in freeway merging situations'. *16th Annual Meeting of the Human Factors Society*, Los Angeles, 70-79, 1972.
Beilby, M.H., 'Road traffic simulation on a small computer'. *Computer Journal* 15(2), 134-137, 1972.
Borch, D.T., 'A computer simulation model of train operations in CTC territory'. In *Proc. AFIPS 1971 Spring Joint Computer Conf.*, AFIPS Press, Montvale, N.J., 93-102.
Burhardt, K.K., & Lee, E.B., 'A simulation technique for traffic systems: validity and applications'. *Proc. 1973 Summer Computation Simulation Conf.*, Quebec, Canada, 485-492, 1973.
Chen, T.C., 'Systems analysis for subway environment'. In *Computers and urban society*, 189-206.
Davis, M., 'Application of fast-time simulation techniques to the study of ATC systems'. *Ergonomics* 14(5), 661-668, 1971.
Deisenroth, M.P., *On simulation methodology in vehicular traffic flow*. Georgia Inst. Technol. Thesis (Univ. Mic. 74-21564), Atlanta, 1974.
Doshay, I., 'Transportation system operability simulation'. *1973 IEEE Region 6 Conference on Minicomputers and their applications*, IEEE, N.Y., 107-111.
Hauser, J.R., 'An efficient model for planning bus routes in communities with populations between 20 000 and 25 000'. *Bull. Oper. Res. Soc. Am.* 21 Supp 2, pB233, 1973. (Abstract only)
Homburger, W.S., 'The role of computers in urban transportation'. In Marois, M., (Ed.), *Man and Computer*, Elsevier, 445-458, 1975.
Hoppe, C.W., 'Using simulation to solve transportation problems'. *Management Controls*, Dec 1970, p253.
Howarth, A. & Powner, E.T., 'A dynamic control strategy and software simulation for multiple traffic intersections'. *Transport Planning and Technology* 2(2), 93-103, 1973.
Jackson, A., 'Modelling problems in air traffic control systems'. In Bekey 1 (1), p49.
Larsson, U. & Lundin, R., *Urban Traffic Simulation*. Univ. Gothenberg, Gothenburg. 1971.
Li, M.C., & Collins, J.T., 'Computer simulation of traffic volume-speed delay model'. In *Computers and Urban Society*, 207-220.

92 Computer Models

Parsons, et al, 'Single-track subway environmental simulation model. Phase 1'. *Government Reports Announcements*, (PB-206 895)(UMTA-DC-MTD-7-71-22), 1971.

Payne, H., 'Models of freeway taffic control'. In Bekey 1(1), p49.

Pollack, M., 'An aircraft scheduling model for air-line planning'. *Bull. Oper. Res. Soc. Am.* 20, Supp 1. pB185, 1972.

Sastry, M.V.R., 'Some computer models of urban transportation systems'. *Traffic Quarterly* 27(2), 269-287, 1973.

Shanks, S.G., Hippler, R.R. & Formica, P.N., 'Urban transportation strategies model'. *1974 Winter Simulation Conf.*, ACM, Edmont, N.Y., 1, 339-348.

Sinha, K.C., 'A computer algorithm for simulation of traffic flow on a section of freeway'. In Sworder, D.D., *Systems and Simulation in the Service of Society*, Simulation Councils, La Jolla, Calif., 61-68, 1972.

Veerapandian, M. & Ramani, S., 'Simulation of a metropolitain bus system'. *Simulation* 24(6), 133-136, June 1975.

World models

Cuypers, J.G.M., 'World dynamics: two simplified versions of Forrester's model'. *Automatica* 9(3), 339-401, 1973.

De Vries, H., 'A critical assessment of the MIT world models'. In Goldberg 2, 149-165.

Favreau, R.R. & McLeod, J., 'CAL-1: a modelling tool for non-programmers'. *Behavioural Science* 20(2), 136-139, 1975.

Forrester, J.W., *World dynamics*. Wright-Allen Press, Cambridge, Mass., 1971.

Krenz, J.H., 'World dynamics - an alternative method'. *IEEE Trans. Syst. Man & Cyber.*, SMC-3(3), 272-275, 1973.

Laska, R.M., 'The world model contoversy: will mankind survive?'. *Computer Decisions* 4(4), 24-27, 1972.

Randers, J. & Meadows, D.H., 'The carrying capacity of the globe'. *Sloan Management Review* 13(2), 11-27, 1972.

Streatfield, G., 'No limit to the growth debate'. *Simulation* 20(6), 210-212, 1973.

6 A Computer Model of Memory

Our objective here is to illustrate how a simple model of memory can be implemented on a computer. The review article by Frijda[1] summarizes the work of psychologists up to 1972 and describes some of the models up to that date. They are usually implemented by means of a special-purpose language such as IPL[2] or LISP[3], which have facilities for easier manipulation of the complex list structures found, but the principles are the same in the FORTRAN version we shall describe.

The Lindsay-Norman model of memory

Lindsay and Norman[4] identify two parts of memory. One part contains the information and is known as the data base; the information stored there is made up of 'concepts' and the links (or inter-relationships) between concepts. The other part is the 'interpretive process', which uses the information stored in the data base and is responsible for evaluating inputs to the memory, for storing new information, for asking questions, for retrieving information to solve problems, and so on.

The data base

Human memory contains a large number of concepts, for example concepts of 'car', 'person', 'house' and so on. There is no absolute definition of a particular concept - each of us understands a concept through its relationship to other concepts in our memory. These relationships are formed when we first encounter the concept and may be modified when we subsequently learn more about it. For example, a child may be given a toy car for his bithday, and his first reaction may be to say that it is blue - he knows what 'blue' is because his cup is blue. So the concepts may be stored in his memory as shown in Fig. 6.1 and a link between 'car' and 'cup' is formed via the common concept 'blue'.

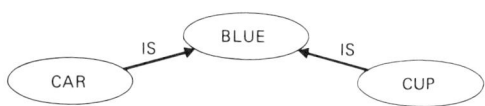

Fig. 6.1: Three concepts (ovals) in memory and their links (arrows)

The reaction of a second child to an identical car may be entirely different. For example, he may notice that the car has wheels because he remembers the wheels of his brother's bicycle which ran over his foot and

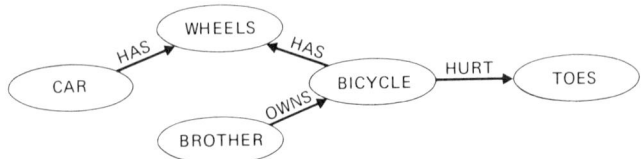

Fig. 6.2: In this memory, car has been linked to wheels. Wheels are memorable as part of the brother's bicycle.

hurt his toes - Fig. 6.2.

The same concept (car) has produced a different reaction in two memory systems and is stored differently in them. Although many types of link are possible, Lindsay and Norman isolate the dominant relationships by which a memory system understands a concept as being:
i) ISA relationship - identifying the class of concepts to which this particular concept belongs, e.g. EMMA ISA PERSON;
ii) IS or HAS relationships - identifying the properties of this particular concept which make it unique, e.g. EMMA IS FIVE, EMMA HAS LONG HAIR. Although we know another EMMA who is seven and has short hair, this particular EMMA is five and has long hair.

These can be represented schematically as shown in Fig. 6.3.

Fig. 6.3: ISA, HAS and IS relationships link the concepts

There are two points to note about the arrows which relate one concept to another. Firstly, they are named - an ISA arrow is different from a HAS arrow. Secondly, they point in a specific direction - if we follow the arrow in the opposite direction, it means something different. Moving from PERSON in the reverse direction along the ISA arrow gives us an 'EXAMPLE' of a PERSON, i.e. EMMA.

Primary and secondary concepts

Suppose our memory system has learned that DAVID is MALE, has a LARGE CAR and is a PERSON. This information would be represented in the model as shown in Fig. 6.4.

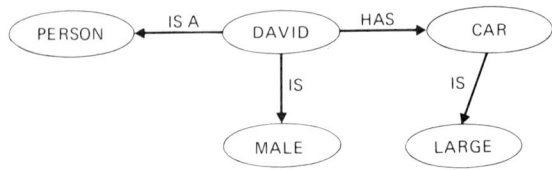

Fig. 6.4: David has a large car

Now suppose that further facts are learned, namely that MARTIN has a SMALL

CAR. Adding this information to the above diagram would be incorrect, if we take it that a car cannot be both large and small.

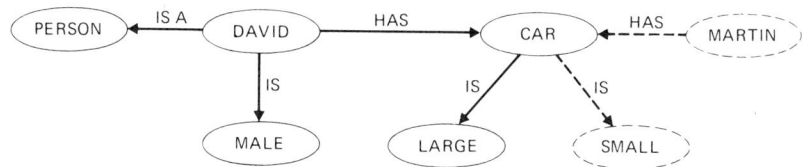

Fig. 6.5: A straightforward attempt to add to Fig. 6.4 the information that Martin has a small car leads to a contradiction

The solution adopted by Lindsay and Norman is to have a single definition of the concept 'car' (known as the *primary definition*), but to allow many instances where the concept is used, perhaps in a modified form. These particular uses, known as *secondary definitions*, are represented by enclosing them in angular brackets, <car>, which can be interpreted as meaning 'this car' - Fig. 6.6.

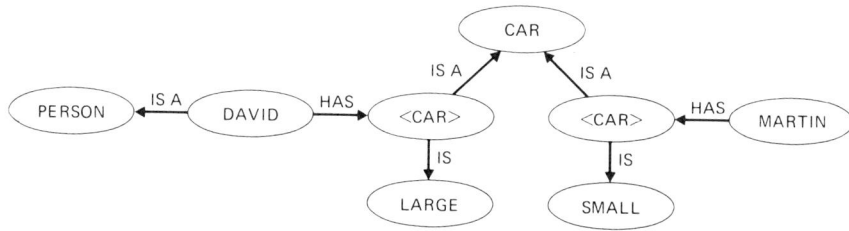

Fig. 6.6: The contradiction is avoided by using secondary concepts to define particular instances of the primary concept

The memory system not only knows of the concept 'car', it also knows that cars may be large or small. It is a large car that David has, whereas Martin's car is small. The addition of each concept is described by additions to the network of arrows; a concept oval in such a network together with the arrows emanating from it is often called a *node*.

The interpretive process

Having developed a basic structure of memory, we turn our attention to the cognitive processes which might operate on it.

Input and output mechanisms

A memory system must be able to communicate with the outside world. It has to accept information from its environment and translate it into a form suitable for storing in the memory structure. In responding to questions, information needs to be retrieved from the structure and translated back into a form that the outside world will understand.

Let us first consider the input mechanism. Suppose our memory system is visiting a zoo and enters the elephant house. It perceives:
SUSIE IS A LARGE GREY ELEPHANT WITH A LONG TAIL.

96 Computer Models

Before this information can be stored in our data base, it must be translated into a standard form capable of being stored:
    SUSIE ISA ELEPHANT
    SUSIE IS LARGE
    SUSIE IS GREY
    SUSIE HAS TAIL
    TAIL IS LONG.
The output mechanism is the converse of this input mechanism.

Making responses

Suppose we have the memory structure as shown in Fig. 6.7; let us explore how the memory system might respond to various queries.

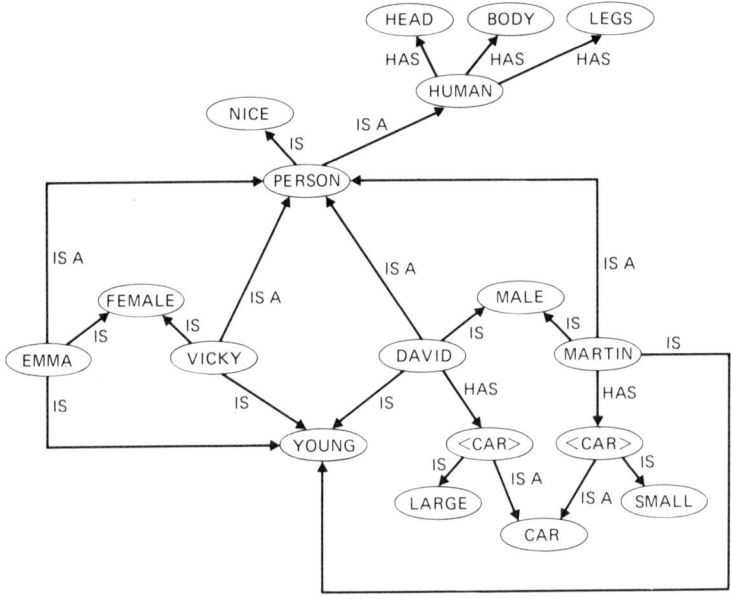

Fig. 6.7: A memory structure with information about four children

A. General query. Suppose the query were of the form 'tell me about ...', for example
        TELL ME ABOUT DAVID.
The memory system might respond something like
> 'David is male. He is young and he has a um, let me see, oh yes, a large car. David is also a person. Now let me tell you about a person. A person is nice, and is also a human. Would you like to know about a human ... ?'

The output is obtained by following the arrows emanating from the concepts. When a secondary definition is encountered it must be examined with care, first following the ISA arrow, and then the other arrows for the qualifiers. On the Lindsay-Norman model this requires time and effort, so they assume that stalling phrases such as 'um', 'let me see' and so on may be used to fill in the time delay.

B. Specific query. A query of the type DOES EMMA HAVE LEGS? would be answered by searching the concept EMMA for the qualifier HAS LEGS. On

failing to find it, the memory system would follow the ISA arrow from EMMA to
the concept PERSON and would search again for the qualifier HAS LEGS. This
process would be repeated on the concept HUMAN, where the qualifier HAS LEGS
would be found. The memory system would then reply 'YES' to the query,
reasoning that a human has legs and, since a person is a human, a person must
also have legs - Emma is a person, so she must have legs too.

Re-organizing memory

A feature of a human memory is that it is continually being reorganized, and
generalization of information may occur. For example, the query 'tell me
about person' might result in the response that EMMA, VICKI, DAVID and MARTIN
are all persons, and then the memory system might review the properties of
these persons. While doing so, it might learn the interesting fact that *all*
persons are young. The memory system might reorganize itself so that the
qualifier 'IS YOUNG' is removed from each of the examples of a person and is
added to the concept PERSON, resulting in the memory structure shown in
Fig. 6.8.

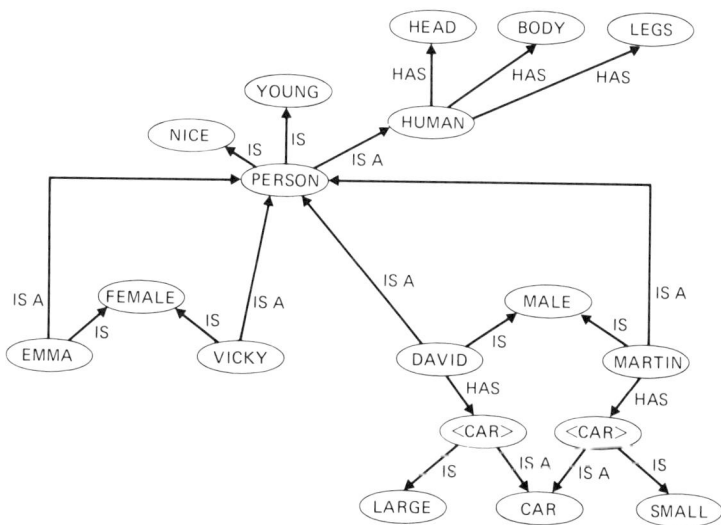

*Fig. 6.8: The memory structure reorganized after making the generalization
that every known person is young, so YOUNG can qualify PERSON*

You will be able to think of other reorganization which could take place,
for example creating secondary concepts MALE PERSON and FEMALE PERSON.

Implementing the model on a computer

Our description of the Lindsay-Norman model of memory has been brief and does
not do its authors full justice. For a fuller introduction, we recommend
their lucid book *Human Information Processing*[4]. Norman and
Rumelhart's *Explorations in Cognition*[5] contains more detail. What we
described in the previous section are the features of the Lindsay-Norman

model we have chosen to include in our computer model. Our choice was governed by the compromise of having sufficient features to provide a reasonable working model, yet at the same time not having so many as to complicate the description unnecessarily.

Even the selected features could lead to a model too detailed for this book and unkindly complicated for a reader to whom all the concepts are new. We have, therefore, imposed further arbitrary limitations on the processing which our computer model will carry out, as follows:

1. Input is in the simple form

    SUSIE ISA ELEPHANT
    SUSIE IS LARGE

    and so on, rather than 'Susie is a large grey elephant with a long tail'. We took it that the problems of extracting the meaning of natural language and recording that meaning in the simple form exemplified were secondary to our present purpose (as well as being very challenging!)
2. We allow only ISA, HAS, IS and EXAMPLE arrows in the model (EXAMPLE, you will recall, is the opposite of ISA). We explain later how, in principle, this limitation can be overcome, so that any relation is allowable.
3. Although the data structure we describe is quite general, considerations of space have obliged us to describe the processing of a model in which only one ISA arrow can come from a given concept. A concept which is pointed to by a HAS arrow may not have ISA or HAS arrows coming from it. A concept which is pointed at by an IS arrow may not have any arrows coming from it. Only arrows of the same type may point at a given concept. (Although these limitations seem severe, the model that results is still quite powerful.)
4. Circular qualification is not allowed, either directly (e.g. PERSON ISA PERSON) or indirectly (e.g. EMMA ISA PERSON, PERSON ISA HUMAN, HUMAN ISA EMMA).

The memory system is designed to be used interactively from a terminal by a user, who holds a 'conversation' with the program. Since it is more natural to hold a conversation with a person, we have adopted the name TIM for the program, and we will refer to the data base as 'TIM's memory' - Fig. 6.9.

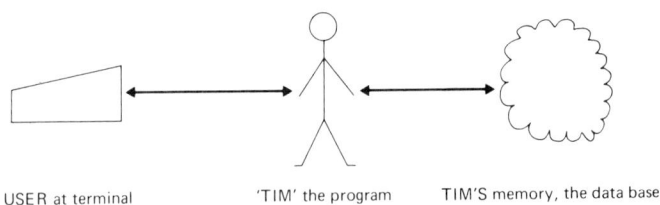

USER at terminal   'TIM' the program   TIM'S memory, the data base

Fig. 6.9: Overview of the model memory system

Simulating TIM's memory in the computer

Each node in the network of concepts is represented by one row of a table called NODES. The table has six columns, as shown in Fig. 6.10.

```
           Concept              Qualifiers
         ┌─────────┐      ┌─────────────────────┐
         NAME  TYPE   IS A   HAS    IS   EXAMPLE
          1     2      3     4      5      6
   1
   2
   3
   ⋮
   99
   100
```

Fig. 6.10: The NODES table which will hold a memory network

Column 1 contains the name of the concept, for example EMMA, PERSON.
Column 2 contains the concept type, which may be one of the following:

```
    1 : ISA  ⎫
    2 : HAS  ⎬  ordinary concepts
    3 : IS   ⎭
   -1 : ISA  ⎫
   -2 : HAS  ⎬  secondary concepts
   -3 : IS   ⎭
```

A zero indicates that the concept has no type (no arrows point *at* it).
Columns 3 to 6 are used for arrows; the details are described below.

Representing arrows in the computer

Our first problem is to decide how to represent the links between concepts. If there were only one arrow of a given type emanating from a node then a solution would be simply to use the appropriate column of the subject concept to point to the object concept; e.g. EMMA IS YOUNG would be represented as shown in Fig. 6.11, where the IS column of EMMA contains the row number of the object concept YOUNG.

	NAME	TYPE	IS A	HAS	IS	EXAMPLE
1	EMMA				2	
2	YOUNG					

Fig. 6.11: Simply identifying the qualifier in the arrow column (EMMA IS YOUNG) would limit the model to one arrow of a type per concept

However, a characteristic of our model of memory is that a node may have several arrows of a given type emanating from it. If the maximum number of IS arrows (for example) were known, we could expand our table so that, instead of having a single IS column, we could have as many as necessary to cater for that maximum number. This would make inefficient use of the computer, obviously, for, even if there were no IS arrows for a particular concept, we would need to allow for the maximum - likewise for ISA and HAS arrows. Since the actual number of arrows from any concept is variable, and we don't wish to impose maximum values, we need an extensible method for representing arrows. Such a method is the Forward-linked List, which has links which chain together the items in a list. Each link contains two fields: the first field points to the object concept (i.e. the field contains the number of the object concept's row in the NODES table) and the second field points to the next link in the chain.

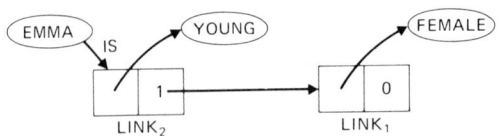

Fig. 6.12: In this linked list, the left field of a link contains the row number of the object concept and the right field contains the number of the next link in the chain

A schematic of a forward-linked list is shown in Fig. 6.12, where the subject concept EMMA is qualified by IS FEMALE and IS YOUNG. The first field of each link points to an object concept; the second field of each link points to the next link in the chain. (This is zero in the case of the last link, link 1, because there are no further links.)

Each link is represented by one row of a table called LINKS. This table has two columns as shown in Fig. 6.13.

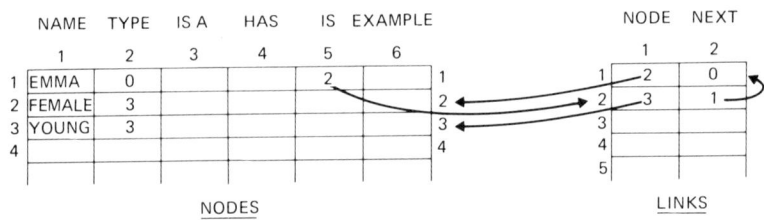

Fig. 6.13: The entries in NODES and LINKS recording the two relations EMMA IS YOUNG, EMMA IS FEMALE

The IS column of row 1 (EMMA concept) of the NODES table contains 2, telling us in which row of the links table our chain starts. The left field in this row contains 3, pointing us back to row 3 of the NODES table which contains the concept YOUNG. The right field contains 1, and this points us to the next link in the chain, row 1 of the LINKS table. Row 1 points to the FEMALE node, and the right-hand field has a zero, telling us we are at the end of the chain. HAS, ISA and EXAMPLE chains are handled in exactly the same way, LINKS being used to hold all the links. If a particular arrow type is not used, the corresponding arrow column for the subject concept concerned holds a zero.

The NODES and LINKS tables for a larger example are shown in Fig. 6.14.

A Computer Model of Memory

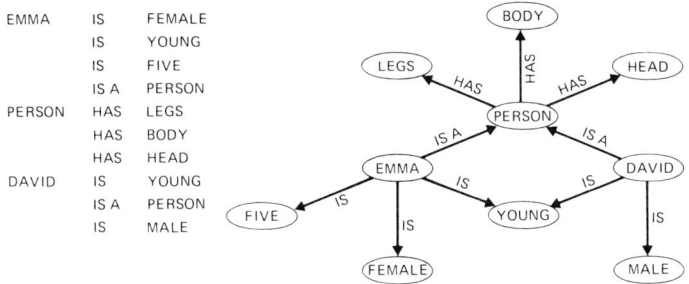

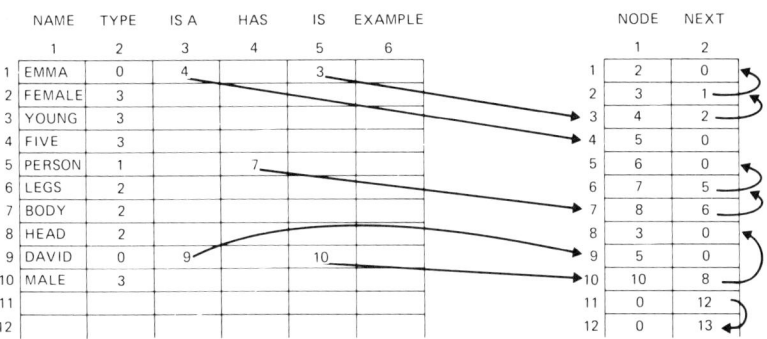

Fig. 6.14: *The NODES and LINKS table entries are made as the concepts are met. LINKS records all the arrows of all types; the NODES entries are updated to point to the latest link in the chain. (For clarity, zero entries for unused qualifiers in the NODES table have been omitted)*

In order to make further entries in the NODES or LINKS tables, it is essential to keep track of where we have got to at any one time. This is done by two further fields. MEMNOW points to the latest row of NODES which currently has a concept entered in it. In the case of LINKS, all the unused links are chained together (the 'free-link chain') and a field called LNKFRE points to the first available link in this chain. The use of these fields will become clearer shortly.

The two fundamental operations that are performed on the memory in our model are 'adding a relation' and 'removing a relation'. Let us consider each in turn.

Adding a relation

Suppose we have entered the relations EMMA IS FEMALE and EMMA IS YOUNG; the NODES and LINKS tables will be as shown in Fig. 6.15.

Now we qualify EMMA by the additional relation EMMA IS FIVE. This can be inserted in the forward-linked list in any position, simply by breaking the chain, inserting the new link and relinking the chain correctly. It is simplest to add the new link at the start of the chain, so that the new link

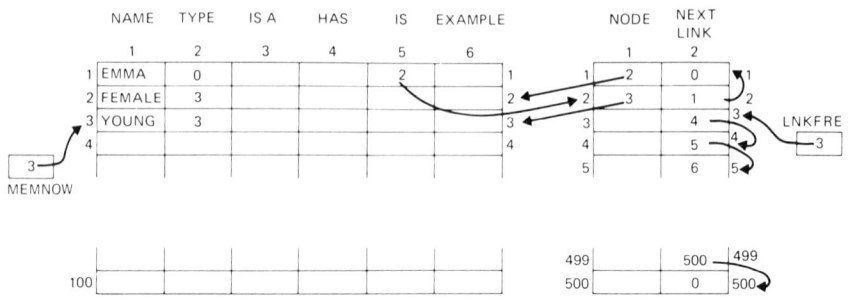

Fig. 6.15: The NODES and LINKS tables prior to the addition of a further relation

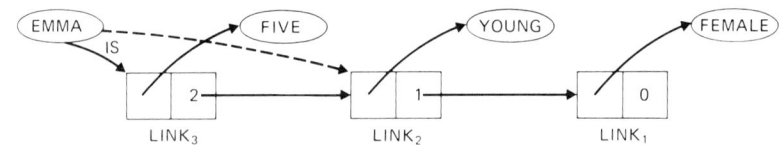

Fig. 6.16: The desired new chain after adding EMMA IS FIVE

becomes the first link in the chain. The new chain will be as shown in Fig. 6.16.
  In our model the relinking is done by the subroutine QUALFY, whose purpose is to qualify a source concept. In principle the processing is:

1. Add the object concept to the NODES table at row (MEMNOW + 1), update MEMNOW.
2. Save the current value of LNKFRE (this will be the number of the first free link - let us call it FIRST) and update LNKFRE to point to the next link in the free-link chain.
3. Change the right-hand field of the link indicated by FIRST so that it points to the same link as is currently pointed to by the appropriate column of the subject concept in NODES (connecting the link to the chain).
4. Change the arrow column of the subject concept so that it points to the link indicated by FIRST (connecting the concept to the link).
5. Set the left-hand field of the link indicated by FIRST to the row number of the object concept.

On completion, the NODES and LINKS tables will be as in Fig. 6.17.

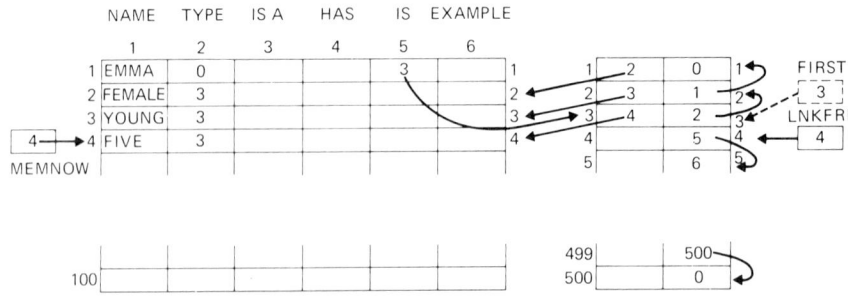

Fig. 6.17: The tables after the addition of the new relation

Removing a relation

After adding the relation EMMA IS FIVE we know that EMMA IS FIVE, YOUNG and FEMALE. Perhaps EMMA ISA PERSON, and we notice that all other persons are young. We may want to remove the qualification IS YOUNG from EMMA so that we can add it to PERSON.

This is achieved by tracing through the chain of relations until the link to be removed is found. Let us call this link NEXT, and the one just before it LAST.

The next step is to remove the link from the chain. Remember we have the situation shown in Fig. 6.18 and we want to reach that shown in Fig. 6.19.

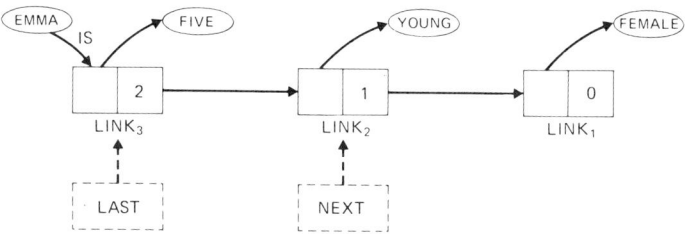

Fig. 6.18: The chain before deleting the link indicated by NEXT

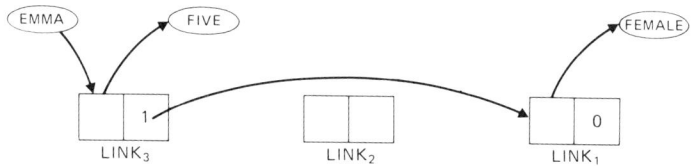

Fig. 6.19: The chain after the deletion

This is achieved by setting the right-hand field of LAST to point to the successor of NEXT, indicated by the right-hand field of NEXT. (A special case arises if the link to be removed happens to be the first link in the chain. In this case, there is no predecessor link, so the arrow column of the NODES table must be changed to point to the successor of NEXT.)

The last step is to return the by-passed, and now unused, link to the free-link chain. This is achieved by adding it to the head of the free-link chain, in the manner described earlier for an addition to an arrow chain.

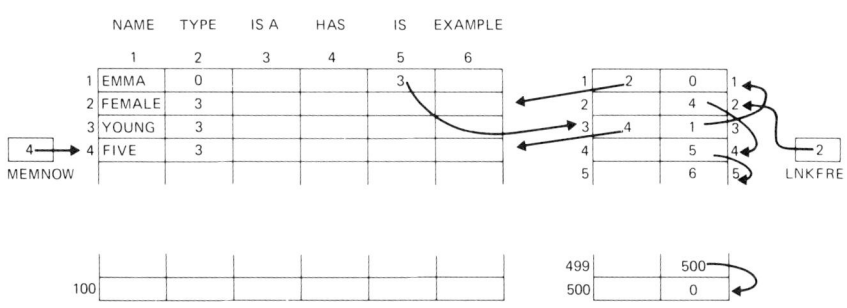

Fig. 6.20: NODES and LINKS after deleting the relation EMMA IS YOUNG

On completion, the NODES and LINKS tables will be as shown in Fig. 6.20. Note that the concept YOUNG still remains in memory - it is just not linked now to the IS chain of EMMA.

Use of a stack

A conversation between two people, A and B, may be something like

A: EMMA ISA PERSON.
B: Oh yes, that's interesting; I don't know this concept PERSON - please tell me more about PERSON.
A: PERSON HAS HEAD.
B: HEAD? That's another concept I haven't come across. Please tell me more about HEAD.
A: HEAD IS LARGE.

And so the conversation continues. When B is satisfied that he knows enough about HEAD (or A declines to provide further information), B may want to backtrack to PERSON, which initially triggered all the discussion about HEAD, and gather further information about PERSON. In a similar way he may backtrack to EMMA when he has exhausted PERSON.

The subject of the original relation EMMA ISA PERSON is EMMA and the object is PERSON. What B does when he goes off exploring PERSON is to make PERSON the subject concept, remembering that EMMA was the previous subject concept. Likewise, after the information PERSON HAS HEAD has been received, B makes HEAD the subject concept and remembers that PERSON is another previous subject concept. At this stage he has two previous subject concepts to remember, EMMA and PERSON, and when he has finished exploring HEAD he will want to retrieve the most recent previous subject, in other words PERSON.

This retrieval order can be achieved by means of a stack, which is simply a list of items which are held in such a way that the items are retrieved in the reverse order to that in which they were stored. A stack is sometimes known as a *Last-In-First-Out* (LIFO) list. The stack of plates at a cafeteria is an everyday example of a stack. Plates are taken from the top by customers and a spring beneath the plates POPs the next plate up, making it available for the next customer. When dirty plates have been collected and washed, they are PUSHed on to the stack, ready for further customers. It is the plates most recently pushed on to the stack which will be the first to be used - those plates at the bottom of the stack, nearest to the spring, may get used only on an exceptionally busy day.

A stack may be implemented by a table with only one column (i.e. a one-dimensional array, in FORTRAN) and a field called TOP, which will be used to point to the top item on the stack. Initially the stack will be empty - Fig. 6.21.

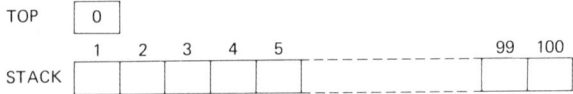

Fig. 6.21: *When the stack is empty, TOP contains zero*

What we PUSH on to the stack in our model is the row number of the NODES table containing the previous subject concept. In the case of EMMA it is 1. So, just prior to making PERSON into the subject concept we would PUSH the

A Computer Model of Memory

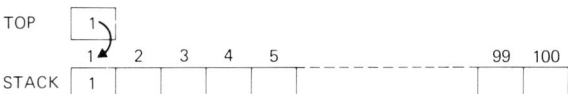

Fig. 6.22: PUSHing an item on the stack increments TOP

value 1 on to the stack, changing it as shown in Fig. 6.22.
Similarly, when we want to explore HEAD further, we need to make PERSON into a previous subject by PUSHing the value 5 (see Fig. 6.14) on to the stack, changing it as shown in Fig. 6.23.

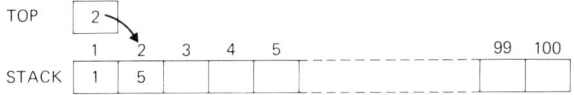

Fig. 6.23: The two items recorded on the stack are
the NODES row numbers of EMMA and PERSON

When we have completed exploring HEAD, we want to return to our most recent previous subject concept. This is achieved by a POP operation on the stack. This operation returns the top value on the stack (in this case, 5) and resets the TOP pointer to the next entry. After this operation the stack appears as in Fig. 6.24.

```
TOP      1
       1   2   3   4   5           99  100
STACK  1
```

Fig. 6.24: PERSON has been POPped, so EMMA is now at the top of the stack

Simulating TIM in the computer

We want TIM to be able to communicate with the user, to perform simple evaluation of information provided by the user, to store new information, to be able to retrieve information for answering questions, and to do some simple thinking, resulting in reorganization of his memory.
At the outset, the user is asked to select from a choice of five options what he would like TIM to do. These options are:

REMEMBER   : puts TIM into 'remember' mode. Thereafter the user is asked to respond to TIM's questions, building up new concepts, and their relationships to other concepts, in TIM' memory.
RECALL   : puts TIM into 'recall' mode. The user may then pose either a general query (of the type 'tell me about DAVID') or a specific query (of the type 'HAS EMMA LEGS?'). TIM will respond appropriately.
DAY-DREAM : TIM is allowed a quiet time to consider the information he has stored in his memory. Some simple reorganization may take place, depending on the precise information in his memory.

106 Computer Models

The next two options do not have a corresponding operation in a real memory, but are provided for the convenience of the user in experimenting with the memory system.

DISPLAY : The total contents of TIM's memory are displayed.
CLEAR : TIM' memory is completely cleared of concepts. It is experimentally convenient for the user to be able to clear memory and start again building up concepts and relationships.

TIM is implemented on the computer by means of a main program which (a) determines the user's choice of what he wants TIM to do and (b) calls an appropriate subroutine (REMEMB for remember, RECALL for recall, DREAM for day-dream, DISPLY for display and CLEAR for clear). These subroutines in turn call the subroutines which manipulate the data base. Figure 6.25 gives a conceptual view of the memory system.

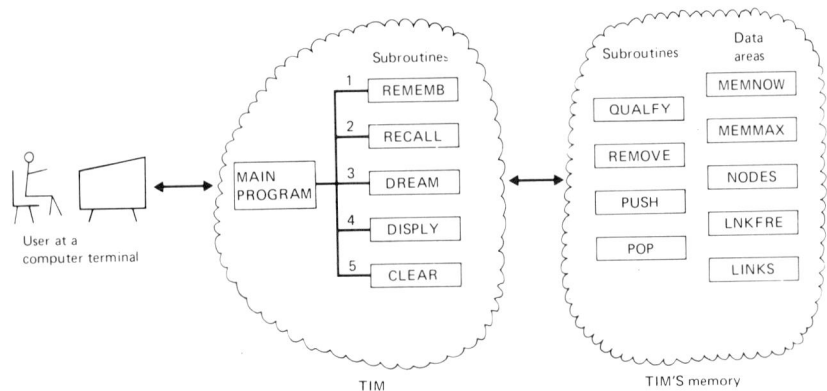

Fig. 6.25: How the memory system is modelled. There are other subroutines in the program, detailed at the end of the chapter.

Let us now look at each of the three principal TIM subroutines in turn. The other two subroutines need no elaboration.

1. REMEMB subroutine

The purpose of the REMEMB subroutine is to prompt the user for information, to validate the information provided (as far as is possible in this simple model), to reject invalid information, and to store valid information in TIM's memory. An outline flowchart showing the principal operations performed by this subroutine is given in Fig. 6.26.

A. Determine the major subject concept. The first task of REMEMB is to determine the subject concept. In this simple model we have imposed the restriction that the initial subject concept (which we term a *major* subject concept) cannot be in memory already. Hence all the information about a particular major subject concept must be ascertained in a single session with the subroutine REMEMB - the user is not allowed to provide TIM with partial information about a major subject concept and then come back at a later time to provide more information about the same concept. The concept is read in from the terminal and is stored in a single computer word (the computer upon which we implemented this model holds six characters per word). This approach, although restricting concepts to six characters or less, leads to a simpler and more easily comprehensible data structure for representing TIM's

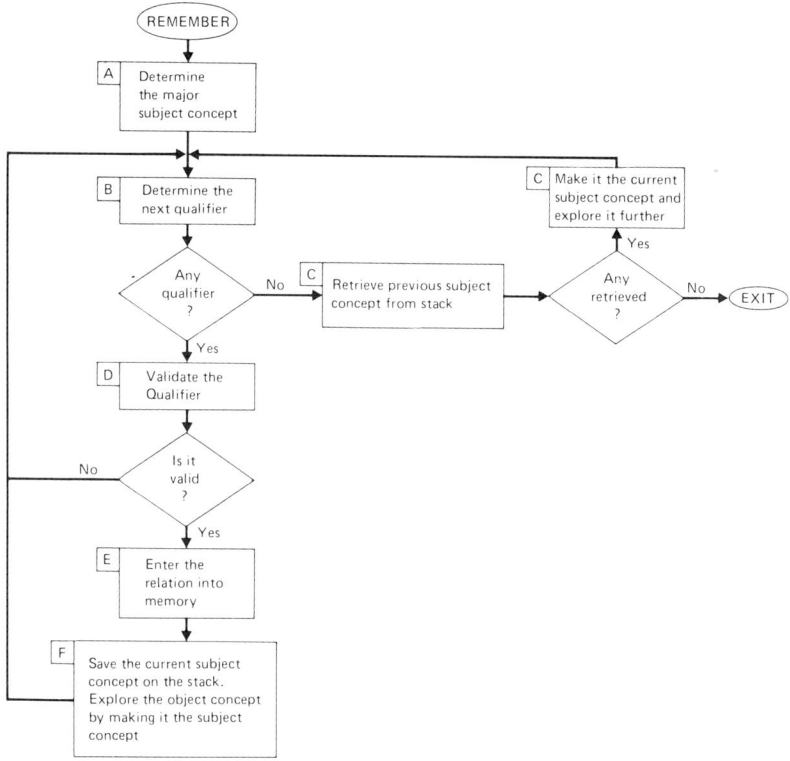

Fig. 6.26: Outline flowchart of the remembering subroutine, REMEMB

memory in the computer. (With computers which hold fewer charcters per word, a similar simplicity can be achieved, without further limiting the length of concept names, by allotting two words per name or three words per name, etc.)
B. Determine the next qualifier. The user is invited to enter more information about the current subject concept - this may be the major subject concept or it may be the previous object concept which TIM is following up. Any restrictions on what he may enter are made clear to the user; for example, if TIM is pursuing a HAS object concept, only IS qualifiers are legal in this simple version. The arrow and the object concept are read and validated.
C. Retrieve previous subject concept. Control passes to this section of the program if the user signifies that he has no further information about the current subject concept. He does this by entering a null response at the terminal (by pressing the return key in response to the prompt given in **B**). This section attempts to get the most recent previous subject concept from the stack, by using the subroutine POP. If successful, this concept becomes the current subject concept, and TIM seeks more information about it.
D. Validate the qualifier. This section checks the validity of the relation and checks that the constraints we have imposed are not being violated. In particular it checks that:

1. The relation is not directly circular, e.g. PERSON ISA PERSON.
2. The object concept is not a major subject concept. This constraint is

applied to prevent major concepts from having secondary definitions. (We avoided this complexity because it does not contribute anything to the understanding of the model - it simply complicates the programs.)
3. The object concept is not a primary concept. (A complexity avoided for the same reason as above.)
4. The arrow is consistent with the type of object concept.
5. The relation is not in memory already.
6. The relation is not indirectly circular, e.g. EMMA ISA PERSON, PERSON ISA HUMAN, HUMAN ISA PERSON. (This condition is detected by the presence of the object concept on the stack.)

Any error detected in this section results in the user being asked to re-enter the object concept.

E. Enter the relation into TIM's memory. On reaching this section, the elation has been validated as far as possible, and TIM is in a position to enter it into his memory. Because TIM is unable to detect spelling errors and because there is no mechanism by which the *user* can delete relations once they have been entered into TIM's memory, TIM first of all checks back to see that his understanding of the relation is what the user intended. He asks

    EMMA ISA PERTON? IS THAT CORRECT?

The user in this case would reply NO (because PERSON has been typed incorrectly) and the relation would not be entered into memory.

On receiving an affirmative reply, TIM gets nodes for the source and object concepts, if necessary. If the object concept is already in memory, TIM then checks with the user that it is the same concept. Suppose the user has entered the relation MARTIN HAS CAR, and the CAR that TIM knows about is BLUE and LARGE. TIM will then output

    CAR IS BLUE
    CAR IS LARGE
    IS THAT CORRECT?

If the user replies YES, the concept CAR that TIM knows will be used as the object concept; on the other hand, if the user replies NO, a secondary definition of CAR will be created. The actual relation is written into memory by calling up the subroutine QUALFY.

F. Explore ISA and HAS object concepts. In this section those object concepts for which further exploration is permitted (ISA and HAS, but not IS) are made into the subject concept, having firstly saved the current subject concept on the stack by a call to the subroutine PUSH.

A sample of the output produced when our program was run is shown below (user's response in italics - a null response is denoted by a blank line following the invitation to ENTER ARROW).

    MEMORY HAS BEEN CLEARED
    0=EXIT 1=REMEMBER 2=RECALL 3=DAY-DREAM 4=DISPLAY 5=CLEAR
    ENTER YOUR REQUIREMENT
    1
    ENTER SUBJECT CONCEPT
    EMMA
    TELL ME MORE ABOUT EMMA   (ISA, HAS OR IS)
    ENTER ARROW
    IS
    ENTER OBJECT CONCEPT
    FEMALE
    EMMA   IS   FEMALE ? IS THIS CORRECT?
    YES

RELATION ENTERED INTO MEMORY

TELL ME MORE ABOUT EMMA   (ISA, HAS OR IS)
ENTER ARROW
ISA
ENTER OBJECT CONCEPT
PERSON
EMMA   ISA PERSON?   IS THIS CORRECT?
YES
RELATION ENTERED INTO MEMORY

TELL ME MORE ABOUT PERSON (ISA, HAS OR IS)
ENTER ARROW
ISA
ENTER OBJECT CONCEPT
HUMAN
PERSON   ISA HUMAN?   IS THIS CORRECT?
YES
RELATION ENTERED INTO MEMORY

TELL ME MORE ABOUT HUMAN   (ISA, HAS OR IS)
ENTER ARROW
HAS
ENTER OBJECT CONCEPT
LEGS
HUMAN HAS LEGS   ? IS THIS CORRECT?
YES
RELATION ENTERED INTO MEMORY

TELL ME MORE ABOUT LEGS   (IS)
ENTER ARROW

TELL ME MORE ABOUT HUMAN   (ISA, HAS OR IS)
ENTER ARROW
HAS
ENTER OBJECT CONCEPT
BODY
HUMAN   HAS BODY   ? IS THIS CORRECT?
YES
RELATION ENTERED INTO MEMORY

TELL ME MORE ABOUT BODY   (IS)
ENTER ARROW

TELL ME MORE ABOUT HUMAN   (ISA, HAS OR IS)
ENTER ARROW
HAS
ENTER OBJECT CONCEPT
HEAD
HUMAN   HAS HEAD   ? IS THIS CORRECT?
YES
RELATION ENTERED INTO MEMORY

TELL ME MORE ABOUT HEAD   (IS)
ENTER ARROW

TELL ME MORE ABOUT HUMAN   (ISA, HAS OR IS)

```
ENTER ARROW

TELL ME MORE ABOUT PERSON  (HAS OR IS)
ENTER ARROW
IS
ENTER OBJECT CONCEPT
NICE
PERSON IS NICE   ?  IS THIS CORRECT?
YES
RELATION ENTERED INTO MEMORY

TELL ME MORE ABOUT PERSON  (HAS OR IS)
ENTER ARROW

TELL ME MORE ABOUT EMMA    (HAS OR IS)
ENTER ARROW
IS
ENTER OBJECT CONCEPT
YOUNG
EMMA    IS YOUNG?  IS THIS CORRECT?
YES
RELATION ENTERED INTO MEMORY

TELL ME MORE ABOUT EMMA    (HAS OR IS)
ENTER ARROW
IS
ENTER OBJECT CONCEPT
FIVE
EMMA    IS FIVE    ?  IS THIS CORRECT?
YES
RELATION ENTERED INTO MEMORY

TELL ME MORE ABOUT EMMA    (HAS OR IS)
ENTER ARROW

0=EXIT  1=REMEMBER  2=RECALL  3=DAY-DREAM  4=DISPLAY  5=CLEAR
ENTER YOUR REQUIREMENT
4
CONCEPT   ISA      HAS      IS       EXAMPLE
=======   ======   ======   ======   ======
EMMA
          PERSON
                            FIVE
                            YOUNG
                            FEMALE
FEMALE
PERSON
          HUMAN
                            NICE
HUMAN
                   HEAD
                   BODY
                   LEGS
LEGS
BODY
HEAD
```

NICE
YOUNG
FIVE

2. RECALL subroutine

An outline flowchart of the principal operations performed by the RECALL subroutine is given in Fig. 6.27.

We will not go into further detail about this subroutine because the reader should now be in a position to fill in the detail himself. A sample of the output produced by our program follows (TIM's memory contains the information shown in Fig. 6.7):

```
1 = TELL ME ABOUT -CONCEPT-
2 = -CONCEPT QUALIFIER CONCEPT- QUESTION
ENTER YOUR REQUIREMENT
2
ENTER SUBJECT CONCEPT
VICKY
ENTER ARROW
HAS
ENTER OBJECT CONCEPT
CAR
VICKY  HAS     CAR   ?  ANSWER IS NO

1 = TELL ME ABOUT -CONCEPT-
2 = -CONCEPT QUALIFIER CONCEPT- QUESTION
ENTER YOUR REQUIREMENT
1
ENTER SUBJECT CONCEPT
DAVID
* DAVID *
        DAVID   IS      MALE
        DAVID   IS      YOUNG
        DAVID   HAS
             ER HMM   LET ME THINK
             OH YES   I KNOW
        DAVID   HAS     CAR
                        CAR    IS    LARGE
        DAVID   ISA     PERSON
DO YOU WANT TO HEAR MORE?
YES
* PERSON *
        PERSON IS      NICE
        PERSON ISA     HUMAN
DO YOU WANT TO HEAR MORE?
NO

1 = TELL ME ABOUT -CONCEPT-
2 = -CONCEPT QUALIFIER CONCEPT- QUESTION
ENTER YOUR REQUIREMENT
2
ENTER SUBJECT CONCEPT
MARTIN
ENTER ARROW
HAS
ENTER OBJECT CONCEPT
LEGS
MARTIN HAS     LEGS  ?  ANSWER IS YES
```

112 Computer Models

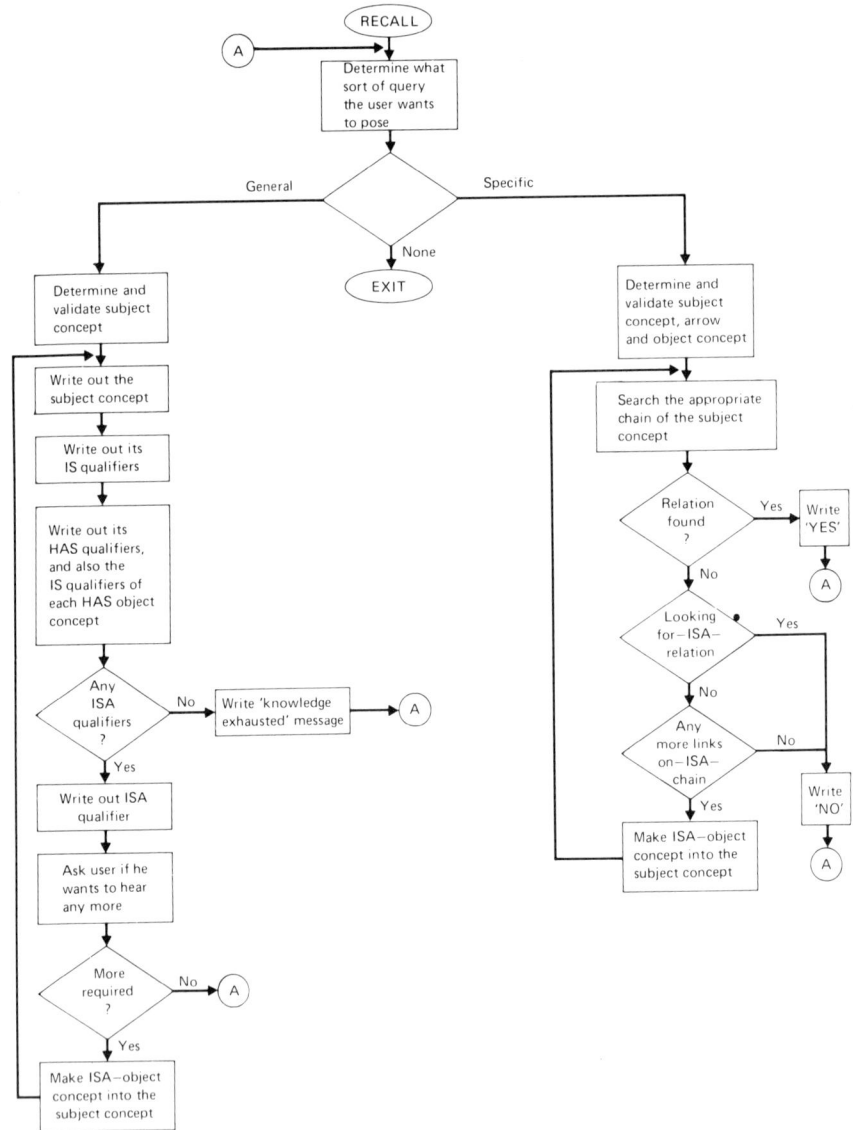

Fig. 6.27: Outline flowchart of the recalling subroutine RECALL

3. DREAM subroutine

The generalization performed by the model can be made as comprehensive as the reader can specify. We have chosen to perform the following simple operations by way of illustration. If all the concepts with the same ISA pointer have a common qualifier, then that qualifier is removed from each of the concepts and added to the ISA object concept;

e.g. EMMA ISA → PERSON ←ISA VICKY
      IS → FEMALE ←IS

would become EMMA ISA→ PERSON ←ISA VICKY
                         IS
                         ↓
                         FEMALE

The EXAMPLE fields of ISA object concepts are then filled in. In the above example, it would be noted that EMMA and VICKY are examples of PERSON.

Those readers who successfully filled in the detail of the RECALL subroutine should also be able to specify the detailed operations which are needed in the DREAM subroutine, so we will not give the flowchart here. We do, though, show the output produced by our program before and after TIM has been day-dreaming.

```
0=EXIT   1=REMEMBER   2=RECALL   3=DAY-DREAM   4=DISPLAY   5=CLEAR
ENTER YOUR REQUIREMENT
4
CONCEPT   ISA      HAS      IS       EXAMPLE
=======   ======   ======   ======   ======
EMMA
          PERSON
                                     FEMALE
FEMALE
PERSON
VICKY
          PERSON
                                     FEMALE

0=EXIT   1=REMEMBER   2=RECALL   3=DAY-DREAM   4=DISPLAY   5=CLEAR
ENTER YOUR REQUIREMENT
3
THAT IS ALL THE DAY-DREAMING I HAVE TIME FOR

0=EXIT   1=REMEMBER   2=RECALL   3=DAY-DREAM   4=DISPLAY   5=CLEAR
ENTER YOUR REQUIREMENT
4
CONCEPT   ISA      HAS      IS       EXAMPLE
=======   ======   ======   ======   ======
EMMA
          PERSON
FEMALE
PERSON
                            FEMALE
                                     VICKY
                                     EMMA
VICKY
          PERSON
```

114 Computer Models

Discussion of the model

Obviously our model is somewhat inarticulate, but we hope nevertheless that we have described clearly the fundamental workings of a computer model of human memory. We do not, of course, say that human memory works by means of linked lists and stacks, only that the behaviour of the model we have implemented is recognizably similar in many respects to the behaviour of a human. The interested and able reader may care to take the skeleton we have presented and cover up the limitations of the model with some more flesh. Examination of the limitations provokes ideas about psychology, as well as about modelling techniques.

Perhaps the severest limitation in our model is the limited number of arrow types (ISA, IS, HAS, EXAMPLE). The separate labels for each arrow, and the fact that we can recognize many other types of relation between concepts with no apparent limit, suggest that our model is lacking some more fundamental part - a 'primitive'. A primitive which suggests itself, and which has the elegant consequence of simplifying the data structure of the model (if not the processing) is the 'forked arrow' where one prong points to the object concept while the other points to the relation concept, as in Fig. 6.28.

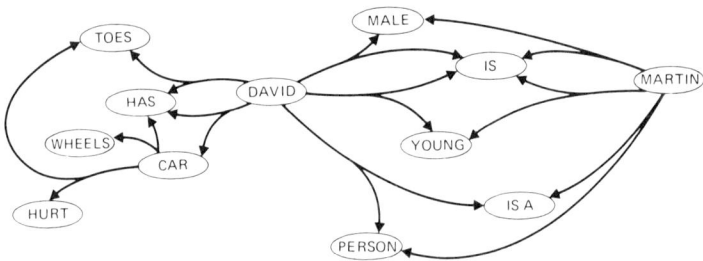

Fig. 6.28: The forked-arrow primitive

This data structure could be represented in simplified NODES and LINKS tables - Fig. 6.29.

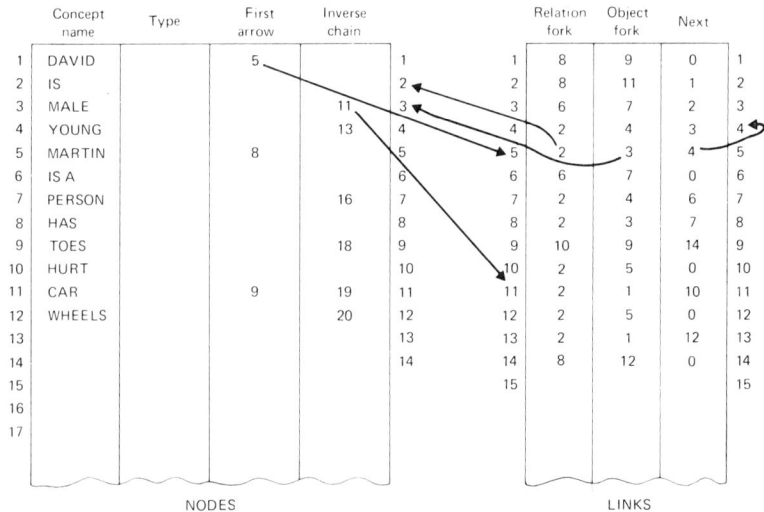

Fig. 6.29: The NODES and LINKS tables for a forked-arrow data structure

We would like to stress that we have not implemented a model with this structure and we cannot forewarn the reader of the difficulties which will be encountered. Speculatively, it should be possible to do away with the *type* column in NODES, (leaving the concept 'typed' by the arrows that point at it), secondary concepts being created with blank concept names. EXAMPLES and the inverse of any relation could be maintained by an inverse chain in the manner of Fig. 6.29. This structure also opens up new possibilities for generalizations (compare, for example, the inverse chains starting at LINKS$_{11}$ and LINKS$_{13}$), for searches on multiple attributes (what HAS WHEELS and HURT TOES?), synonyms, intransitive relationships, and so on. Interesting though these speculations are, they take us somewhat beyond our present purpose and we must leave them to others to develop. Some of the more important subroutines used in our simple model are listed below for the convenience of programmer readers.

References

1. Frijda, N.H., 'Simulation of human long-term memory'. *Psychological Bulletin* 77(1), 1-31, 1972.
2. Newell, A. & Simon, H.A., 'Computers in psychology'. In R.D. Luce, R.R. Bush, & E. Galant (Eds), *Handbook of mathematical psychology 1*, Wiley, 1963, New York.
3. McCarthy, J., et al, *LISP 15 programming manual*. MIT Computation Center. Cambridge, Mass., 1962.
4. Lindsay, P.H. & Norman, D.A., *Human Information Processing*. Academic Press, N.Y., 1972.
5. Norman, D.A., Rumelhart, D.E. & the LNR Research Group, *Explorations in Cognition*. W.H. Freeman, San Francisco, 1975.

Some of TIM's key subroutines

```
      SUBROUTINE REMEMB
C-
C-      THIS SUBROUTINE STORES CONCEPTS, AND THEIR RELATIONSHIP TO
C-      OTHER CONCEPTS, IN TIM'S MEMORY
C-
C
C-      S     :  THE NUMBER OF THE ROW IN THE NODES ARRAY
C-               CONTAINING THE CURRENT SUBJECT CONCEPT
C-               (ZERO IF NOT IN MEMORY)
C-      SCEPT :  THE ALPHABETIC NAME OF THE CURRENT SUBJECT
C-               CONCEPT
C-      STYPE :  CONTAINS THE TYPE OF THE CURRENT SUBJECT CONCEPT
C-                   -3 = -IS - SECONDARY CONCEPT
C-                   -2 = -HAS   SECONDARY CONCEPT
C-                   -1 = -ISA- SECONDARY CONCEPT
C-                    0 = MAJOR SUBJECT CONCEPT
C-                    1 = -ISA- CONCEPT
C-                    2 = -HAS- CONCEPT
C-                    3 = -IS - CONCEPT
C-                   11 = PRIMARY CONCEPT POINTED AT BY A SECONDARY CONCEPT
C-
C-      OB,OCEPT AND OTYPE ARE AS ABOVE, BUT FOR THE OBJECT CONCEPT
C-
```

116 Computer Models

```
C-
      IMPLICIT INTEGER(A-Z)
      LOGICAL SAMCPT,OK,INSTCK,YESNO,EXISTS
      COMMON MEMNOW,MEMMAX,NODES(100,6),LNKFRE,LINKS(500,2)
      COMMON/LITRAL/BLANK,ARROWS(3),IDUMMY(8),TWOS
      COMMON/IO/JIN,JOUT
C-
C- **********************************************************************
C- *                                                                    *
C- *    A.   DETERMINE THE MAJOR SUBJECT CONCEPT                        *
C- *                                                                    *
C- **********************************************************************
      STYPE=0
  100 WRITE(JOUT,110)
  110 FORMAT(1H0,8X,21HENTER SUBJECT CONCEPT)
      CALL GETCON(SCEPT,OK)
      IF(.NOT. OK) RETURN
      S=SEARCH(SCEPT)
      IF(S .EQ. 0) GO TO 200
      WRITE(JOUT,120)
  120 FORMAT(1H ,40H*** ERROR ***  CONCEPT ALREADY IN MEMORY)
      GO TO 100
C-
C- **********************************************************************
C- *                                                                    *
C- *   B. DETERMINE NEXT QUALIFIER                                      *
C- *                                                                    *
C- **********************************************************************
  200 IF(STYPE.EQ.2.OR.STYPE.EQ.-2) GO TO 240
C-          WE HAVE EITHER A MAJOR SUBJECT OR AN -ISA- CONCEPT
      IF(NODES(S,3).NE.0) GO TO 220
      WRITE(JOUT,210) SCEPT
  210 FORMAT(1H0,8X,19HTELL ME MORE ABOUT ,A6,17H (ISA, HAS OR IS))
      IARROW=1
      GO TO 260
  220 WRITE(JOUT,230) SCEPT
  230 FORMAT(1H0,8X,19HTELL ME MORE ABOUT ,A6,12H (HAS OR IS))
      IARROW=2
      GO TO 260
C-          WE HAVE A -HAS- CONCEPT
  240 WRITE(JOUT,250) SCEPT
  250 FORMAT(1H0,8X,19HTELL ME MORE ABOUT ,A6,5H (IS))
      IARROW=3
C-          GET THE ARROW
  260 WRITE(JOUT,270)
  270 FORMAT(1H ,8X,12HENTER ARROW )
      CALL GETARR(IARROW,OK)
      IF(.NOT.OK) GO TO 300
C-          GET THE OBJECT CONCEPT
      OTYPE=IARROW
  280 WRITE(JOUT,290)
  290 FORMAT(1H ,8X,21HENTER OBJECT CONCEPT )
      CALL GETCON(OCEPT,OK)
      IF(.NOT.OK) GO TO 200
      OB=SEARCH(OCEPT)
      GO TO 400
```

```
C-
C- ***********************************************************************
C- *                                                                     *
C- *  C.  RETRIEVE PREVIOUS SUBJECT CONCEPT AND MAKE IT THE               *
C- *      CURRENT SUBJECT CONCEPT                                         *
C- ***********************************************************************
  300 CALL POP(S,OK)
      IF(.NOT.OK) RETURN
      STYPE=NODES(S,2)
      SCEPT=NODES(S,1)
      IF(SCEPT.EQ.TWOS) SCEPT=NODES(LINKS(NODES(S,3),1),1)
      GO TO 200
C-
C- ***********************************************************************
C- *                                                                     *
C- *  D.  VALIDATE THE QUALIFIER                                          *
C- *                                                                     *
C- ***********************************************************************
  400 IF(.NOT.(SCEPT.EQ.OCEPT)) GO TO 410
      WRITE(JOUT,405)
  405 FORMAT(1H ,49H*** ERROR ***  CONCEPT DEFINED IN TERMS OF ITSELF,
     *19H : RE-ENTER CONCEPT)
      GO TO 280
  410 IF(OB.EQ.0) GO TO 500
C-        OBJECT CONCEPT IS IN MEMORY
      OTYPE=NODES(OB,2)
C-
      IF(OTYPE.NE.0) GO TO 430
      WRITE(JOUT,425) OCEPT
  425 FORMAT(1H ,15H*** ERROR ***  A6,27H IS A MAJOR SUBJECT CONCEPT,
     *19H : RE-ENTER CONCEPT)
      GO TO 280
C-
  430 IF(OTYPE.GT.0.AND.OTYPE.LE.3) GO TO 440
      WRITE(JOUT,435) OCEPT
  435 FORMAT(1H ,15H*** ERROR ***   ,A6,21H IS A PRIMARY CONCEPT,
     *19H : RE-ENTER CONCEPT)
      GO TO 280
C-
  440 IF(IARROW.EQ.OTYPE) GO TO 450
      WRITE(JOUT,445) ARROWS(IARROW),ARROWS(OTYPE)
  445 FORMAT(1H ,15H*** ERROR ***   ,A6,19H ARROW POINTING TO ,A6,
     *27H CONCEPT : RE-ENTER CONCEPT)
      GO TO 280
C-
  450 IF(.NOT.EXISTS(S,IARROW,OB)) GO TO 460
      WRITE(JOUT,455) SCEPT,ARROWS(IARROW),OCEPT
  455 FORMAT(1H ,15H*** ERROR ***   ,A6,3X,A6,9H ALREADY,
     *19H : RE-ENTER CONCEPT)
      GO TO 280
C-
  460 IF(.NOT.INSTCK(OB)) GO TO 500
      WRITE(JOUT,465)
  465 FORMAT(1H ,38H*** ERROR ***  CIRCULAR QUALIFICATION ,
     *19H : RE-ENTER CONCEPT)
      GO TO 280
```

```
C-
C-     ************************************************************
C-     *    E.   ENTER THE RELATION INTO TIM'S MEMORY              *
C-     *                                                           *
C-     ************************************************************
   500 WRITE(JOUT,505) SCEPT,ARROWS(IARROW),OCEPT
   505 FORMAT(1H ,8X,A6,3X,A6,3X,A6,21H ?  IS THIS CORRECT ?)
       IF(YESNO(ICHAR)) GO TO 520
       WRITE(JOUT,510)
   510 FORMAT(1H ,8X,32HRELATION NOT ENTERED INTO MEMORY)
       GO TO 200
C-           IF NECESSARY GET NODE FOR SUBJECT CONCEPT
   520 IF(S.NE.0) GO TO 530
       CALL GETMEM(S)
       NODES(S,1)=SCEPT
       NODES(S,2)=STYPE
C-           IF NECESSARY GET NODE FOR OBJECT CONCEPT
   530 IF(OB.NE.0) GO TO 540
       CALL GETMEM(OB)
       NODES(OB,1)=OCEPT
       NODES(OB,2)=OTYPE
       GO TO 550
C-           SEE IF THE OBJECT CONCEPT HAS THE SAME QUALIFICATION AS
C-           THE ONE ALREADY IN MEMORY
   540 IF(SAMCPT(OB)) GO TO 550
C-           NOT THE SAME - SO GENERATE A SECONDARY CONCEPT
       CALL SECOND(OB)
C-
   550 CALL QUALFY(S,IARROW,OB)
       WRITE(JOUT,560)
   560 FORMAT(1H ,8X,28HRELATION ENTERED INTO MEMORY)
C-
C-     ************************************************************
C-     *    F.   EXPLORE -ISA- AND -HAS- OBJECT CONCEPTS           *
C-     *                                                           *
C-     ************************************************************
   600 IF(OTYPE.EQ.3) GO TO 200
       CALL PUSH(S,OK)
       IF(OK) GO TO 620
       WRITE(JOUT,610)
   610 FORMAT(1H ,29H*** ERROR ***  STACK OVERFLOW)
       STOP
   620 S=OB
       STYPE=NODES(S,2)
       SCEPT=OCEPT
       GO TO 200
       END
```

```
      BLOCK DATA
      IMPLICIT INTEGER(A-Z)
      COMMON/IO/JIN,JOUT
      DATA JIN,JOUT/5,6/
      COMMON/LITRAL/BLANK,ARROWS(3),KYES,KNO,K0,K1,K2,K3,K4,K5,TWOS
      DATA BLANK,ARROWS,KYES,KNO,K0,K1,K2,K3,K4,K5,TWOS
     */1H ,3HISA,3HHAS,2HIS,3HYES,2HNO,1H0,1H1,1H2,1H3,1H4,1H5,6H222222/
      COMMON/STACKS/TOP,MAXSTK,STACK(100)
      DATA TOP,MAXSTK/0,100/
      END
```

Initialises the labelled COMMON blocks. The unlabelled COMMON block is initialised in the main program by calling the subroutine CLEAR.

```
      SUBROUTINE CLEAR
      IMPLICIT INTEGER(A-Z)
      COMMON MEMNOW,MEMMAX,NODES(100,6),LNKFRE,LINKS(500,2)
C-
      MEMNOW=0
      MEMMAX=100
      DO 1 J=2,6
        DO 1 I=1,100
    1     NODES(I,J)=0
C-
      LNKFRE=1
      LNKMAX=500
      ILAST=LNKMAX-1
      DO 2 I=1,ILAST
        LINKS(I,1)=0
    2   LINKS(I,2)=I+1
      LINKS(LNKMAX,1)=0
      LINKS(LNKMAX,2)=0
C-
      RETURN
      END
```

Clears TIM's memory by resetting the values of the variables in the unlabelled COMMON block.

```
      LOGICAL FUNCTION EXISTS(S,IARROW,OB)
      IMPLICIT INTEGER(A-Z)
      COMMON MEMNOW,MEMMAX,NODES(100,6),LNKFRE,LINKS(500,2)
      EXISTS=.FALSE.
      NEXT=NODES(S,IARROW+2)
   10 IF(NEXT.EQ.0) RETURN
      IF(LINKS(NEXT,1).EQ.OB) GO TO 20
      NEXT=LINKS(NEXT,2)
      GO TO 10
   20 EXISTS=.TRUE.
      RETURN
      END
```

Determines whether or not the relation subject concept - arrow - object concept specified by S, IARROW and OB is in memory. The chain defined by S and IARROW is searched for the object concept OB. If found, the value .TRUE. is returned, otherwise .FALSE. is returned.

```
      SUBROUTINE GETARR(ISTART,OK)
      IMPLICIT INTEGER(A-Z)
      LOGICAL OK
      COMMON/LITRAL/BLANK,ARROWS(3)
      COMMON/IO/JIN,JOUT
      OK=.FALSE.
   10 READ(JIN,20) ICHAR
   20 FORMAT(A6)
      IF(ICHAR.EQ.BLANK) RETURN
      DO 30 IARROW=ISTART,3
         IF(ICHAR.EQ.ARROWS(IARROW)) GO TO 50
   30    CONTINUE
      WRITE(JOUT,40) ICHAR
   40 FORMAT(1H ,15H*** ERROR ***   ,A6,
     *28H IS INVALID : RE-ENTER ARROW)
      GO TO 10
   50 OK=.TRUE.
      ISTART=IARROW
      RETURN
      END
```

Accepts and validates an arrow entered by the user. If the arrow is valid, control is returned to the calling program with OK set to .TRUE.; otherwise the user is informed his input is invalid and asked to re-enter the arrow. A null response causes a return to the calling program with OK set to .FALSE.

The value passed in ISTART specifies which arrows are valid. If it is 1, ISA, HAS and IS arrows are valid; if 2, HAS and IS arrows are valid; if 3, only IS arrows are valid. On return, ISTART is set to 1 for an ISA arrow, 2 for a HAS arrow and 3 for an IS arrow.

```
      SUBROUTINE GETCON(CNCEPT,OK)
      IMPLICIT INTEGER(A-Z)
      LOGICAL OK
      COMMON/LITRAL/BLANK
      COMMON/IO/JIN,JOUT
      OK=.FALSE.
   10 READ(JIN,20) CNCEPT
   20 FORMAT(A6)
      IF(CNCEPT.EQ.BLANK) RETURN
      IF(VALCPT(CNCEPT)) GO TO 40
      WRITE(JOUT,30) CNCEPT
   30 FORMAT(1H ,15H*** ERROR ***   ,A6,
     *30H IS INVALID : RE-ENTER CONCEPT)
      GO TO 10
   40 OK=.TRUE.
      RETURN
      END
```

Accepts and validates a concept entered by the user. If the concept is valid, control is returned to the calling program with OK set to .TRUE.; otherwise the user is informed his input is invalid and asked to re-enter the concept. A null response causes a return to the calling program with OK set to .FALSE.

```
      SUBROUTINE GETLINK(INDEX)
      IMPLICIT INTEGER(A-Z)
      COMMON/IO/JIN,JOUT
      COMMON MEMNOW,MEMMAX,NODES(100,6),LNKFRE,LINKS(500,2)
      IF(LNKFRE.NE.0) GO TO 20
      WRITE(JOUT,10)
   10 FORMAT(1H ,29H*** ERROR ***   LINKS OVERFLOW)
      STOP
   20 INDEX=LNKFRE
      LNKFRE=LINKS(LNKFRE,2)
      RETURN
      END
```

Returns the index of the next free link in the LINKS array. The program stops with an appropriate message if no link is available.

```
      SUBROUTINE GETMEM(INDEX)
      IMPLICIT INTEGER(A-Z)
      COMMON/IO/JIN,JOUT
      COMMON MEMNOW,MEMMAX,NODES(100,6),LNKFRE,LINKS(500,2)
      MEMNOW=MEMNOW+1
      INDEX=MEMNOW
      IF(INDEX.LE.MEMMAX) RETURN
      WRITE(JOUT,10)
   10 FORMAT(1H ,29H*** ERROR ***   NODES OVERFLOW)
      STOP
      END
```

Returns the index of the next free node in the NODES array. The program stops with an appropriate message if no node is available.

```
      LOGICAL FUNCTION INSTCK(OB)
      IMPLICIT INTEGER(A-Z)
      COMMON/STACKS/TOP,MAXSTK,STACK(100)
      INSTCK=.FALSE.
      IF(TOP.EQ.0) RETURN
      DO 10 I=1,TOP
         IF(OB.NE.STACK(I)) GO TO 10
         INSTCK=.TRUE.
         RETURN
   10    CONTINUE
      RETURN
      END
```

Returns the value .TRUE. if the value passed in OB is on the stack, otherwise it returns the value .FALSE.

```
      SUBROUTINE POP(S,OK)
      IMPLICIT INTEGER(A-Z)
      LOGICAL OK
      COMMON/STACKS/TOP,MAXSTK,STACK(100)
      OK=.FALSE.
      IF(TOP.EQ.0) RETURN
      OK=.TRUE.
      S=STACK(TOP)
      TOP=TOP-1
      RETURN
      END
```

POPs the value off the top of the stack and returns it in S with OK set to .TRUE. If the POP operation cannot be performed because the stack is empty, the subroutine returns with OK set to .FALSE.

```
      SUBROUTINE PUSH(S,OK)
      IMPLICIT INTEGER(A-Z)
      LOGICAL OK
      COMMON/STACKS/TOP,MAXSTK,STACK(100)
      OK=.FALSE.
      IF(TOP.EQ.MAXSTK) RETURN
      OK=.TRUE.
      TOP=TOP+1
      STACK(TOP)=S
      RETURN
      END
```

PUSHes the value passed in S onto the stack and returns with OK set to .TRUE. If the PUSH operation cannot be performed because the stack is full, the subroutine returns with OK set to .FALSE.

```
      SUBROUTINE QUALFY(S,IARROW,OB)
      IMPLICIT INTEGER(A-Z)
      COMMON MEMNOW,MEMMAX,NODES(100,6),LNKFRE,LINKS(500,2)
      CALL GETLNK(FIRST)
      NEXT=NODES(S,IARROW+2)
C-          INSERT AT HEAD OF CHAIN
      NODES(S,IARROW+2)=FIRST
      LINKS(FIRST,1)=OB
      LINKS(FIRST,2)=NEXT
      RETURN
      END
```

Establishes in TIM's memory the relation subject concept - arrow - object concept specified by S, IARROW and OB.

```
      SUBROUTINE REMOVE(S,IARROW,OB)
      IMPLICIT INTEGER(A-Z)
      COMMON MEMNOW,MEMMAX,NODES(100,6),LNKFRE,LINKS(500,2)
C-        FIND THE LINK
      LAST=0
      NEXT=NODES(S,IARROW+2)
   10 IF(NEXT.EQ.0) RETURN
      IF(LINKS(NEXT,1).EQ.OB) GO TO 30
      LAST=NEXT
      NEXT=LINKS(NEXT,2)
      GO TO 10
C-        REMOVE LINK FROM CHAIN
   30 IF(LAST.NE.0) GO TO 40
      NODES(S,IARROW+2)=LINKS(NEXT,2)
      GO TO 50
   40 LINKS(LAST,2)=LINKS(NEXT,2)
C-        RETURN LINK TO FREE LINK CHAIN
   50 LINKS(NEXT,2)=LNKFRE
      LNKFRE=NEXT
      RETURN
      END
```

Removes from TIM's memory the relation subject concept - arrow - object concept specified by S, IARROW and OB.

```
      LOGICAL FUNCTION SAMCPT(INDEX)
      IMPLICIT INTEGER(A-Z)
      LOGICAL YESNO
      COMMON/LITRAL/IDUMMY,ARROWS(3)
      COMMON/IO/JIN,JOUT
      COMMON MEMNOW,MEMMAX,NODES(100,6),LNKFRE,LINKS(500,2)
      SAMCPT=.TRUE.
      ICOUNT=0
      CNCEPT=NODES(INDEX,1)
      DO 40 IARROW=2,3
        NEXT=NODES(INDEX,IARROW+2)
        IF(NEXT.EQ.0) GO TO 40
        ICOUNT=1
C-        FOLLOW THE CHAIN
   20   WRITE(JOUT,30) CNCEPT,ARROWS(IARROW),NODES(LINKS(NEXT,1),1)
   30   FORMAT(1H ,8X,A6,3X,A6,3X,A6)
        NEXT=LINKS(NEXT,2)
        IF(NEXT.NE.0) GO TO 20
   40 CONTINUE
      IF(ICOUNT.EQ.0) RETURN
C-        THERE ARE QUALIFICATIONS - CHECK FOR CORRECTNESS
      WRITE(JOUT,10)
   10 FORMAT(1H ,8X,17HIS THAT CORRECT ?)
      IF(YESNO(CHAR)) RETURN
      SAMCPT=.FALSE.
      RETURN
      END
```

Determines whether the concept in row INDEX of the nodes array has the same qualifiers as the concept the user has in mind. All the qualifications (if any) are output and the user is asked if they are all correct. If he replies YES, the function returns with the value .TRUE., otherwise the value is .FALSE.

124 Computer Models

```
      INTEGER FUNCTION SEARCH(CNCEPT)

      COMMON MEMNOW,MEMMAX,NODES(100,6),LNKFRE,LINKS(500,2)
      SEARCH=0
      IF(MEMNOW.EQ.0) RETURN
      DO 10 I=1,MEMNOW
         IF(CNCEPT.EQ.NODES(I,1)) GO TO 20
   10 CONTINUE
      RETURN
   20 SEARCH=I
      RETURN
      END
```

Searches the first column of the nodes array for the concept passed in CNCEPT (MEMNOW contains the number of the last row of NODES currently being used to hold a concept). If a match is found, the appropriate row number is returned; otherwise, zero is returned.

```
      SUBROUTINE SECOND(OB)

      COMMON/LITRAL/IDUMMY(12),TWOS
      COMMON MEMNOW,MEMMAX,NODES(100,6),LNKFRE,LINKS(500,2)
C-
C-       CREATE PRIMARY NODE
C-
      CALL GETMEM(IPRIME)
      NODES(IPRIME,1)=NODES(OB,1)
      NODES(IPRIME,2)=11
      NODES(IPRIME,3)=NODES(OB,3)
C-
C-       MAKE PREVIOUS NODE INTO A SECONDARY
C-
      NODES(OB,1)=TWOS
      NODES(OB,2)=-NODES(OB,2)
C-       SET -ISA- POINTER TO POINT TO PRIMARY
      CALL GETLNK(K)
      NODES(OB,3)=K
      LINKS(K,1)=IPRIME
      LINKS(K,2)=0
C-
C-       CREATE NEW SECONDARY
C-
      CALL GETMEM(ISEC)
      NODES(ISEC,1)=NODES(OB,1)
      NODES(ISEC,2)=NODES(OB,2)
      NODES(ISEC,3)=NODES(OB,3)
      OB=ISEC
      RETURN
      END
```

Handles the creation of primary and secondary nodes. The node passed in OB contains an ordinary concept. Firstly a primary of node OB is created with the ISA chain from node OB attached to it. Then node OB is made into a secondary node, with its ISA pointer pointing to the primary node. Finally, a new secondary node is created and OB points to this new secondary node on return to the calling program.

```
      LOGICAL FUNCTION VALCPT(CNCEPT)
```

Validates the concept passed in CNCEPT. If it comprises only upper case letters the value .TRUE. is returned, otherwise .FALSE. is returned. No listing is provided as VALCPT is machine-dependent.

```
      LOGICAL FUNCTION YESNO(ICHAR)
      IMPLICIT INTEGER(A-Z)
      COMMON/LITRAL/IDUMMY(4),KYES,KNO
      COMMON/IO/JIN,JOUT
      YESNO=.TRUE.
   10 READ(JIN,20) ICHAR
   20 FORMAT(A6)
      IF(ICHAR.EQ.KYES)RETURN
      IF(ICHAR.EQ.KNO) GO TO 40
      WRITE(JOUT,30)
   30 FORMAT(1H ,48H*** ERROR ***    INVALID REPLY : ANSWER YES OR NO)
      GO TO 10
   40 YESNO=.FALSE.
      RETURN
      END
```

Returns the value .TRUE. if the user types YES at the terminal and the value .FALSE. if the user types NO. All other responses by the user are reported as errors.

7 Bed Usage in a Hospital Surgical Suite

Introduction

An influx of people into a development area will produce an increase in the demand for hospital facilities in that area. During the planning stage of such a development, one question that might be asked is 'can the existing hospitals cope with the increased demand? If not, can they be extended and the services they provide expanded, or is a new hospital needed?' A computer model can play an important part in providing quantitative information upon which decisions can be based.

This chapter describes the hospital surgical suite of Deaconness Hospital in Saint Louis, Missouri, and the models which were developed to assist in management decisions concerning the expansion of the hospital facilities. In this hospital the basic procedure for surgery is that a patient undergoes an operation, after which he spends a period in a recovery room receiving post-operative care before being returned to one of the general wards. A model of the hospital surgical suite was constructed by Schmitz and Kwak[1].

The simulation, which was done by hand in a manner similar to that used in our airport example, was conducted using three, four, five, six operating theatres. Based on twenty-seven operations per day, which was the predicted new surgical load due to the increased bed complement, the optimum number of operating theatres was found to be five and there was a need for *at least twelve* recovery-room beds.

A computer model was later developed by Kwak, Kuzdrall and Schmitz[2] using a computer language specifically designed for simulation, GPSS (General Purpose Simulation System - IBM Corporation, New York). The purpose of this model was to determine the minimum number of recovery beds which would be needed in the Deaconness Hospital to ensure that no patient would have to wait for a recovery bed to become available if there were five operating theatres performing twenty-seven operations per day. (From here on we will refer to the work of Schmitz and Kwak by the initials SK, and we will use the initials KKS to refer to the later work by Kwak, Kuzdrall and Schmitz.)

The remainder of this chapter is devoted to constructing a computer model of a hospital similar to the Deaconness Hospital, following the eight steps suggested in Chapter 3.

Step 1 - the question for which an answer is sought

We shall adopt the same objective as KKS used, namely, to find the number of beds required in the recovery room consistent with there being no queueing at the recovery room, i.e. a patient in need of recovery care should not be denied access because all the recovery beds are occupied.

Step 2 - the queues, queueing entities and inter-arrival times

Operations begin at 7.30 a.m. and twenty-seven are performed during any day. Patients are admitted to hospital prior to the day of their operation, so that they are on hand when their operation day arrives. These twenty-seven can be thought of as 'arriving' for their operation at 7.30 a.m. and, since there are only five operating theatres, having to form a queue. The first five may enter an operating theatre immediately, but the remaining twenty-two must wait in the queue until such time as a theatre becomes free. So the first queue we have identified in the system is the operating-theatre queue. The inter-arrival times are all zero, which is to say that all patients arrive at the same time, 7.30 a.m.

On completion of their operations, most patients pass into the recovery room, where they will spend some time coming out from the anaesthetic and receiving specialized post-operative treatment before being returned to a general ward. (A few patients who have undergone particular minor operations may not require the intensive post-operative care and so by-pass the recovery room, being returned straight to the general ward from the operating theatre.) It is convenient to think of there being a queue outside the recovery room which patients join on leaving the operating theatre and which they leave as and when a recovery bed becomes available. Recalling that the objective of the model is to find the number of beds in the recovery room which will ensure that a patient is not denied access to a bed because they are all occupied, we will be achieving this objective if *all* patients spend zero time in the recovery-room queue. The inter-arrival time of patients at this queue is not known, being dictated by what happens to the patients earlier in the system (i.e. in the operating-theatre queue and in the operating theatre).

Step 3 - the channels and their related service times

There are two kinds of service channel in this system: the operating theatres, of which there are five, and the recovery beds, for which we are trying to determine the minimum number consistent with no denial of service. Fig. 7.1 gives a schematic representation of our present understanding of the system.

A typical path of a patient through the system might be general ward to operating-theatre queue to operating theatre 4 to recovery-room queue to

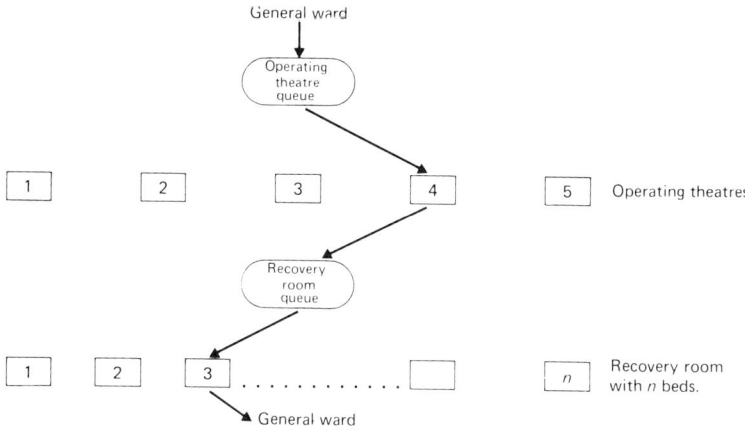

Fig. 7.1: Channels and queues in the system

recovery bed 3 to general ward, the particular operating theatre and recovery bed simply depending on what happens to be available at the time.

It should be apparent from Fig. 7.1 that we have a composite system, made up from two multi-channel, single-queue systems arranged so that the ouput from one (the operating-theatre system) forms the input to the other (the recovery-room system).

The time each patient spends in the operating theatre is noted on a charge ticket which accompanies the patient through the system and which is later used by the accounts office for charging the patient. In order to find the distribution of times that patients spent in an operating theatre, SK took a sample of 445 patients, extracted their operating-theatre times from the charge tickets and grouped these times into half-hour intervals, with the result shown in Table 7.1.

Duration of operation (hours)	Frequency
0.01-0.50	181
0.51-1.00	103
1.01-1.50	64
1.51-2.00	42
2.01-2.50	22
2.51-3.00	13
3.01-3.50	8
3.51-4.00	5
more than 4.00	7
	445

Table 7.1: Distribution of duration of operations

The times have been expressed in hours and hundredths of an hour. The table shows that out of a total of 445 operations, 181 took half an hour or less, 103 took more than half an hour but less than (or exactly) one hour, and so on.

SK went one stage further and looked for a theoretical distribution which would fit the measured data. They concluded that the observed frequencies were described by a negative exponential distribution with a mean of 1.03 hours. We will not dwell on how this fitting was done - for the moment we will accept their conclusions, and use them in our model - but we will return to the observed data of Table 7.1 when we are validating our computer model. We shall only stress at this point that SK did not argue an empirical hypothesis about the distribution of operation times - they proceeded on the basis that a negative exponential distribution of mean 1.03 hours was so close to the observed distribution that they might as well use it as a substitute for the observed distribution.

The length of stay in the recovery room is related to the type of operation the patient has just undergone - operations lasting half an hour or less are classified as minor, whereas those requiring longer than half an hour come into the category of major operations. A sample of 1531 patients requiring recovery-room facilities was taken, and their times were grouped into half-hour intervals according to their surgery classification - the resulting probability distributions are shown in Table 7.2.

In their analysis of the sampled data, SK did not attempt to fit a theoretical distribution but used the approximation that patients spent the mean of their time cell in the recovery room. In other words, patients who had undergone major operations spent 2, 2½, 3, 3½ or 4 hours in the recovery

Bed Usage in a Hospital Surgical Suite

	Mean time in recovery room (hours)	Probability	
Minor:	0.50	0.010	
	1.00	0.635	1.00
	1.50	0.355	
Major:	2.00	0.222	
	2.50	0.014	
	3.00	0.598	1.00
	3.50	0.024	
	4.00	0.142	

Table 7.2: Distribution of durations of recovery after minor and major surgery

room, with a probability of 0.222 that it would be 2 hours, 0.014 that it would be $2\frac{1}{2}$ hours, and so on. It is evident from the low probability of spending either $2\frac{1}{2}$ or $3\frac{1}{2}$ hours recovering that recovery-room procedures were such as to bias patients towards a stay of a whole number of hours. We shall follow the method of SK in our computer model, if only to demonstrate the technique of sampling from a measured distribution rather than from a distribution fitted to the measured data (as with the negative exponential distribution of the operating times). What is not made clear in the original papers is why a sample of 1531 patients was used to determine the recovery-time distribution, whereas an earlier sample of 445 was used to determine the distribution of times in the operating theatre. Perhaps it was just a question of accepting the largest samples of data that were available.

Step 4 - the states of the entities

Each patient can be in one of the following states:

1. waiting in the operating-theatre queue,
2. undergoing an operation in one of the five operating theatres,
3. moving from the operating theatre,
4. waiting in the recovery-room queue,
5. recovering in one of the beds in the recovery room.

A patient is regarded as being in one of the general wards if he is not in one of the above states. As in the airport example described in Chapter 3, other states can be identified, but they are not central to the model.

Each operating theatre can be in one of the following states:

1. busy, being occupied by a patient undergoing an operation,
2. being cleaned after an operation and made ready for the next operation,
3. free - no operation going on, nor is it being cleaned.

Similarly, each recovery bed can be in one of the following states:

1. busy, being occupied by a patient recovering from an operation,
2. being cleaned and made ready for the next patient,
3. free, not occupied by a patient nor being cleaned.

Step 5 - the rules for state transitions

The purpose of this step is to identify the conditions which must prevail before an entity undergoes a transition from one state to another. Let us

130 Computer Models

first of all examine the state-transition diagrams shown in Fig. 7.2. The transitions for the operating theatres and the recovery beds are fairly straightforward, being simply 'free' to 'busy', 'busy' to 'being cleaned' and 'being cleaned' back to 'free'. The transitions are labelled A, B and C respectively for the case of operating theatres and E, F and G respectively for recovery beds. Included in Fig. 7.2 are the five explicit states defined for patients in step 4, together with the implicit state 'general ward', which is shown in broken lines. The transitions a patient may undergo are summarized in the state-transition matrix in Fig. 7.3 (the letters next to the √ relate to the corresponding patient transitions shown in Fig. 7.2).

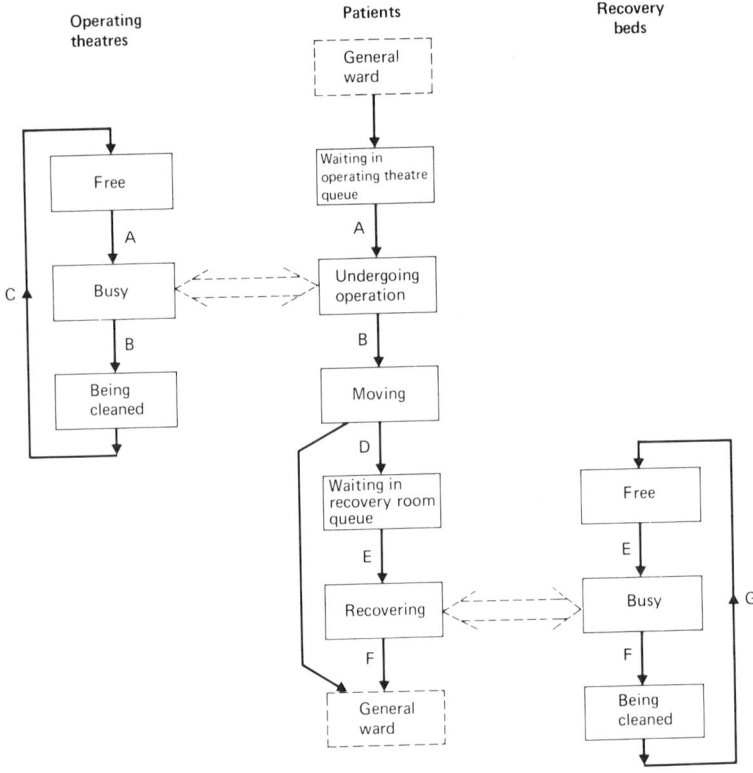

Fig. 7.2: State-transition diagrams for patients and service channels

'FROM' state \ 'INTO' state	General ward	Operating theatre queue	Operating theatre	Moving	Recovery room queue	Recovery room
General ward		√				
Operating theatre queue			√A			
Operating theatre				√B		
Moving	√D				√D	
Recovery room queue						√E
Recovery room	√F					

Fig. 7.3: State-transition matrix for patients

The alert reader may have noticed in Fig. 7.2 that some transition identification letters appear twice. This is explained by the fact that there is a one-to-one correspondence between the state 'having operation' and the operating-theatre state 'busy' - the operating theatre can be 'busy' only when a patient is undergoing an operation. An operating theatre moves from 'free' to 'busy' at exactly the same time as a patient moves from 'waiting' to 'undergoing operation', so we can test whether the necessary conditions hold for the patient transition and, if they do, we can perform both transitions. A similar argument applies to the patient state 'recovering' and the recovery-bed state 'busy'. (Another way of looking at this diagram is in terms of *events*, which trigger off transitions. For example, event B is 'completion of operation'; when this event occurs, the two transitions labelled B - the patient transition 'undergoing operation' to 'moving' and the operating-theatre transition 'busy' to 'being cleaned' - take place.)

The conditions which determine the state transitions are:

A (Event: start operation)
A1. There must be a patient waiting in the operating-theatre queue.
A2. There must be an operating theatre free.

B (Event: complete operation)
B1. A time equal to the duration of the operation (determined by a random sample from a negative exponential distribution with mean 1.03 hours) has elapsed since the operation started.

C (Event: complete cleaning operating theatre)
C1. A time equal to the length of time necessary to clean a theatre (assumed constant at 0.25 hours) has elapsed since the cleaning began.

D (Event: complete moving patient)
D1. A time equal to the length of time necessary to move a patient (assumed constant at 0.08 hours) has elapsed since the moving began. The destination of all major-operation patients, and of 63 per cent of minor-operation patients, is the recovery room; the remaining minor-operation patients are moved directly to the general ward.

E (Event: enter recovery room)
E1. There must be a patient waiting in the recovery-room queue.
E2. There must be a recovery bed free.

F (Event: complete recovery)
F1. A time equal to the length of time necessary for the patient to recover has elapsed since the patient entered the recovery room. Recovery times depend on whether the patient has undergone a major or minor operation, and the respective distributions are shown in Table 7.2.

G (Event: complete cleaning recovery bed)
G1. A time equal to the length of time necessary to clean a recovery bed and make it ready for the next patient (assumed constant at 0.25 hours) has elapsed since the cleaning began.

Step 6 - construct the model

We are now in a position to construct a computer model of our hospital surgical suite. We will use FORTRAN as our programming language and make use of the EDSIM subroutines described in Appendix C - this combination is called an EDSIM program. Those readers less experienced in programming may prefer to scan quickly over this section, acquiring the general flavour but omitting the details, before going on to step 7.

132 Computer Models

An EDSIM program for modelling an event-based discrete simulation, such as our present case, is made up of four sections: declarations, initialisation, transitions and termination.

Declarations section

Classes and sets. In any day, twenty-seven patients undergo operations, so our first declaration will be a CLASS of entity called PEOPLE, comprising twenty-seven PERSONs:

```
      INTEGER PEOPLE,PERSON
      CALL DCLASS(PEOPLE,PERSON,27)
```

In EDSIM, a SET is the means of keeping track of all the entities in a given state. For example, if at a certain time PERSON 3, PERSON 5 and PERSON 18 were all waiting in the queue for the recovery room, then the recovery-room-queue set would contain the values 3, 5 and 18. A set is needed for every state in which PERSON may be. Let us call the sets to hold those patients in the operating-theatre queue, in the operating theatre, being moved, queuing for the recovery room, and in the recovery room OPQ, OP, MOVE, RECQ and REC respectively, and then prefix the letter P to remind ourselves that these sets are for Persons:

```
      INTEGER POPQ(29),POP(7),PMOVE(7),PRECQ(16),PREC(15)
      CALL DSET(POPQ,29)
      CALL DSET(POP,7)
      CALL DSET(PMOVE,7)
      CALL DSET(PRECQ,16)
      CALL DSET(PREC,15)
```

Two points must be remembered when declaring sets in EDSIM programs:
1. the programmer must reserve memory for all sets he needs, by using either an INTEGER or a DIMENSION statement;
2. the amount of memory which must be reserved for each set is given by the maximum number of entities the set will ever hold, plus 2; so, because POPQ will never hold more than 27 PERSONs, we need to reserve 27 + 2 = 29 memory locations.

The sets POP and PMOVE have both been declared for a maximum of 5 PERSONs. In the case of POP this is because there are only five operating theatres – no more than five persons can be undergoing an operation at any one time. The reason for the size of PMOVE is somewhat different. Suppose that five operations terminate at the same time: five PERSONs would be transferred from the set POP into the set PMOVE and the five operating theatres would be transferred to their state 'being cleaned'. No more operations can begin (thereby precluding any more operations finishing, with the subsequent transfer of the patient to the set PMOVE) before the theatres have been cleaned (which takes 0.25 hours), but moving a patient takes only 0.08 hours, so all patients will have been moved before the operating theatres have been cleaned. Different relative times could modify this analysis.

The number of recovery beds has been set at 13, the figure that the model of SK gave as the minimum required. It then follows that a maximum of 14 (27 less 13) persons can be in the recovery-room queue PRECQ. We have adopted these specific set sizes in order to illustrate some of the interrelationships between the sets; there is little reason, apart from requiring more computer memory, why all the PERSON sets (other than PREC, the one whose minimum size we are trying to determine) could not have been declared for a maximum of 27 PERSONs. (There is a slight argument against declaring sets unnecessarily large, since it gives a slightly increased opportunity for a programming error to go unnoticed.)

Bed Usage in a Hospital Surgical Suite

The full class and set declarations appear in the listing of the program at the end of the chapter. The set names for operating theatres are prefixed by the letter O, while those for recovery beds are prefixed by the letter R.

Time cells. In an EDSIM program, all time cells are held in COMMON in an array called ITIMES. The first cell of this array is reserved for the EDSIM clock. In our model we need 27 person time cells, 5 operating-theatre time cells and 13 time cells associated with the recovery beds. The declarations are:

```
INTEGER PTIME,OTIME,RTIME
COMMON ICLOCK,PTIME(27),OTIME(5),RTIME(13),ITIMCT
ITIMCT=47
DIMENSION ITIMES(47)
EQUIVALENCE (ITIMES(1),ICLOCK)
CALL ITIMOK(ITIMES,ITIMCT)
```

ICLOCK is the EDSIM clock. Following the 27 person time cells (PTIME), the 5 operating-theatre time cells (OTIME) and the 13 recovery-bed time cells (RTIME) there is the mandatory count, called ITIMCT, of the number of cells which appear in COMMON. A more detailed explanation of the time-cell declarations can be obtained by reference to Appendix C.

Histograms. Histograms are also defined in the declarations section.

If we wish to obtain a histogram of the times of day when patients start their operation, grouping all patients who start between 7.30 a.m. and 8.00 a.m. into the first cell, those patients who start between 8.00 a.m. and 8.30 a.m. into the second cell, and so on, the distribution would be declared using the EDSIM subroutine DHIST (*D*eclare *HIST*ogram) and the following statements:

```
INTEGER HINOP(38)
CALL DHIST(HINOP,33,7750,500)
```

The name of the histogram is INOP (*IN*to *OP*erating theatre), and we have adopted the convention of prefixing all histograms by the letter H to remind us that they are histograms. The call to the subroutine DHIST declares HINOP to be a histogram containing 33 cells, the variate value associated with the first being 7750 and the variate values associated with subsequent cells being 500 more than the previous one. We have adopted one thousandth of an hour as our unit of time, so 7.30 a.m. is represented as 7500, 8.00 a.m. is represented as 8000 and 1.15 p.m. is represented as 13250. We have declared the mid-value of the first cell to be 7750, so all values up to (but not including) 8000 will be tallied into the first cell, values 8000 and above up to (but not including) 8500 will be tallied into the second cell, and so on.

The programmer must reserve memory space for all the histograms he wishes to have, using either an INTEGER or a DIMENSION statement. The space needed for an EDSIM histogram is the number of cells in the histogram, plus 5. In the example above, HINOP has 33 cells, so we reserve 33 + 5 = 38 cells.

The reader may remember that the time a patient spends in the recovery room is to be sampled from a distribution of measured times (Table 7.1). Taking the distribution for major surgery as an example, it would be represented in our program as a histogram. It requires 5 cells, so we need to declare 10 memory locations. The first variate value is 2000 (2 hours) and successive values are 500 (half an hour) more than the previous one. Our declaration is

```
INTEGER HMAJOR(10)
CALL DHIST(HMAJOR,5,2000,500)
```

HMAJOR must be initialized from the data given in Table 7.1 and to do this we need to know that the data cells of an EDSIM histogram are preceded by five control cells. So locations 6-10 of the array HMAJOR contain data values, which can be set by:

        DATA (HMAJOR(I),I=6,10)/222,14,598,24,142/

The remaining histogram declarations can be seen in the full listing at the end of the chapter.

Initialization section

The initialization falls into two parts: that required at the outset of the simulation and that required at the start of every day.

```
C-
C-          **********   INITIALIZATION SECTION    **********
C-
      READ(5,10) NDAYS,ISEED1,ISEED2
C-
      IDAY=1
      CALL LOAD(OPROOM,5,OFREE)
      CALL LOAD(RECBED,13,RFREE)
      CALL CLEAR(HINOP)
      CALL CLEAR(HOUTOP)
      CALL CLEAR(HINREC)
      CALL CLEAR(HOUTREC)
      CALL CLEAR(HOPQ)
      CALL CLEAR(HRECQ)
      CALL CLEAR(HINUSE)
      CALL CLEAR(ZOPTIM)
      CALL CLEAR(ZMAJOR)
      CALL CLEAR(ZMINOR)
C-
C-          INITIALIZATION AT THE START OF EACH DAY
C-
   50 CALL LOAD(PERSON,27,POPQ)
      ICLOCK=7500
      DO 60 I=1,PEOPLE
   60 PTIME(I)=0
```

In order to avoid recompiling the program to rerun the model over a different period, or using different seeds, the appropriate values are input at run-time using a READ statement. Two separate seeds are used for sampling from the operating-theatre time distribution (ISEED1) and the recovery-bed time distributions (ISEED2), following the recommendations made in Chapter 4. NDAYS is the number of days over which the simulation is to be run. IDAY is used to hold the current day; it is initialised to 1 and incremented by 1 at the end of a day's operations, until it finally exceeds the value in NDAYS. All histograms are cleared to zero using the subroutine CLEAR - this is unnecessary on a computer which initializes all variables and arrays to zero on loading the program.

Careful consideration needs to be given to the state of the SETs at the start of a day. DSET ensures that all sets are initially empty. Setting ICLOCK to the value 7500 models the day beginning at 7.30 a.m. At this time our 27 patients arrive in the operating-theatre queue, achieved in the program by the statement:

        CALL LOAD(PERSON,27,POPQ)

meaning 'load the first 27 persons into the set POPQ'.

Also, at the start of the simulation, we need to ensure that operating theatres and recovery beds are in the state 'free'. This is achieved by:

    CALL LOAD(OPROOM,5,OFREE)
    CALL LOAD(RECBED,13,RFREE)

These two statements do not need to be executed at the start of each day because all operating theatres and recovery beds will have been left in the state 'free' at the end of the previous day.

The person time cells are all initialized to zero at the start of each day, so that they can be used to measure the length of time each person waits in the operating-theatre queue.

PEOPLE is set by DCLASS to contain the number of PERSONs in the class 'people', i.e. 27. The variables PEOPLE, OPRMS and RECBDS could have been used in the three calls to LOAD above, instead of the constants 27, 5 and 13 respectively - using variables rather than constants reduces the number of places where modifications need to be made if the class sizes are changed.

It is worth mentioning that errors can be easily introduced into a computer model of this sort by incorrect initialization, particularly if the programmer relies on the contents of the sets at the end of one day for the initial conditions of the sets for the next day. Cases could arise where the results of significance to the programmer from a one-day run might be correct, but similar results from a two-day run incorrect. It would be unfortunate if the programmer checked only the results from the one-day run and, because these were correct, assumed the longer run to be correct too.

Transitions section

Before looking in detail at the procedures for state transitions, it may be as well to remind the reader of the general structure of the transitions section of an event-based discrete simulation program. This is shown in Fig. 7.4. The transitions section is made up of a series of procedures, one for each event. When an event occurs (i.e. the conditions for the event are all satisfied) the transitions associated with the event are performed. After the question 'has the event occurred?' has been asked for every event, the clock is advanced to the next event and the sequence is repeated until the end of the simulation is reached.

In cases where more than one event may occur in a single pass through the transitions section, the order in which the transitions are performed becomes important. The conditions which must be satisfied before event E (enter recovery room) occurs are
1. there must be a patient in the recovery-room queue,
2. there must be a recovery bed free.

Suppose the programmer tested for event E before testing for event D (complete moving patient). If the recovery-room queue was empty, event E would not occur. Moving on to test for event D, it might be that the condition was satisfied, so that a patient now joined the recovery-room queue. If event E had been tested after event D, event E would have occurred (remember there are no clock changes during the cycling through and testing of events); hence the ordering of the events can determine whether a particular event can occur. Similarly, event G (complete recovery-bed cleaning) should be tested before event E. It is left to the reader to decide for himself how the remaining events should be ordered - the general rule is that END-OF-SERVICE should be tested before BEGIN-SERVICE.

A typical event. Let us examine in more detail one of the events of our hospital simulation: event A (start operation). The conditions for event A to occur are that there should be an operating theatre free and that there

136 Computer Models

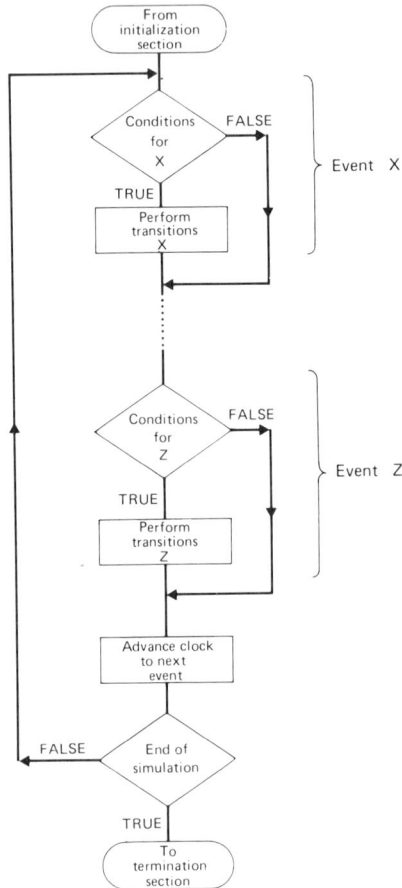

Fig. 7.4: General structure of the transitions section

should be a patient waiting in the operating theatre queue. If either of these two conditions are not satisfied the transitions associated with the event are not performed.

```
242    C-
243    C-       EVENT A          PERSON      OPQ  TO  OP
244    C-                        OPROOM      FREE TO  BUSY
245    C-
246        700 I=FIRST(OFREE)
247            IF(I.EQ.0) GO TO 800
248            J=FIRST(POPQ)
249            IF(J.EQ.0) GO TO 800
250            CALL FROM(OPROOM,I,OFREE)
251            CALL INTO(OPROOM,I,BUSY)
252            CALL FROM(PERSON,J,POPQ)
253            CALL INTO(PERSON,J,POP)
254            CALL TALLY(HOPQ,-PTIME(J))
255            CALL TALLY(HINOP,ICLOCK)
```

```
256             OPERS(I)=J
257             PMINOR(J)=.FALSE.
258             ITIME=NEGEXP(1030,ISEED1)
259             IF(ITIME.GT.500) GO TO 710
260             ITIME=490
261             PMINOR(J)=.TRUE.
262         710 OTIME(I)=ITIME
263             CALL TALLY(ZOPTIM,ITIME)
264             GO TO 700
```

Lines	Purpose
246-9	A jump to the next event (labelled 800) is made if either of the conditions is not fulfilled.
250-3	OPROOM I is moved from the set FREE (line 250) into the set BUSY (line 251). PERSON J is moved from the set OPQ into the set OP. These are the transitions associated with the event.
254	The length of time the patient spends in the operating-theatre queue is the negated value contained in that patient's time cell (his time cell was set to zero when he entered the queue). This statement updates HOPQ, the histogram of waiting times in the operating-theatre queue.
255	The histogram of times of day at which patients enter the operating theatres (HINOP) is updated.
256	OPERS is an array of size 5, one element for each of the operating theatres, which is used to keep track of which particular theatre is occupied by which patient.
257-62	How long is the patient going to spend in the theatre? This is found in line 258 by sampling from a negative exponential distribution with mean 1030 time units (1.03 hours). A logical array PMINOR containing 27 elements is used to record which patients are undergoing minor surgery, and the appropriate element is set .TRUE. if the sampled time is half an hour or less. It was found by SK that there was an upward biasing of times of operations lasting for half an hour or less, the observed times being consistent with using a mean time of 0.49 hours. This is catered for in the computer program by line 260.
263	The sampled durations of the operations are tallied in histogram ZOPTIM, which is discussed in detail in the section on validation.
264	The final step is to return and ask whether the event can re-occur, i.e. is there still an operating theatre free and a person in the queue?

Advancing the clock to the next event.

```
265     C-
266     C-          TIME ADVANCE
267     C-
268         800 IF(EMPTY(POPQ)   .AND.EMPTY(POP)   .AND.EMPTY(PMOVE) .AND.
269           *    EMPTY(PRECQ) .AND.EMPTY(PREC)  .AND.EMPTY(OCLEAN).AND.
270           *    EMPTY(RCLEAN)) GO TO 850
271             CALL TIMADV(ITIMES,ITIMCT)
272             GO TO 100
273     C-
274     C-          START NEW DAY
275     C-
276         850 IDAY=IDAY+1
277             IF(IDAY.LE.NDAYS) GO TO 50
```

138 Computer Models

268-70   This FORTRAN line tests whether the day's patients have completely passed through the system (all person sets are empty) and all the operating theatres and recovery beds have been cleaned and are now free. If these conditions are true, a new day is begun (lines 276-7).

271-2   The day has not yet been completed - advance the clock to the next event and go to start another cycle through the procedures.

276-7   Increment the day. If the required number of days have not yet been simulated, go to the statement labelled 50, which is the first line of the initialization for the start of the day. Otherwise continue to the termination section.

The complete transition section can be seen in the full listing of the program at the end of the chapter.

Termination section

This section is entered when the simulation is complete. Its function is to report the results and validation information accumulated during the simulation. In this particular program this is achieved by means of calls to the EDSIM subroutine PRHIST (PRint HISTogram).

Step 7 - validate the model

The stage of validating the model is concerned with investigating whether the model we have constructed is a valid representation of the real-world situation. We will follow the guidelines given in Chapter 4.

The logic of the model

The basic idea is to trace through the defined procedures to ensure that the model behaves in the way the real world behaves. To do this, the modeller needs to conjecture circumstances and combinations of circumstances which can arise in the real world and then, by inspection of the procedures of the model, satisfy himself that the model handles these circumstances in the correct way. Of course, these circumstances are the same as those the modeller should have envisaged when he was constructing the model. For example, we discussed in step 6 the case of two events occurring simultaneously and found that we needed to give careful consideration to the ordering of our procedures. However, it is likely that the modeller will have forgotten to cater for certain circumstances when he was constructing the model. By having a definite phase where the modeller stands back from being engrossed in the detail of designing the procedures and reorientates his mind to the real-world situation, it is possible that he may think of further cases which should be catered for. In practice it is too time-consuming to inspect *every* case, but the modeller should identify the major cases, which test the program at crucial points. In the hospital simulation our list was as follows.

1. At the start of a day the first five patients should go into the operating theatre at 7.30 a.m.
2. To test the events, trace the path of one major-operation patient through the whole system.
3. To test the remaining transition, test event D with a minor-operation patient who does not require recovery-room facilities.
4. To test the remaining paths, test events A and E with a minor-operation patient who does require recovery-room facilities.
5. To test combinations of events, make a pass through all the procedures for the case of:

no recovery beds free,
no patients in the recovery-room queue,
event D (complete moving patient)
event G (complete cleaning recovery bed) } occur simultaneously.

We found one logic error in our original program while working through this list.

Checking the computer program

Some programs can be checked by running the program with a particular set of input values and comparing the results with those obtained by performing hand calculations using the same set of data. Stochastic simulation programs do not come into this category - there are usually no *precise* answers which can be checked; rather, there is a range over which answers are reasonable.

EDSIM provides facilities for ouputting intermediate values, contents of sets and so on, and these can be used to advantage. For example, the modeller is well advised to output checking information for each of the events by running the program in CHECK mode (see Appendix C for further information) for the first few dozen transitions. This check information can then be traced by hand and any errors located. However, because of the large number of transitions (and hence a large volume of output) involved in a simulation lasting even a single day, it becomes impracticable (and probably unnecessary) to extend this approach beyond a few dozen transitions. Selective checking of critical values (for example, the contents of the sets at the end of a day's simulation) is likely to pay better dividends in identifying errors. When it has been established that an error exists in the program, selective checking, i.e. printing the values of variables or sets which are likely to contribute to locating the error, can be invaluable.

Once we have the detail sorted out to our satisfaction (this does not mean that the program is now correct), we should stand back again, look at the program output and ask ourselves 'would we expect these results?' To help answer this question, we included three extra histograms (ZOPTIM, ZMAJOR and ZMINOR) and an extra variable (ZNOREC) in our program, purely for validation purposes. The purpose of these extra variables is described in the listing of the program at the end of the chapter.

We simulated patients undergoing operations over a thirty-seven-day period. Data were aggregated into histograms, which were printed at the end of the run. Some of the 'reasonableness' tests and consistency checks we applied are now discussed.

Histogram of times into the operating theatre. The histogram output by our program is shown in Fig. 7.5. This histogram is tallied in event A to record the time of day that a patient enters the operating theatre. The numbers in the column on the left-hand side are the variate values for the half-hour time cells; the length of the line of asterisks corresponds to the frequency of occurrences in a given cell; and the numbers in the column on the right-hand side give the actual frequency of occurrences in a given cell. For example, there were 185 patients who entered the operating theatre between 7500 time units (7.30 a.m.) and 8000 time units (8.00 a.m.). A total of 999 patients were processed.

After having laboured hard and long to design our model, convert it into a computer program and run it on the computer, when we finally get histograms being output it is very tempting to accept them as being correct. Avoid the temptation - start asking questions. For example, how many patients would we expect to have been processed? Simple - 27 per day for 37 days gives 999. So far so good. 185 patients entered an operating theatre between 7.30 a.m. and 8.00 a.m. We know that each day five patients enter an operating theatre

```
          FREQUENCY.
          O        40        80       120       160       200
          +---------+---------+---------+---------+---------+
 7750  I**************************************************        185
 8250  I**************************                               103
 8750  I**************                                            56
 9250  I****************                                          62
 9750  I*****************                                         67
10250  I*******************                                       75
10750  I*****************                                         68
11250  I*******************                                       74
11750  I****************                                          64
12250  I******************                                        71
12750  I****************                                          63
13250  I*********                                                 33
13750  I*********                                                 33
14250  I*******                                                   26
14750  I*****                                                     17
15250  I*                                                          2
15750  I                                                           0
16250  I                                                           0
17250  I                                                           0
TIME INTO OPERATING THEATRE.

NUMBER OF ENTRIES =         999
              MEAN =    10273.38
STANDARD DEVIATION =     2099.82
```

Fig. 7.5: Histogram HINOP - time of day a patient begins his operation

at 7.30 a.m., which over a period of 37 days makes a total of 37 x 5 = 185. This agrees with the histogram. But would we have expected more than 185? Can another operation start before 8 a.m.? No. The minimum duration of an operation is 0.49 hours (see the notes on event A in the transitions discussion of step 6) and cleaning the theatre takes a further 0.25 hours. The answers to a few such simple questions can increase our confidence in the model.

Breakdown of patients into major/minor. The histograms output by the program showed the following breakdown of patients:

```
                    ⎧ 600 major
   999 patients  ⎨
                    ⎩ 399 minor  { 256 used recovery room
                                  143 did not require recovery room
```

These figures show that 39.9 per cent of patients underwent minor surgery, and of these patients 64.2 per cent did require the recovery room. What percentages would we have expected? A minor operation is defined as lasting half an hour or less, so the percentage of minor operations can be determined theoretically by looking in tables at a negative exponential distribution of mean 1030 time units and seeing what fraction occurs at a value of 500 or less. The theoretical value is 38.5 per cent, which compares favourably with our observed value. We may remember that 63 per cent of minor-operation patients need to use the recovery-room facilities - this value was obtained from the original data. Again, this agrees reasonably well with our observed value of 64.2 per cent. Without going into statistical tests and levels of significance, we can see that our model produces a breakdown of patients which is quite close to the values in the real world.

Goodness of fit: operating-theatre times

You may remember that in step 3, when we were discussing the distribution of times a patient spent in an operating theatre, we accepted the finding of SK that a negative exponential distribution fitted the observed data, but we promised to return and take another look at the observed data. We are now in a position to fulfil that promise. Fig. 7.6 shows the distribution of operation times as sampled in our computer run. We want to answer the question 'are our computer-run data and the observed data significantly different?' To simplify the comparison we show the two sets of data side by side in Table 7.3. Applying the 'two-sample chi-square test' described on page 68, we obtain a value of chi-square equal to 1.5 with 8 degrees of freedom.

```
                FREQUENCY.
        O        80       160       240       320       400
        +---------+---------+---------+---------+---------+
    250 I*****************************************************     399
    750 I******************************                             229
   1250 I******************                                         142
   1750 I************                                                90
   2250 I*********                                                   62
   2750 I*****                                                       34
   3250 I**                                                           9
   3750 I**                                                          16
   4250 I*                                                            7
   4750 I*                                                            3
   5250 I*                                                            2
   5750 I*                                                            2
   6250 I*                                                            1
   6750 I*                                                            2
   7250 I                                                             0
   7750 I                                                             0
   8250 I                                                             0
   8750 I                                                             0
   9250 I                                                             0
   9750 1*                                                            1
  10250 I                                                             0
  10750 I                                                             0
  11250 I                                                             0
TIME IN OPERATING THEATRE QUEUE.

    NUMBER OF ENTRIES =          999
                 MEAN =         1114.52
    STANDARD DEVIATION =         953.55
```

Fig. 7.6: Distribution of duration of operations obtained from the computer model (HOPQ)

The value of chi-square indicates a 'suspiciously good fit', which we expect since we know that SK looked for and chose a theoretical distribution which was practically the same as that observed. So we can be satisfied that the results of our model are virtually the same as we would have got had we sampled from the observed distribution directly. You may have noticed that the mean value of the distribution shown in Fig. 7.6 is 1115 time units (1.115 hours) - yet this distribution was obtained by sampling from a

Duration (hours)	Frequency Real world	Computer model
0.0-0.5	181	399
0.5-1.0	103	229
1.0-1.5	64	142
1.5-2.0	42	90
2.0-2.5	22	62
2.5-3.0	13	34
3.0-3.5	8	9
3.5-4.0	5	16
more than 4.0	7	18
	445	999

Table 7.3: Distribution of operation times in the real world and the computer model

negative exponential distribution with a mean of 1.03 hours. Why the difference? Can it be accounted for simply by statistical fluctuations? It turns out that the two values are not significantly different, particularly when you remember that in the computer model we bias upwards (to a value of 490 time units) those times which are less than 500 time units. A similar analysis can be done for durations of times in the recovery room (which were also sampled from a measured distribution), i.e. we expect a 'suspiciously good' fit between the samples drawn in the model and the observed distribution.

Goodness of fit: output distribution

Of the twelve histograms we generate in our computer model, only two - HRECQ (waiting times in the recovery-room queue) and HINUSE (number of recovery beds in use) - relate directly to achieving our objective of determining the minimum number of recovery beds required. The remainder of the histograms are for validating the model: they are used for comparison with what happens in practice in the real hospital. Unfortunately, we do not have all the data available to us, being remote from the hospital, but we are in the position of having the simulation data of KKS, who also went through the procedure of validating their model. In fact their results 'closely duplicated the hospital's experience, and were accepted by management as the basis for deciding the capacity of the recovery room...' - this statement nicely summarizes the whole purpose of validation: the model should reflect the real world. For the purpose of this case study, we compared our results with those of KKS and found no features in which the two models significantly disagreed. The comparison is shown in Table 7.4.

	Our model value	'Real world' (KKS model) value
No. of patients	999	999
No. of patients using recovery room	856	856
Mean time in operating-theatre queue	2.77 h	2.79 h
Mean time in recovery-room queue	0.20 h	0.00 h
Mean time patients enter op. theatre	10.273 (2.01 h)	10.020 (2.10 h)
Mean time patients leave op. theatre	11.388 (2.32 h)	11.390 (2.28 h)
Mean time patients enter rec. room	11.570 (2.36 h)	11.460 (2.32 h)
Mean time patients leave rec. room	13.997 (2.72 h)	14.030^3 (2.65 h)

Table 7.4: Comparison of our computer model with that of KKS. The figures in parentheses are the corresponding standard deviations

The comparison shows that the two models produce remarkably close results. Let us assume that we (and, more importantly, the hospital management) are satisfied that our model closely duplicates the real hospital. We can now experiment with it.

Step 8 - experimenting with the model

The objective of writing this program was to determine the minimum number of beds required in the recovery room. To quote KKS, 'no queueing at the recovery room is permitted since it would represent undercapacity, a situation in which a patient who needs recovery care is denied entrance because it is totally occupied. The reasons for this policy are obvious.' KKS concluded, on the basis of 37 trial days, that the optimum number of beds was thirteen, and the hospital's management established the capacity of the recovery room at thirteen on the basis of their model.

The results from our simulation are broadly in agreement with those of KKS. Of the 856 patients who utilized the recovery room, 855 spent no time in the recovery-room queue, and one patient spent less than nine minutes waiting. The histogram (HINUSE) of the number of beds in use in the recovery room, at a time just prior to a patient leaving the room, is shown in Fig. 7.7.

```
           FREQUENCY.
    O         40         80        120       160       200
    +---------+---------+---------+---------+---------+
 1  I**********                                                       39
 2  I***********                                                      40
 3  I**************                                                   51
 4  I**********************                                           83
 5  I*********************                                            81
 6  I*****************************                                   110
 7  I**************************************                          143
 8  I********************************                                123
 9  I*************************                                        94
10  I*************                                                    52
11  I********                                                         25
12  I***                                                              11
13  I*                                                                 4
RECOVERY BEDS IN USE.

    NUMBER OF ENTRIES =        856
                 MEAN =        6.40
    STANDARD DEVIATION =       2.62
```

Fig. 7.7: Histogram of the number of beds in use in the recovery room just prior to a patient leaving

The mean number of beds occupied is 6.4. On four occasions all thirteen beds were occupied, and it was obviously during one of these occasions that another patient arrived at the recovery-room queue and was obliged to wait.

It is now evident that the hospital management were rather imprecise in setting their objective: it should not have been that a patient should *never* have to wait, but that there should be a low probability (say 1 in 1000) that a patient should have to wait. Let us return to this point in a moment. Meanwhile, it is easy to conjecture how a queue for the recovery room might form. Suppose our first thirteen patients are major-operation patients, whose operation time is 501 time units, but who all occupy the recovery beds for the maximum time of 4000 time units, and suppose the last fourteen patients are all minor-operation patients, whose operation time is 490 time units. This combination of patients represents the worst possible case we can imagine in that all the recovery beds become occupied at the earliest possible moment in the day and are occupied for as long as possible and on top of this the remaining patients pass through the system to the recovery-room queue as quickly as possible. Figure 7.8 shows the number of patients in the recovery room and the recovery-room queue as a function of time of day (up to 12 noon).

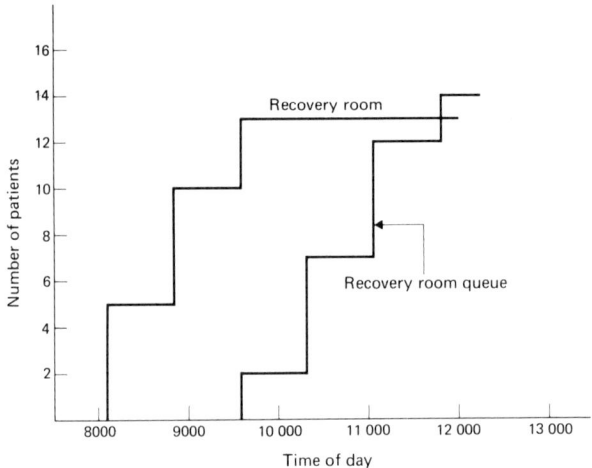

Fig. 7.8: *The contrived 'worst case'. Number of patients in the recovery room and the recovery-room queue as a function of time of day.*

It is evident from this figure that if the hospital management wanted to be absolutely sure that a patient would *never* have to wait, they would need to provide twenty-seven recovery beds - one for each patient - and, of course, our simulation model does not allow for the malfunction of the equipment associated with a recovery bed, so maybe we would need more recovery beds just in case!

Returning to realities (so often concerned with balancing cost with benefit), suppose the management wanted to know how many beds they should provide so that a patient had less than one chance in a thousand of having to wait for a recovery bed.

In our single computer run with 13 recovery beds and 856 patients we have only one observation of a wait. This is approximately one chance in a thousand, but before we can say more about the probability of waits with thirteen beds we need to repeat the trials with different seeds until we make a few more such observations (or make so many trials without again observing a wait that we are convinced the chances are less than 1 in 1000 - in this case it would be wise to reduce the number of beds and rerun the program).

One last point before we leave this case study. The worst build-up of patients in the recovery-room queue arises when there are several patients with long recovery room times followed by several patients with short operation times. Perhaps we can avoid this situation by carefully scheduling patients into the operating theatres instead of choosing them at random as in the model. If the situation is beginning to develop where a large number of beds is going to be occupied for a relatively long time, then we could counterbalance by assigning the operating theatres to either minor-operation patients who are less likely to require recovery-room facilities or to major-operation patients who will probably occupy the operating theatre for relatively long times. To understand more precisely the effect of one or other of these policies would require a modified computer model. It is often the case with simulation models that, while exploring one path, a whole new avenue for investigation is opened up.

References and notes

1. Schmitz, H.H. & Kwak, N.K., 'Monte Carlo simulation of operating-room and recovery-room usge'. *Operations Research* 20, 1171-1180, 1972.
2. Kwak, N.K., Kuzdrall, P.J. & Schmitz, H.H., 'Simulating the use of space in a hospital surgical suite'. *Simulation* Nov 1975, 147-152.
3. 0.250 was deducted from the figure published by KKS, because the recovery-bed cleaning time was included.

The program

```
C-        **********   DECLARATIONS SECTION    **********
      CALL EDINIT(6)
      INTEGER FIRST,RANDUM,COUNT,SAMPLE
      LOGICAL DONE,EMPTY
      COMMON/EDSIMZ/DONE,IDUMMY(105)
C-
C- CLASS : PEOPLE     27 PATIENTS FOR OPERATIONS
C-
C-   SET  : POPQ       PATIENTS AWAITING OPERATION
C-        : POP        PATIENTS UNDERGOING OPERATION
C-        : PMOVE      PATIENTS BEING MOVED AFTER OPERATION
C-        : PRECQ      PATIENTS AWAITING RECOVERY BED
C-        : PREC       PATIENTS IN RECOVERY ROOM
C-
C- ARRAY : PMINOR     TRUE IF THE GIVEN PERSON IS UNDERGOING A MINOR
C-                    OPERATION, OTHERWISE FALSE
C-
      INTEGER PEOPLE,PERSON
      CALL DCLASS(PEOPLE,PERSON,27)
      INTEGER POPQ(29),POP(7),PMOVE(7),PRECQ(16),PREC(15)
      CALL DSET(POPQ,29)
      CALL DSET(POP,7)
      CALL DSET(PMOVE,7)
      CALL DSET(PRECQ,16)
      CALL DSET(PREC,15)
      LOGICAL PMINOR(27)
C-
C- CLASS : OPRMS      5 OPERATING THEATRES
C-
C-   SET  : OFREE      OPERATING THEATRES WHICH ARE FREE
C-        : OBUSY      OPERATING THEATRES WHICH ARE BEING USED
C-        : OCLEAN     OPERATING THEATRES WHICH ARE BEING CLEANED
C-
C- ARRAY : OPERS      HOLDS THE INDEX OF THE PERSON IN A GIVEN THEATRE
C-
```

```
      INTEGER OPRMS,OPROOM
      CALL DCLASS(OPRMS,OPROOM,5)
      INTEGER OFREE(7),OBUSY(7),OCLEAN(7)
      CALL DSET(OFREE,7)
      CALL DSET(OBUSY,7)
      CALL DSET(OCLEAN,7)
      INTEGER OPERS(5)
C-
C- CLASS : RECBDS     13 RECOVERY BEDS
C-
C-    SET : RFREE     RECOVERY BEDS WHICH ARE FREE
C-        : RBUSY     RECOVERY BEDS WHICH ARE BEING USED
C-        : RCLEAN    RECOVERY BEDS WHICH ARE BEING CLEANED
C-
C- ARRAY : RPERS      HOLDS THE INDEX OF THE PERSON IN A GIVEN RECOVERY BED
C-
      INTEGER RECBDS,RECBED
      CALL DCLASS(RECBDS,RECBED,13)
      INTEGER RFREE(15),RBUSY(15),RCLEAN(15)
      CALL DSET(RFREE,15)
      CALL DSET(RBUSY,15)
      CALL DSET(RCLEAN,15)
      INTEGER RPERS(13)
C-
C-
C-      ITIMES ARRAY
C-
C-
C-      PTIME       27 TIME CELLS, ONE FOR EACH    PERSON
C-      OTIME        5 TIME CELLS, ONE FOR EACH    OPERATING THEATRE
C-      RTIME       13 TIME CELLS, ONE FOR EACH    RECOVERY BED
C-
      INTEGER PTIME,OTIME,RTIME
      COMMON ICLOCK,PTIME(27),OTIME(5),RTIME(13),ITIMCT
      ITIMCT=47
      DIMENSION ITIMES(47)
      EQUIVALENCE(ITIMES(1),ICLOCK)
      CALL ITIMOK(ITIMES,ITIMCT)
C-
C-
C- HISTOGRAMS : HINOP  : TIME PATIENT ENTERS OPERATING THEATRE
C-            : HOUTOP : TIME PATIENT LEAVES OPERATING THEATRE
C-            : HINRC  : TIME PATIENT ENTERS RECOVERY ROOM
C-            : HOUTRC : TIME PATIENT LEAVES RECOVERY ROOM
C-            : HOPQ   : WAITING TIMES IN QUEUE FOR OPERATIONS
C-            : HRECQ  : WAITING TIMES IN QUEUE FOR RECOVERY ROOM
C-            : HMAJOR : DISTRIBUTION OF RECOVERY TIMES AFTER MAJOR OPS
C-            : HMINOR : DISTRIBUTION OF RECOVERY TIMES AFTER MINOR OPS
C-            : HINUSE : NUMBER OF RECOVERY BEDS IN USE
C-
      INTEGER HINOP(38),HOUTOP(38),HINREC(38),HOUTREC(38)
      INTEGER HOPQ(38),HRECQ(38),HMAJOR(10),HMINOR(8),HINUSE(18)
      CALL DHIST(HINOP,33,7750,500)
      CALL DHIST(HOUTOP,33,7750,500)
      CALL DHIST(HINRC,33,7750,500)
      CALL DHIST(HOUTRC,33,7750,500)
```

```
      CALL DHIST(HOPQ,33,0,500)
      CALL DHIST(HRECQ,33,0,100)
      CALL DHIST(HINUSE,13,1,1)
      CALL DHIST(HMAJOR,5,2000,500)
      CALL DHIST(HMINOR,3,500,500)
      DATA (HMAJOR(I),I=6,10)/222,14,598,24,142/
      DATA (HMINOR(I),I=6,8)/10,635,355/
C-
C-
C-       THE FOLLOWING HISTOGRAMS AND VARIABLES ARE FOR VALIDATING
C-       THE SIMULATION PROGRAM - ALL START WITH THE LETTER Z
C-
C-
C-       ZNOREC  :  COUNT OF THE NUMBER OF PATIENTS NOT REQUIRING
C-                  THE RECOVERY ROOM
C-       ZOPTIM  :  HISTOGRAM OF SAMPLED OPERATION TIMES
C-       ZMAJOR  :  HISTOGRAM OF SAMPLED TIMES IN RECOVERY
C-                  ROOM AFTER MAJOR OPERATIONS
C-       ZMINOR  :  HISTOGRAM OF SAMPLED TIMES IN RECOVERY
C-                  ROOM AFTER MINOR OPERATIONS
C-
C-
      INTEGER ZNOREC,ZOPTIM(38),ZMAJOR(10),ZMINOR(8)
      ZNOREC=0
      CALL DHIST(ZOPTIM,33,250,500)
      CALL DHIST(ZMAJOR,5,2000,500)
      CALL DHIST(ZMINOR,3,500,500)
C-
C-       **********    INITIALISATION SECTION    **********
C-
      READ(5,10) NDAYS,ISEED1,ISEED2
   10 FORMAT(I2,2I10)
      WRITE(6,20) NDAYS
   20 FORMAT(1H1,50H HOSPITAL SIMULATION. 27 OPERATIONS PER DAY OVER A,
     *11H PERIOD OF ,I3,5H DAYS)
      WRITE(6,30) ISEED1,ISEED2
   30 FORMAT(1H0,8HSEED1 = ,I15,5X,8HSEED2 = ,I15)
C-
      CALL CLEAR(HINOP)
      CALL CLEAR(HOUTOP)
      CALL CLEAR(HINRC)
      CALL CLEAR(HOUTRC)
      CALL CLEAR(HOPQ)
      CALL CLEAR(HRECQ)
      CALL CLEAR(HINUSE)
      CALL CLEAR(ZOPTIM)
      CALL CLEAR(ZMAJOR)
      CALL CLEAR(ZMINOR)
      IDAY=1
      CALL LOAD(OPROOM,OPRMS,OFREE)
      CALL LOAD(RECBED,RECBDS,RFREE)
C-
C-       INITIALISATION AT START OF EACH DAY
C-
   50 CALL LOAD(PERSON,PEOPLE,POPQ)
      ICLOCK=7500
      DO 60, I=1,PEOPLE
   60 PTIME(I)=0
```

148 Computer Models

```
C-
C-         **********    TRANSITIONS SECTION    **********
C-
C-
C- EVENT F          PERSON      REC   TO   GENERAL WARD
C-                  RECBED      BUSY  TO   CLEAN
C-
  100 DO 110 I=1,RECBDS
      IF(RTIME(I).NE.0) GO TO 110
      CALL FROM(RECBED,I,RBUSY)
      IF(.NOT.DONE) GO TO 110
      CALL TALLY(HINUSE,COUNT(RBUSY)+1)
      CALL INTO(RECBED,I,RCLEAN)
      RTIME(I)=250
      J=RPERS(I)
      CALL FROM(PERSON,J,PREC)
      CALL TALLY(HOUTRC,ICLOCK)
  110 CONTINUE
C-
C- EVENT G          RECBED     CLEAN  TO   FREE
C-
  200 DO 210 I=1,RECBDS
      IF(RTIME(I).NE.0) GO TO 210
      CALL FROM(RECBED,I,RCLEAN)
      IF(.NOT.DONE) GO TO 210
      CALL INTO(RECBED,I,RFREE)
  210 CONTINUE
C-
C- EVENT D          PERSON     MOVE  TO   RECQ / GENERAL WARD
C-
  300 J=FIRST(PMOVE)
      IF(J.EQ.0) GO TO 400
      IF(PTIME(J).NE.0) GO TO 400
      CALL FROM(PERSON,J,PMOVE)
      IF(.NOT.PMINOR(J)) GO TO 305
      IF(RANDUM(100,ISEED1).GT.63) GO TO 310
  305 CALL INTO(PERSON,J,PRECQ)
      GO TO 300
  310 ZNOREC=ZNOREC+1
      GO TO 300
C-
C- EVENT E          PERSON     RECQ  TO   REC
C-                  RECBED     FREE  TO   BUSY
C-
  400 J=FIRST(PRECQ)
      IF(J.EQ.0) GO TO 500
      I=FIRST(RFREE)
      IF(I.EQ.0) GO TO 500
      CALL FROM(RECBED,I,RFREE)
      CALL INTO(RECBED,I,RBUSY)
      CALL FROM(PERSON,J,PRECQ)
      CALL TALLY(HRECQ,-PTIME(J))
      CALL INTO(PERSON,J,PREC)
      CALL TALLY(HINRC,ICLOCK)
      RPERS(I)=J
      IF(PMINOR(J)) GO TO 410
```

```
          ITIME=SAMPLE(HMAJOR,ISEED2)
          CALL TALLY(ZMAJOR,ITIME)
          GO TO 420
     410  ITIME=SAMPLE(HMINOR,ISEED2)
          CALL TALLY(ZMINOR,ITIME)
     420  RTIME(I)=ITIME
          GO TO 400
C-
C- EVENT B             PERSON        OP    TO     MOVE
C-                     OPROOM        BUSY  TO     CLEAN
C-
     500  DO 510 I=1,OPRMS
          IF(OTIME(I).NE.0) GO TO 510
          CALL FROM(OPROOM,I,OBUSY)
          IF(.NOT.DONE) GO TO 510
          CALL INTO(OPROOM,I,OCLEAN)
          OTIME(I)=250
          J=OPERS(I)
          CALL FROM(PERSON,J,POP)
          CALL TALLY(HOUTOP,ICLOCK)
          CALL INTO(PERSON,J,PMOVE)
          PTIME(J)=80
     510  CONTINUE
C-
C- EVENT C             OPROOM        CLEAN TO     FREE
C-
     600  DO 610 I=1,OPRMS
          IF(OTIME(I).NE.0) GO TO 610
          CALL FROM(OPROOM,I,OCLEAN)
          IF(.NOT.DONE) GO TO 610
          CALL INTO(OPROOM,I,OFREE)
     610  CONTINUE
C-
C- EVENT A             PERSON        OPQ   TO     OP
C-                     OPROOM        FREE  TO     BUSY
C-
     700  I=FIRST(OFREE)
          IF(I.EQ.0) GO TO 800
          J=FIRST(POPQ)
          IF(J.EQ.0) GO TO 800
          CALL FROM(OPROOM,I,OFREE)
          CALL INTO(OPROOM,I,OBUSY)
          CALL FROM(PERSON,J,POPQ)
          CALL TALLY(HOPQ,-PTIME(J))
          CALL INTO(PERSON,J,POP)
          CALL TALLY(HINOP,ICLOCK)
          OPERS(I)=J
          PMINOR(J)=.FALSE.
          ITIME=NEGEXP(1030,ISEED1)
          IF(ITIME.GT.500) GO TO 710
          ITIME=490
          PMINOR(J)=.TRUE.
     710  OTIME(I)=ITIME
          CALL TALLY(ZOPTIM,ITIME)
          GO TO 700
C-
```

```
C-         TIME ADVANCE
C-
  800 IF(EMPTY(  POPQ).AND.EMPTY(   POP).AND.EMPTY( PMOVE).AND.
     *    EMPTY( PRECQ).AND.EMPTY(  PREC).AND.EMPTY(OCLEAN).AND.
     *    EMPTY(RCLEAN)) GO TO 850
      CALL TIMADV(ITIMES,ITIMCT)
      GO TO 100
C-
C-         START NEW DAY
C-
  850 IDAY=IDAY+1
      IF(IDAY.LE.NDAYS) GO TO 50
C-
C-         **********    TERMINATION SECTION    **********
C-
      WRITE(6,900)
  900 FORMAT(1H0,17HEND OF SIMULATION)
      CALL PRHIST(HINOP,10HFREQUENCY.,28HTIME INTO OPERATING THEATRE.)
      CALL PRHIST(HOUTOP,10HFREQUENCY.,28HTIME FROM OPERATING THEATRE.)
      CALL PRHIST(HINRC,10HFREQUENCY.,24HTIME INTO RECOVERY ROOM.)
      CALL PRHIST(HOUTRC,10HFREQUENCY.,24HTIME FROM RECOVERY ROOM.)
      CALL PRHIST(HOPQ,10HFREQUENCY.,32HTIME IN OPERATING THEATRE QUEUE.)
      CALL PRHIST(HRECQ,10HFREQUENCY.,28HTIME IN RECOVERY ROOM QUEUE.)
      CALL PRHIST(HINUSE,10HFREQUENCY.,21HRECOVERY BEDS IN USE.)
      WRITE(6,910)
  910 FORMAT(1H1,41HSIMULATION VALIDATION INFORMATION FOLLOWS)
      WRITE(6,920) ZNOREC
  920 FORMAT(1H0,I8,39H PATIENTS DID NOT REQUIRE RECOVERY ROOM)
      CALL PRHIST(ZOPTIM,10HFREQUENCY.,17HSAMPLED OP TIMES.)
      CALL PRHIST(ZMAJOR,10HFREQUENCY.,14HSAMPLED MAJOR.)
      CALL PRHIST(ZMINOR,10HFREQUENCY.,14HSAMPLED MINOR.)
      STOP
      END
```

8 An Educational Economic Model

Introduction

The attempts by national economic-policy makers to achieve full employment, price stability, and a satisfactory rate of economic growth constitute one of the more interesting real-life dramas. Instructors in economics courses have long recognized this fact and attempted to foster interest in macroeconomic theory by relating the theoretical models to the current economic situation. This chapter describes a computer program, DYNKEYNES, which was designed by William B. Stronge of Florida Atlantic University to aid students bridge this gap between theory and reality. Our chapter, up to the discussion section at the end, is adapted from the original paper with the permission of its author and the publishers and copyright-holders, Sage Publications, Inc.

General features and objectives

Although sufficiently general to allow consideration of a variety of hypotheses about aggregate consumer behaviour and the structure of the economy, DYNKEYNES is designed to give students an operational insight into the following concepts and theorems:

equilibrium income,
the autonomous spending multiplier,
the Phillips curve,
the inflationary gap,
the balanced budget theorem,
the macroeconomic implications of the national debt,
exogenous and endogenous variables,
alternative consumption theories,
built-in stabilizers,
the full-employment budget,
the conflict between internal and external balance,
the macroeconomic implications of trade warfare,
the full-employment current-account balance of international payments
comparative statics and dynamics.

To this end, the output of the program includes:

1. equilibrium values of gross national product, employment, the budget balance, the current account of the balance of payments, and a disequilibrium price change;
2. multipliers showing the effect on gross national product, employment, the budget balance, and the current account of the balance of payments, of changes in autonomous spending, government purchases, exports, imports, taxes and business saving. These multipliers enable the student to examine the effects of alternative specifications of the equations and are especially oriented toward the analysis of fiscal policy.

152 Computer Models

The current version of the program is geared to the analysis of US economic policy during the period 1960-1970; therefore the equations employed are based upon data from that period. However, the program is sufficiently general to allow similar analysis for any economy or time period.

The underlying mathematical model

The underlying mathematical model is specified by the following six behavioural equations and six identities:

GNP identity:
$$GNP_t = C_t + A_t + G_t + X_t - M_t \tag{1}$$
Consumption function:
$$C_t = a_0 + a_1 DY_t + a_2 DY_{t-1} + a_3 C_{t-1} \tag{2}$$
Import function:
$$M_t = b_0 + b_1 GNP_t \tag{3}$$
Tax function:
$$TN_t = c_0 + c_1 GNP_t \tag{4}$$
Business saving function:
$$SB_t = f_0 + f_1 GNP_t \tag{5}$$
Definition of aggregate demand at full employment:
$$AD_t^F = C_t^F + A_t + G_t + X_t - M_t^F \tag{6}$$
Definition of inflationary gap:
$$GAP_t = AD_t^F - GNP_t^F \tag{7}$$
Production function:
$$GNP_t = d_0 + d_1 E_t \tag{8}$$
Inflation function:
$$\Delta P_t = e_1 \Delta P_{t-1} + e_2 GAP_t \tag{9}$$
Full employment budget:
$$BB_t^F = TN_t^F - G_t - GTRF_t \tag{10}$$
Full employment balance of payments:
$$ICAB_t^F = X_t - M_t^F \tag{11}$$
Disposable income identity:
$$DY_t = GNP_t - TN_t - SB_t \tag{12}$$

An explanation of the symbols is given in Table 8.1. The subscript t refers to the year, and superscript F indicates that the variable is evaluated at the full employment level. All variables are expressed in billions of 1958 dollars except employment and the price change. Employment is in millions and the price deflator has 1958 = 100.

Full employment is defined to be 96% of the total labour force. The user finds potential GNP by evaluating equation 8 at the full employment level. Full employment levels of other variables are found by evaluating their associated equations at the full employment GNP level.

Input options

A major feature of the model and program design is the flexibility allowed in the use of the program for analyzing the effect of alternative

Endogenous variables	Symbol	Parameters	Symbol
Gross national product	GNP	Autonomous consumption	a_0
Consumption	C	Marginal propensity to	
Imports	M	consume	a_1
Disposable income	DY	Lagged income coefficient	a_2
Net taxes	TN	Lagged consumption	
Business saving	SB	coefficient	a_3
Aggregate demand	AD	Autonomous imports	b_0
Inflationary gap	GAP	Marginal propensity to	
Employment	E	import	b_1
Price change	ΔP_t	Autonomous taxes	c_0
Budget balance	BB	Marginal tax rate	c_1
Current account of the		Autonomous business	
balance of inter-		saving	f_0
national payments	ICAB	Marginal propensity to	
		business save	f_1
Exogenous variables		Production intercept	d_0
		Productivity of labour	d_1
Autonomous aggregate		Lagged price change	
demand	A	coefficient	e_1
Government purchases	G	Inflationary gap	
Exports	X	coefficient	e_2
Potential output	GNP^F		
Government transfers to		Subscripts	
foreigners	GTRF		
Lagged price change	ΔP_{t-1}	Current year	t
		Previous year	t-1

Table 8.1: Explanation of symbols

specifications of the equations, and for evaluating the effect of alternative fiscal policies on the targets traditionally considered by economic policy makers.

The student is required to make three fundamental decisions when using the input options:

1. whether to consider a fiscal policy
2. whether to consider a foreign sector
3. which consumption function to use.

Figures 8.1 to 8.3 are designed to show the steps followed by the computer as the input options are specified.

When the user of the model does not wish to consider fiscal policy, the coefficients of the net taxes and business savings functions (c_0 and c_1 in equation 4, f_0 and f_1 in equation 5) are set to zero. Further, G_t is set to zero in equations 1, 6 and 10. The autonomous aggregate demand (A_t) entered by the user should then include the value of government purchases (G_t). If the student chooses to consider fiscal policy, he can either have an income tax or assume taxes to be exogenous. In the case where there is no income tax, the marginal tax rate is set to zero and the autonomous level of taxes is read in as c_0. Once again, autonomous aggregate demand (A_t) should include the value of government purchases (G_t) when fiscal policy is not considered. The program reacts in a similar fashion to the options specified in the foreign sector section.

The consumption function in the model (equation 2) contains three separate consumption theories as special cases. If $a_2 = a_3 = 0$, equation 2 is the familiar Keynesian consumption function. If $a_0 = a_3 = 0$, equation 2 is a

154 Computer Models

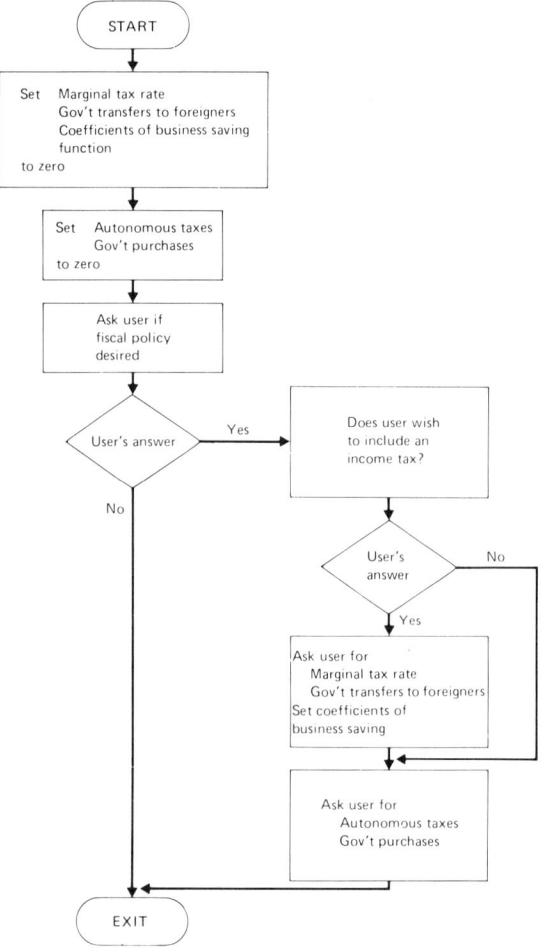

Fig. 8.1: Input options for the fiscal sector

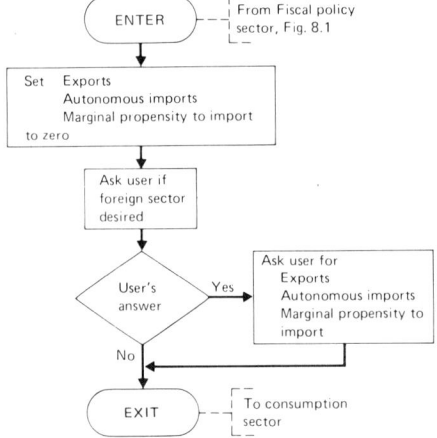

Fig. 8.2: Input options for the foreign sector

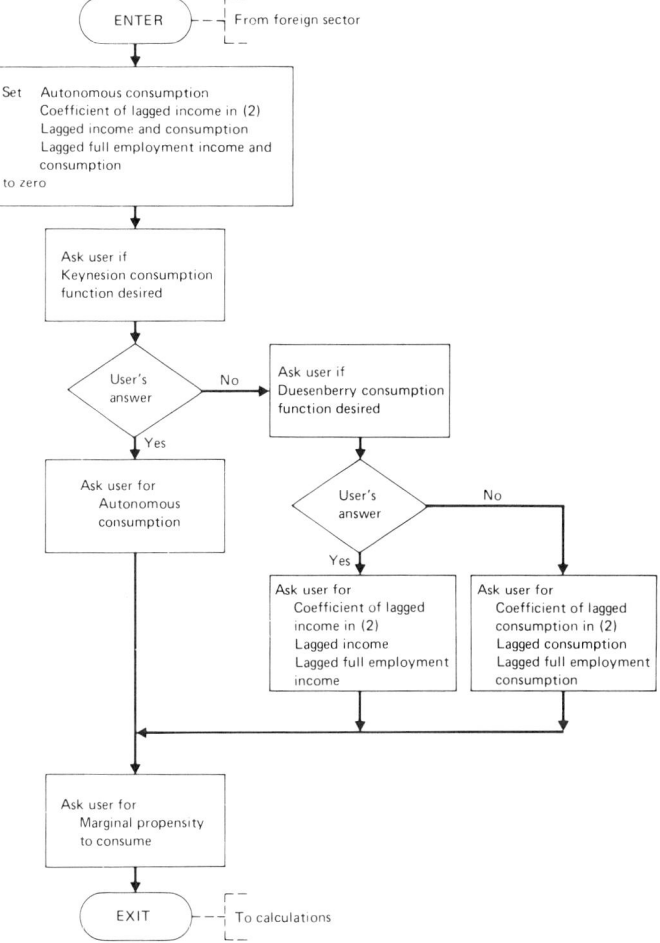

Fig. 8.3: Consumption sector input options

Duesenberry consumption function under the assumption that previous peak income equals last period's income. This assumption was true throughout the period analysed by the model. If $a_0 = a_2 = 0$, then equation 2 is a Friedman consumption function, where permanent income is measured as a distributed lag of past values of measured income. Finally, it should be noted that the income variable in the consumption function can be either GNP or disposable income, depending on whether net taxes and business saving are included in the model or not.

In cases where the user answers 'yes' to any of the three questions above, the program responds by asking for the appropriate values of the exogenous variables and parameters (except the coefficients of the production and inflation functions, which are permanently stored in the program because no assignments are given which call for changing them; DYNKEYNES is sufficiently general, however, to allow such modification).

The program is designed to allow the student to run alternative model economies using actual data for any time span. The assignments developed by Stronge require the student to do just this for the 1960-1970 decade. To this

156 Computer Models

end, considerable care was taken to ensure that the measures of the variables used are the same as the national accounts. This involved some aggregation of existing data. Net taxes were defined as total tax receipts plus social insurance contributions minus government transfers to resident persons, government interest, and government subsidies. Business saving is defined to ensure that the official measure of disposable income (prior to deflation) is the same as that used in the model. It includes undistributed corporate profits, capital consumption allowances, the statistical discrepancy and inventory valuation adjustment less consumer interest payments.

Output options

Figure 8.4 is a flowchart showing which results of the model are printed out, according to which input options were selected. In a similar way, the multipliers printed out depend on the model specified. The price change printed out is the change in the first year of the dynamic path. This is because the system never reaches the long-run equilibrium rate of inflation. After the first run, no further multipliers are printed out unless a change is made to the parameters or the model. This is because the multipliers remain the same when a model is solved for a series of years. Since many assignments involve simulating the economy over a given period, printing the multipliers each year would unnecessarily slow down the process. Table 8.2 presents the endogenous and exogenous variables for which multipliers are printed. Thus, in the most complicated model ('yes' to fiscal policy, 'yes' to income tax, 'yes' to foreign sector), the multipliers for the effect of changes in each of the exogenous variables on each of the endogenous variables are printed. Subsets of these multipliers are printed for the less complicated models; the appropriate subset is determined by the input options in the same way that the subset of equilibrium values printed out is determined.

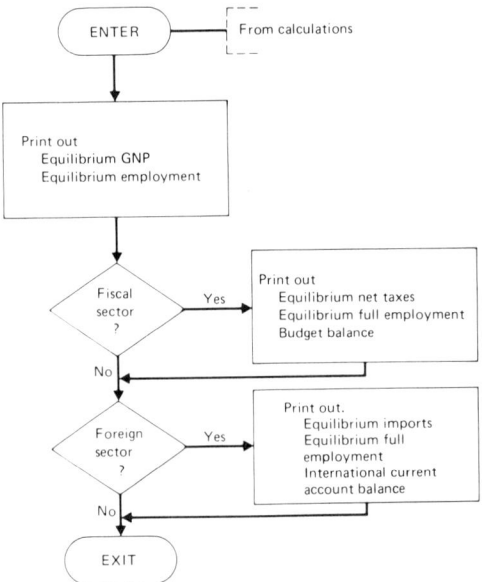

Fig. 8.4: Equilibrium output options for the model

Endogenous	*Exogenous*
GNP	Autonomous spending
Employment	Government purchases
Net taxes	Exports
Full employment budget	Autonomous consumptiom
Imports	Autonomous imports
Full employment trade	Autonomous taxes
	Autonomous business saving

Table 8.2: Variables for which multipliers are printed

There is also an output option to provide the dynamic path of the system. This takes on added importance because of the instability of the price equation. If the user wishes the dynamic path to be printed out, he must specify how many years he wishes to see.

Example of an assignment with the model

```
DO YOU WANT A FISCAL POLICY?  NO
DO YOU WANT A FOREIGN SECTOR?  NO
DO YOU WANT A KEYNESIAN CONSUMPTION FUNCTION?  YES
TYPE THE VALUE FOR AUTONOMOUS CONSUMPTION
24.5
TYPE THE VALUES FOR MARGINAL PROPENSITY TO CONSUME
AND AUTONOMOUS SPENDING, SEPARATED BY COMMAS
0.5912,172.6
TYPE THE VALUE FOR FULL EMPLOYMENT GNP
571.7
TYPE THE VALUE FOR LAGGED PRICE CHANGE
1.6
```

(The value of autonomous spending given above is the sum of business investment, government purchases, and net exports in 1960 - namely, 172.6. The value for full-employment GNP is also the 1960 value (571.7), and the lagged price change is the 1959 implicit deflator for GNP minus the 1958 implicit price deflator for GNP.)

The input options chosen by the student lead to the following model:

(1) $GNP_t = C_t + A_t = C_t + 172.6$
(2) $C_t = a_0 + a_1 DY_t = 24.5 + 0.5912 DY_t$
(3) $AD_t^F = C_t^F + A_t = C_t^F + 172.6$
(4) $GAP_t = AD_t^F - GNP_t^F = AD_t^F - 571.7$
(5) $GNP_t = d_0 + d_1 E_t = -678.2 + 18.06 E_t$
(6) $\Delta P_t = e_1 \Delta P_{t-1} + e_2 GAP_t = 1.15 \Delta P_{t-1} + 0.006 GAP_t$
(7) $DY_t = GNP_t$

The coefficients in equations 5 and 6 are automatically specified by the program.

Once the input variables are specified, the computer executes the appropriate calculations and prints the following output:

```
EQUILIBRIUM GNP = 482.143
INFLATIONARY GAP = -36.6110
EQUILIBRIUM EMPLOYMENT = 64.2493
PRICE CHANGE = 1.62033

THE FOLLOWING IS THE TABLE OF MULTIPLIERS
                              GNP         EMP
AUTONOMOUS SPENDING         2.44618     0.135448
AUTONOMOUS CONSUMPTION      2.44618     0.135448
```

The program is designed to allow the student to retain this model and use it over the decade of the 1960s. Using the data in Table 8.3, the solution for 1961 can be obtained as follows:

```
DO YOU WISH TO CHANGE MODELS?    NO
DO YOU WISH TO CHANGE VARIABLES? YES
DO YOU WISH TO CHANGE PARAMETERS? NO
TYPE THE VALUE FOR AUTONOMOUS SPENDING
176.6
TYPE THE VALUES FOR FULL EMPLOYMENT GNP AND LAGGED
PRICE CHANGE, SEPARATED BY COMMAS
587.9,1.7
```

The computer responds with

```
EQUILIBRIUM GNP = 491.928
INFLATIONARY GAP = -39.2335
EQUILIBRIUM EMPLOYMENT = 64.7911
PRICE CHANGE = 1.71960
```

Note that the table of multipliers is not repeated because none have changed.

In a similar manner, the equilibrium values for 1960-1971 can be generated. The data needed and results are presented in Table 8.3.

Year	A_t	GNP_t^F	ΔP_{t-1}	Actual GNP_t	Model GNP_t	E_t	ΔP_t
1960	172.6	571.7	1.6	487.6	482.1	64.2	1.6
1961	176.6	587.9	1.7	497.2	491.9	64.8	1.7
1962	194.1	595.2	1.3	529.6	534.7	67.2	1.3
1963	201.1	615.0	1.2	550.8	551.9	68.1	1.2
1964	212.5	636.7	1.4	581.2	579.7	69.7	1.5
1965	227.3	660.2	1.6	617.6	615.9	71.7	1.7
1966	248.9	689.1	2.1	658.4	668.8	74.6	2.4
1967	256.7	723.4	3.0	675.1	687.9	75.6	3.4
1968	268.3	748.7	3.7	706.7	716.2	77.2	4.2
1969	272.7	781.2	4.7	724.7	727.0	77.8	5.3
1970	264.9	811.9	5.9	720.1	707.9	76.8	6.5
1971	271.7	828.1	7.1	739.5	724.6	77.7	7.9

Table 8.3: Exogenous values, actual GNP and equilibrium values 1960-1971. (Note: ΔP_{t-1} in the 1961 figures is the actual price change in 1960, obtained from published data and input into the model. ΔP_t in the 1960 figures is the model's predicted price change for 1960.)

To exit from the program, the student must answer 'no' to all questions, as follows:

    DO YOU WISH TO CHANGE MODELS?   NO
    DO YOU WISH TO CHANGE VARIABLES? NO
    DO YOU WISH TO CHANGE PARAMETERS? NO

With the results obtained from using DYNKEYNES, the student is required to submit written answers to the questions below.

1. Compare the equilibrium values of GNP with the actuals and list some reasons why they are not the same.
2. Compute the equilibrium unemployment rate (U_t), rate of inflation (INF_t) and the growth rate of full-employment GNP for 1961-1971 ($GRWTH_t$).
3. Suppose the economic policy makers had the following goals:
   (a) unemployment less than or equal to 4 per cent;
   (b) inflation less than or equal to 2 per cent;
   (c) growth rate of full-employment GNP greater than or equal to 3 per cent.
   In what years was the government successful in achieving some or all of its goals?
4. Plot the rate of inflation against the unemployment rate. Does there appear to be a tradeoff between the two goals?
5. Find the deviation of equilibrium employment from EF. Using the multipliers, by how much would you change A_t in each year 1960-1971 to achieve E^F? What would be the rates of inflation if autonomous spending reached the levels you specified necessary to achieve E^F?

Discussion

Although it is a fascinating topic - and one which is of great importance to all of us - this is not the place for a general discussion of the validity of the traditional macroeconomic models and we must leave the interested reader to follow this topic up in the economics literature. As to the validity of the particular model presented as an example, or of the general models which can be constructed using DYNKEYNES, we would only remind you that the models have an *educational*, not an economic, purpose.

We would like to explain one or two practical points about building models such as this one on a computer. At its heart is a set of simultaneous equations - a straightforward approach to programming these is to first manipulate them by hand so that the unknown quantities - the desired results - are expressed in terms of the 'knowns' - the input variables and constants. This is called the *reduced form* of the equations and the simplest method of finding the reduced form is by repeated substitution of other expressions for the unknowns. This is not difficult for a model the size of Stronge's, but it is rather long, so we show below how to determine the reduced form of the specific model given in the example assignment.

From equation 1, and for the sake of clarity showing the 'knowns' in terms of the input values to distinguish them from the unknowns,

$$GNP_t = C_t + 172.6$$

Therefore, from equation 2,

$$GNP_t = 24.5 + 0.5912 DY_t + 172.6$$

and from equation 7,

$$GNP_t = 24.5 + 0.5912 GNP_t + 172.6$$

Therefore, $(1 - 0.5912)\text{GNP}_t = 24.5 + 172.6$

and
$$\text{GNP}_t = \frac{24.5 + 172.6}{(1 - 0.5912)}$$

Expressed in terms of the input variables, the reduced form for GNP_t is therefore

(8) $$\text{GNP}_t = \frac{a_0 + A_t}{(1 - a_1)}$$

In this next example, instead of dealing with the actual numbers input in the example assignment, we will use the symbols for the variables but set the 'knowns' in bold to distinguish them from the unknowns.

From (4), $\text{GAP}_t = \text{AD}_t^F - \mathbf{GNP}_t^F$

From (3), $\text{GAP}_t = \mathbf{C}_t^F + \mathbf{A}_t - \mathbf{GNP}_t^F$

From (2), $\text{GAP}_t = \mathbf{a}_0 + \mathbf{a}_1 \mathbf{GNP}_t^F + \mathbf{A}_t - \mathbf{GNP}_t^F$

Therefore
(9) $\text{GAP}_t = \mathbf{a}_0 + (\mathbf{a}_1 - 1)\mathbf{GNP}_t^F + \mathbf{A}_t$

The reduced form for employment is obtained from equation 5.

(10) $$E_t = \frac{\text{GNP}_t - \mathbf{d}_0}{\mathbf{d}_1}$$

At this stage, of course, GNP_t is a 'known' since we have already determined its reduced form, so no further substitution is needed. It will also be seen that equation 6 requires no reduction.

The program to solve this smaller version of the model is very simple:

```
C-            INPUT VARIABLES AND PARAMETERS HAVE BEEN STORED IN
C-            AT,AO,A1,GNPFT,DO,D1,E1,E2,LAGP RESPECTIVELY
      GNPT = (AO+AT)/(1-A1)
      GAPT = AO+(A1-1)*GNPFT+AT
      ET = (GNPT-DO)/D1
      PT = E1*LAGP+E2*GAPT
C-            THE ANSWERS MAY NOW BE PRINTED OUT
```

The reader may care to verify for himself that the reduced form of GNP of the complete model is:

$$\text{GNP}_t = \frac{a_0 - b_0 - a_1(c_0 + f_0) + a_2 DY_{t-1} + a_3 C_{t-1} + A_t + G_t + X_t}{1 - a_1(1 - c_1 - f_1) + b_1}$$

The 'time path' of the model can be found in the program by substituting the current answers of the model (time t) for the lagged variables (time t-1) and repeating the solution of the equations.

The formulae for calculation of the multipliers could be determined by inspection of the reduced form of the equations. For example, in the simplified model above, we can inspect equation 8 and ask 'what increase in GNP_t will result if we increase autonomous spending (A_t) by 1?' GNP_t will increase by $1/(1-a_1)$ and this is the GNP multiplier of autonomous spending, say m. Inspecting equation 10, we ask 'what increase in E_t will occur if A_t increases by 1?' We know that GNP_t will go up by m, the GNP multiplier, so E_t will go up by m/d_1. This is the employment multiplier. By doing things this way, we could actually write the formulae for the multipliers into the program - but this hand analysis tends to get complicated if the model is complex. A better method of finding multipliers is to 'conduct an experiment' within the program, by storing the calculated results of the model, increasing an input variable by 1 and re-calculating the results. The increase in each result is its multiplier for the input variable changed. The program can repeat this process for each input variable and print out the multipliers.

A more general method of solving the equations

Finding the reduced form by hand as above leads to an easily implemented and quickly executed computer solution. The only disadvantage is that the amount of hand manipulation entailed with a large system of equations takes time and may result in a clerical slip. The reader who is facing the practical problems of solving models like these may like to learn a variation of the method which can be used either to double-check the hand solutions found by substitution or which, with a little more programming effort, can be built into the program so that the computer does the work of manipulation.

The first step is to re-write the equations so that all the unknowns and their coefficients are on the left, leaving only the knowns on the right. Taking the limited version of Stronge's model by way of example (and simplifying equation 2 by substituting GNP_t for DY_t, thereby eliminating equation 7), we get

$$GNP_t - C_t = A_t$$
$$C_t - a_1 GNP_t = a_0$$
$$ADF_t - C_t^F = A_t$$
$$ADF_t - GAP_t = GNPF_t$$
$$GNP_t - d_1 E_t = d_0$$
$$\Delta P_t - e_2 GAP_t = e_1 \Delta P_{t-1}$$

It will be appreciated that this system of equations is incomplete as it is short of an expression for full employment consumption. Stronge suggests we take this as

$$C_t^F = a_0 + a_1 GNP_t^F$$

The second step is to prepare a table which in effect expresses each 'known' (right-hand side) as a function of all the unknowns. We list all the unknowns across the top and enter in the body of the table the known coefficients that correspond to each of the equations, as in Table 8.4.

You will be able to see that if, for example, we want to find GNP_t from row (i), we could do this if we could eliminate the coefficient of C_t in the same row. One method of doing this would be by adding or subtracting any row that looks suitable for the purpose - of course, any operation done to the left of the equals sign must also be done to the right. So one possibility to solve for GNP_t would be to add row (ii) to row (i), giving a

162 Computer Models

Unknowns:	AD^F_t	C_t	C^F_t	E_t	GAP_t	GNP_t	ΔP_t	=	Knowns
(i)		-1			1			=	A_t
(ii)		1				$-a_1$		=	a_0
(iii)	1		-1					=	A_t
(iv)	1				-1			=	GNP^F_t
(v)				$-d_1$		1		=	d_0
(vi)					$-e_2$		1	=	$e_1 \Delta P_{t-1}$
(vii)				1				=	$a_0 + a_1 GNP^F_t$

Table 8.4: The table of coefficients (blank entries are to be taken as coefficients of zero)

revised row (i) - let us call this (i)' -

(i)' $\qquad\qquad\qquad\qquad 1 - a_1 \qquad\qquad = a_0 + A_t$

We now have an expression where GNP_t is the only unknown, and we need to divide the row by the coefficient of GNP_t so that it is scaled to a coefficient of 1: i.e. dividing by $1-a_1$ gives

(i)'' $\qquad\qquad\qquad\qquad 1 \qquad\qquad = (a_0 + A_t)/(1-a_1)$

Similarly, to find C_t now we need to eliminate the coefficient of GNP_t from row (ii). There is not another GNP_t coefficient of the right size, so we must scale another row suitably, e.g. multiplying row (i)'' by $-a_1$ gives

(i)''' $\qquad\qquad\qquad\qquad -a_1 \qquad\qquad = -a_1(a_0 + A_t)/(1-a_1)$

and subtracting row (i)''' from row (ii) gives

(ii)' $\qquad 1 \qquad\qquad\qquad\qquad\qquad = a_0 + a_1(a_0+A_t)/(1-a_1)$

The reader who is unfamiliar with this approach may care to solve for the other unknowns before proceeding to the discussion that follows.

This method becomes lengthy if each equation in the system uses a large number of unknowns (unlike our example), in which case it becomes preferable to follow the procedure described below for a computer program. This procedure works on the same principle except that the unwanted coefficients are eliminated from the columns, instead of the rows.

The program procedure is not difficult to understand when one knows that the trick is to work towards a sort of ideal table in which all the coefficients along a diagonal, say top left to bottom right, are 1 and all the others are zero, thereby ensuring that a solution (if there is one) is found for each unknown in turn. Assuming the coefficients of the unknowns and the values of the knowns have been inserted into the table by the program, a straightforward procedure is:

1. Consider each position in the diagonal in turn (say, row j column j), starting from the top left-hand corner
2. If the coefficient at row j column j is zero, we must arrange to get something there, so exchange row j for another row further down that has a non-zero coefficient in column j (see later for more detail about this)
3. Eliminate the non-zero coefficients in the rest of column j *below* the diagonal (again, see later for more detail).

After completion of these steps, we hope it is clear that all the coefficients *below* the diagonal will be zero. At this point, it will be more convenient to consider a simpler case, so take the three unknowns with three knowns of Table 8.5 by way of example.

Unknowns:	x_1	x_2	x_3	=	Knowns
(i)	a	b	c	=	y_1
(ii)	0	d	e	=	y_2
(iii)	0	0	f	=	y_3

Table 8.5: *A simplified table after eliminating coefficients below the diagonal*

It will be realized that we already have a solution for x_3, the unknown whose coefficient is in the bottom right-hand corner, because all the other coefficients in that row are zero. So dividing the bottom row by f gives us the answer for x_3. Knowing x_3, we can see that $d.x_2 = y_2 - e.x_3$, that is $x_2 = (y_2 - e.x_3)/d$, so we have a solution for x_2. Knowing x_2 and x_3, we can see that $a.x_1 = y_1 - b.x_2 - c.x_3$, so $x_1 = (y_1 - b.x_2 - c.x_3)/a$. We need not actually go through the process of eliminating the coefficients above the diagonal - we can get the answers directly by this method. The general rules for this procedure are:

4. Divide the known on the right-hand side of the bottom row by the coefficient in the bottom right-hand corner, giving the answer for the right-most unknown. Leave this answer in the right-hand side.
5. Consider each remaining position in the diagonal in turn, working up from right to left (say, row j, column j). The answer for the unknown of column j is found by subtracting, from the known on the right-hand side of row j, an amount equal to the other unknowns in row j (i.e. to the right of the diagonal), and dividing the result by the coefficient at row j column j (FORTRAN programmers should note that the variable which holds the result of the subtractions should be declared DOUBLE PRECISION to preserve precision in the answer). These unknowns to the right of the diagonal are found by considering each position to the right of row j column j in turn (say, row j column k) and multiplying the known at row k by the coefficient at row j column k.

To understand the elimination at step 3, suppose there is a non-zero coefficient to be eliminated at row k, column j. We must scale the coefficient on the diagonal (row j column j) so that it is equal to the coefficient to be eliminated (row k column j) and then subtract row j from row k. The scaling can be done by multiplying row j by a scaling factor equal to: the coefficient at row k column j, divided by the coefficient at row j column j. If this scaling factor is very large, there may be a loss of precision in the answer, so it is desirable that in the previous step, step 2, row j is exchanged for the row with the *largest* coefficient (in absolute terms, i.e. ignoring any sign) in column j - this will ensure that the scaling factor is always less than (or equal to) 1, so there will be no loss of precision in the answer from this cause.

Naturally, this method can be applied to a system of equations of any size, although the time taken by the computer becomes a limitation with very large systems of equations. Finding the multipliers by 'experiment' in the program, as previously described, is still the most efficient method.

Reference

1. Stronge, W.B., 'A simulation model for introducing Keynesian economics'. *Simulation and Games* 4(4), Dec 1973, 411-428.

Appendix A
Statistical Concepts

Histograms

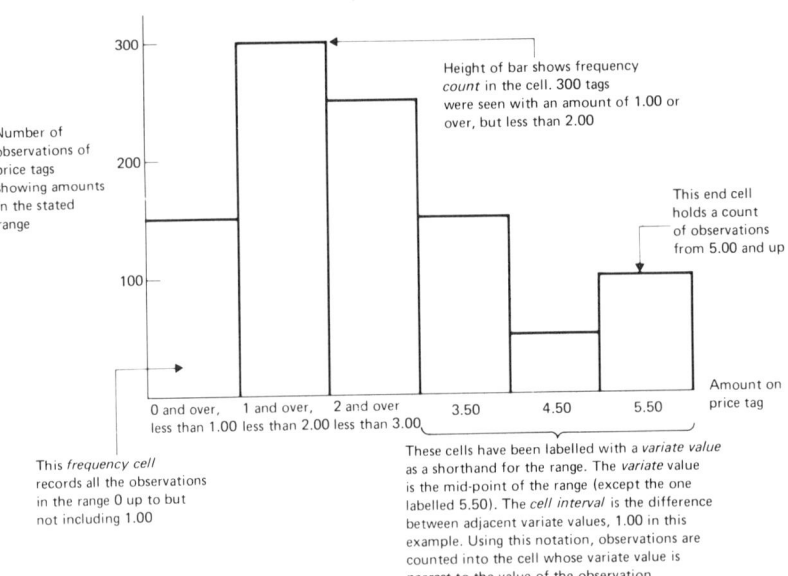

Fig. A1: 1000 observations of price tag amounts in department stores recorded in a histogram

Probability distribution

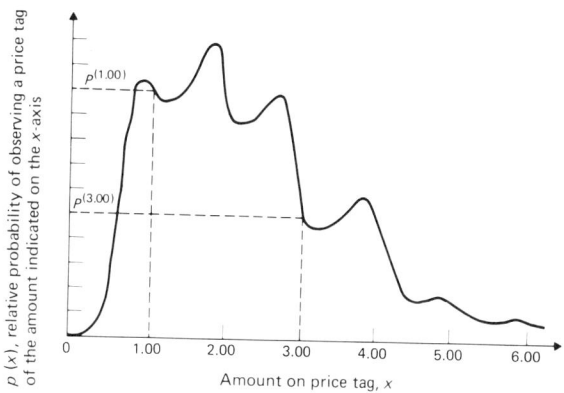

Fig. A2: A graph predicting the relative probability of observing a price tag of the amount shown on the horizontal axis. The graph says, for example, that in the long run you will see twice as many tags for 1.00 as you will for 3.00.

Random, or uniform, distribution

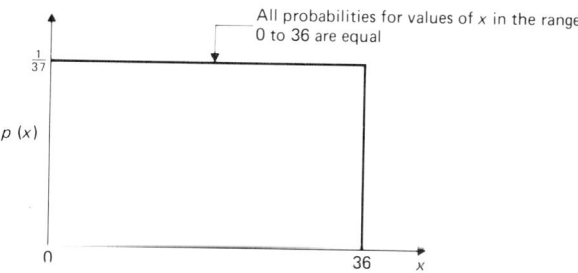

Fig. A3: The relative probability of the numbers on the horizontal axis 'coming up' on a roulette wheel. (A person with a precise mind might say that this graph should not show that a number like 1.25 or 31.337 is as likely as the integers. This limitation is usually taken as 'understood' when the observations are known to take only certain values - the same applied in Fig. A2 if the interval between adjacent prices was never less than 0.01.) The scale of the $p(x)$ axis is normally chosen so that the sum of the probabilities of all the possible x values is unity. For the case of a roulette wheel, $p(x) = 1/37$.

Normal distribution

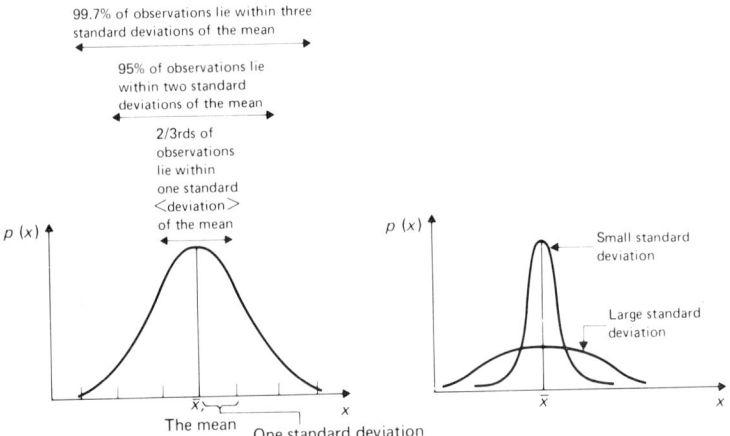

Fig. A4: The relative probability graph of a normal distribution has this bell shape. The mean (i.e. the average of all the values which will be observed in the long run) and the mode (i.e. the value which will be observed most often in the long run) are the same. A normal distribution can be completely described by specifying its mean value and its standard deviation (the measure of the distribution's 'spread').

Negative exponential distribution

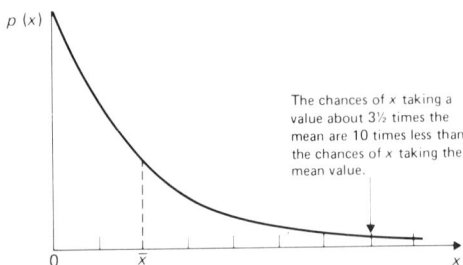

Fig. A5: The negative exponential distribution describes the probable interval between random numbers. The distribution can be completely described by specifying its mean, i.e. the average interval. If ten people arrive at a shop at random points of time within each hour, the average interval between arrivals will be 60/10 = 6 minutes, while the intervals you would observe in the long run are distributed as in this figure.

Suppose you try the roulette wheel of Fig. A3 above 37 times. You would get a shock if each of the numbers 0-36 came up exactly once. With just 37 goes, you would expect some numbers to come up twice, or even three times say, and some not to come up at all.

Imagine you have done this experiment and you have recorded all the numbers you got, in ascending order. Now suppose you start tallying up a histogram of the *interval* between one number in your list and the number next following. An interval of 0 will be recorded quite often, so will an interval of 1. You are not so likely to find you are dealing with a larger interval, say 5 or 10, while a really big interval like 30 is highly improbable.

If you repeated the experiment with another 37 numbers, and another, and so on (still tallying in the same histogram), you would find that your histogram was tending towards the shape shown in Fig. A5. Remembering that you are generating 37 numbers in a range of 37 you would expect the long-run *average interval* (i.e. the mean of the intervals) to be 1. (If, at each experiment, you generated 74 numbers, you would expect the mean to be 0.5, and so on.)

Appendix B
Computer Concepts

Organisation of a computer

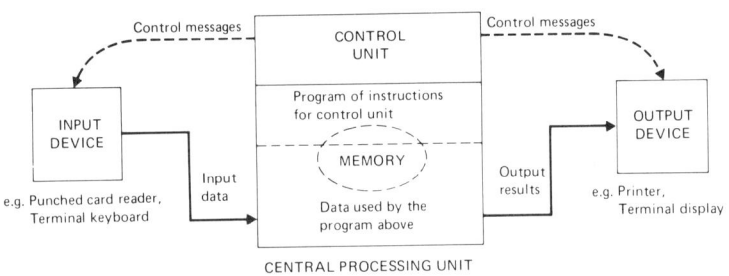

Fig. B1: Organisation of a computer

The computer comprises a collection of electronics called a central processing unit (CPU) connected by wires to input and output devices. Data is sent along the wires as electronic signals.
 The central processing unit has two important parts - a memory and a control unit.

Stored program

The program of instructions which the computer is to follow is stored in the memory, together with the data used by the program.
 The instructions and data can be thought of as being held in numbered boxes in memory, each box holding one instruction or piece of data.

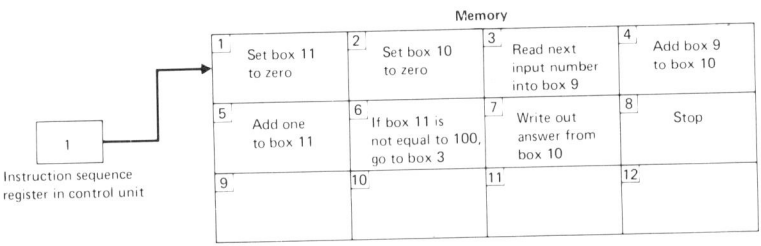

Fig. B2: A computer memory holding a program to read in and add up 100 input numbers

Computer Concepts

Instruction execution cycle

The control unit can cause activity on input or output devices and can cause arithmetic to take place on the data. (Although the instructions in Fig. B2 are written in English, for illustration, they are in fact recorded electronically and only a limited number of well-defined types of instruction allowed.)

The control unit contains an index to the boxes in memory, called the Instruction Sequence Register. When a program starts, the control unit sets this register to point to the first instruction (box 1 in our example). It then slavishly executes the following cycle:

Step 1: Get the instruction indicated by the sequence register. Go to step 2.
Step 2: Add 1 to the sequence register. Go to step 3.
Step 3: Do what the instruction tells you. Go back to step 1.

If the reader cares to pretend he is the control unit he can work the program in Fig. B2 with a pencil and eraser, and appreciate just how unthinking and mechanical the control unit is. Just slavishly follow the steps above (at box 6, interpret 'go to box 3' as meaning 'set the value of the instruction sequence register to 3') until you get to the point where you realize how dull it is to be a control unit.

The power of the machine lies in the human imagination, skill or inventiveness in specifying the program.

Symbolic languages - FORTRAN

In writing a program of any complexity, it is tedious and error-prone to use box numbers in instructions. In a symbolic programming language, the programmer can use names he makes up instead of box numbers and leave to the computer the task of translating his names into numbers. The most widely used symbolic language for scientific work is FORTRAN (*FOR*mula *TRAN*slation language). In FORTRAN, instructions requiring arithmetic are written as assignments in which the box to the left of an 'equals' sign (=) is to receive the result of the calculation specified on the right of the sign. The program of Fig. B2 could appear in FORTRAN:

```
        COUNT = 0
        TOTAL = 0
    999 READ(5,/) NUMBER
        TOTAL = TOTAL + NUMBER
        COUNT = COUNT + 1
        IF (COUNT.NE.100) GO TO 999
        WRITE(6,/) TOTAL
        STOP
```

There is an exact correspondence between this FORTRAN program and the internal machine program of Fig. B2. COUNT, TOTAL and NUMBER are the symbolic names of boxes 11, 10 and 9 respectively, while '999' is the symbolic 'name' of box 3. (The numbers in the READ and WRITE instructions simply specify the input or output device concerned, and .NE. means 'not equal'.)

Subroutines

A subroutine is a small program which has to be written and tested only once, after which it can be called into use by other programs as often as they require. If you find a subroutine somebody else has written which is useful to your present purpose, you may save a lot of effort. Even when there is no labour saving in this sense, large programs are always broken down into smaller subroutines, each of which has a clear purpose, so that proper testing may be carried out.

Suppose we wish to write a subroutine which will find the percentage that one number is of another. In FORTRAN, this subroutine could appear:

```
SUBROUTINE PCENT(ANUM1,ANUM2,ANSWER)
ANSWER = (ANUM1/ANUM2)*100
RETURN
```

The name PCENT can be used in other programs later on to invoke the subroutine. The names ANUM1, ANUM2 and ANSWER are the subroutine's names for the boxes it will need to use whenever it is invoked. RETURN means 'go back to the program that called me up'. The asterisk is used in FORTRAN to signify multiplication, and the oblique stroke signifies division.

Once the subroutine is declared and available, it can be called up from any program, for example:

```
X = 2
Y = 4
CALL PCENT(X,Y,RESULT)
WRITE(6,/) RESULT
```

would cause '50' to be written out. Note that the symbolic names used in the calling program do not have to be the same as those in the subroutine - the names are private to each program. When the instructions are executed inside the computer, they will all be in terms of box numbers and the computer's translation of the instruction to CALL will ensure that the right boxes are used.

Another useful type of subroutine is called a *function*. With this type, the name of the subroutine is also the name of the box that holds the answer. This often allows for simpler programs, e.g. the previous example could be written:

```
FUNCTION PCENT(ANUM1,ANUM2)
PCENT = (ANUM1/ANUM2)*100
RETURN
```

and the calling program can then invoke the function simply by using its name (i.e. it is not necessary to CALL it), for example:

```
X = 2
Y = 4
RESULT = PCENT(X,Y)
WRITE(6,/) RESULT
```

Appendix C
EDSIM Subroutines

Introduction

EDSIM (Event-based Discrete SIMulation) is a method of implementing simulation models on a computer using the general-purpose language FORTRAN. EDSIM is a library of subroutines for commonly needed simulation requirements which can be called from a FORTRAN main program. This method has the advantage over many of the special-purpose simulation languages available – there are over fifty of these – in that

i) it is easily learnt and used by a person with some programming experience in FORTRAN;
ii) it can easily be made available to that person, whatever the computer he uses, providing it has a FORTRAN compiler;
iii) it offers facilities approximately equivalent to those of a powerful simulation language Extended CSL[1], but it is substantially faster in execution and requires no special software.

Declarations

The data which the EDSIM subroutines manipulate are provided by the programmer, mainly in the form of arrays. Although the simulation programmer does not need to know how EDSIM works internally, he must be partially aware of the structure of the arrays. It is the programmer's responsibility to declare the entities of the simulation, the states to which these entities can belong, the time cells, and any histograms required; he does this by means of the following declarations:

Classes. The term CLASS is used in EDSIM to refer to a group of entities, with the class name being the plural of the entity name. For example we may require a class SHIPS comprising 48 of the entities called SHIP. This would be achieved by:

            INTEGER SHIPS,SHIP
            CALL DCLASS(SHIPS,SHIP,48)

Class names and entity names are represented in EDSIM as FORTRAN INTEGER variables. The call to the EDSIM subroutine DCLASS (Declare CLASS) defines SHIPS as being a class of 48 entities called SHIP (i.e. SHIP 1, SHIP 2 ,..., SHIP 48). On return from DCLASS, SHIPS has the value 48. The variables SHIPS and SHIP must not be changed by the programmer.

Sets. The term SET refers to an array which is used to keep track of the entities in a particular state. For example the entities SHIP 1, SHIP 3 and SHIP 27 may be in the state 'at sea', in which case the array ATSEA would contain the values 1, 3 and 27. The declaration which establishes the set would be:

            INTEGER ATSEA(50)
            CALL DSET (ATSEA,50)

Sets are represented as FORTRAN INTEGER arrays, and the size of the array is the maximum number of entities that the set may hold, plus 2. In this case 48 ships may be in the state 'at sea', so the size of the array is 48 + 2 = 50. The call to the EDSIM subroutine DSET (Declare SET) defines ATSEA as a set capable of holding 48 entities. (Experienced programmers will also appreciate that by using the class name instead of a constant, fewer changes may be needed if the program is amended to cater for a different class size, e.g. CALL DSET(ATSEA,SHIPS+2) could be a substitute for the previous example.)

The number of entities a set may hold does not have to be the same as the class size. For example, if the dock facilities deal with a maximum of three ships, the following set declaration would suffice:

> INTEGER DOCKED(5)
> CALL DSET(DOCKED,5)

A set may hold only entities belonging to the class defined just prior to the declaration of the set; the programmer would be notified of an error if, for example, he tried to put the entity PERSON 15 into the set ATSEA - only SHIPs may go in it.

The two extra cells the programmer declares for the set, over and above those necessary to hold the maximum number of entities, are control cells used by EDSIM and are the *last two* cells of the array. Figure C1 shows the array ATSEA.

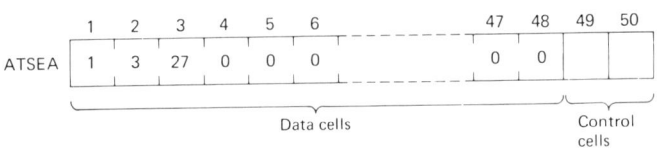

Fig. C1: An EDSIM set array. Entities in the set are recorded in the data cells. The last two cells are control cells used by the subroutines.

Temporary sets. Temporary sets are practically identical to sets, the only difference being that a temporary set is not tied to a specific class - it may hold entities from *any* class, provided that *at any one time* all the entities in the set belong to the same class. An example of the use of temporary sets is described later, when the subroutine ANY has been defined. The declaration of a temporary set, capable of holding a hundred entities, uses the EDSIM subroutine DTEMP (Declare TEMPorary set), for example:

> INTEGER TEMP(102)
> CALL DTEMP(TEMP,102)

Time cells. A time-cell array (ITIMES) is used in an EDSIM program to hold all the time cells needed for the simulation. Suppose we want a time cell associated with every ship, and a time cell associated with each dock; the declaration would be:

> INTEGER TSHIP,TDOCK
> COMMON ICLOCK,TSHIP(48),TDOCK(3),ITIMCT
> ITIMCT = 53
> DIMENSION ITIMES(53)
> EQUIVALENCE (ITIMES(1),ICLOCK)

Time cells are in COMMON (to ensure that they are all contiguous) and are all INTEGER variables. The first cell is reserved for the EDSIM clock. Then follow the 48 ship time cells and the 3 dock time cells. Finally there is a mandatory cell ITIMCT, which is set to the number of cells in the time-cells common block (including ICLOCK and ITIMCT itself), in this example, 53. The DIMENSION and EQUIVALENCE statements simply allow the whole time-cells common block to be referenced by the single name ITIMES. Because of the possibility of errors creeping in when declaring the time cells (particularly in counting the time cells in a large simulation program) EDSIM provides a subroutine to validate the time declarations; this also initializes all time cells to zero. The time declarations should be followed by:

```
                    CALL ITIMOK(ITIMES,ITIMCT)
```

Histograms. Histograms are a convenient way to display results from a simulation model. In an EDSIM program, all histograms are stored as integer arrays. For example, in the model of Chapter 2 a histogram of receipts at the barbecue is required, and this is declared as:

```
                    DIMENSION BARBQ(14)
                    CALL DHIST(BARBQ,9,0,1000)
```

Remembering that all the variables have been implicitly declared of type INTEGER at the start of this program, the first line of the foregoing declaration reserves fourteen memory locations for an integer array BARBQ. The first five of these locations are used as control cells by EDSIM and must not be altered by the programmer; the frequency counts are stored in the remaining cells. The call to the EDSIM subroutine DHIST(Declare HISTogram) declares BARBQ to be a histogram containing nine cells, the variate value associated with the first being zero, and the variate values associated with the subsequent cells being 1000 more than the previous variate value.

Histograms can be initialized - for example, for the purpose of sampling from a measured distribution - by means of a READ or DATA statement. Perhaps it is worth emphasizing that the first FIVE cells of an EDSIM histogram are control cells and hence not available to the programmer: the first cell specified in a READ or DATA statement is 6, for example:

```
                    READ(6,10)  (BARBQ(I),I=6,14)
```

More realistic examples can be found in the hospital simulation of Chapter 7.

Miscellaneous. The EDSIM subroutines use a block of COMMON labelled EDSIMZ, of size 106 memory locations. The first location of this common block is for a logical variable called DONE - we will see the use of this variable when the EDSIM subroutines are defined later. EDSIM contains some integer functions (FIRST, RANDUM, COUNT, SAMPLE) and logical functions (EMPTY) which must be declared appropriately if used. For example:

```
                    INTEGER FIRST,RANDUM,COUNT,SAMPLE
                    LOGICAL DONE,EMPTY
                    COMMON/EDSIMZ/DONE,IDUMMY(105)
```

Finally, preceding all class, set, time cell and histogram declarations, there may be a call to the EDSIM initialization routine EDINIT. This takes the form:

```
                    CALL EDINIT(6)
```

where 6 is the device number of the peripheral on which EDSIM output is to be written. This call may be omitted on computers which initialize all memory locations to zero on loading a program.

Complete examples of short EDSIM programs are given on pages 46 and 145.

Modes of running EDSIM programs

EDSIM programs can be run in one of two modes - CHECK mode or NOCHECK mode. The former is used during the development stage of a simulation program, when the programmer may need to know intermediate contents of specified sets, time cell values and so on, for checking or debugging his program - CHECK mode makes this sort of information easily available. The EDSIM subroutines to facilitate this checking are described in the next section.

During the development stage there is a greater chance of one part of a program corrupting another part to produce erroneous results, for example by an array overflowing (on a computer which does not perform array bound checking). In particular, corruption of classes or sets could lead to formidable problems for the programmer to solve, when the routines which manipulate these data areas are not his own but are provided from the EDSIM library. Consequently, in CHECK mode, classes, sets and histograms are checked for errors of this sort, as far as possible. Examples of internal checking performed by EDSIM are:

1. the specified entity is valid (e.g. SHIP 49 would be invalid);
2. the class and set are compatible (e.g. an attempt to put PERSON 21 into ATSEA would be invalid);
3. the current members of a set are valid (e.g. set ATSEA may have been corrupted and now contains SHIP 483).

When the programmer has validated his model and is satisfied that the program is performing correctly, he will use the model for experimenting. This stage is often the most time-consuming, in terms of computer usage. During this stage the program will normally be run in NOCHECK mode, which by-passes the checking facilities and results in substantially shorter execution times (by a factor of two or three, depending on the actual simulation).

EDSIM subroutines and functions

Key:
- E = entity name, e.g. PERSON, SHIP. This is the singular name specified in the DCLASS call.
- I = index, an integer variable or constant identifying a particular entity in a class
- S = set name, e.g. ATSEA
- V = integer variable or constant, e.g. ICLOCK
- D = distribution (histogram) name, e.g. BARBQ
- literal = a Hollerith constant of the form nH followed by n characters, the last of which is a full stop, e.g. 5HFREQ. . The maximum value of n is 30.
- DONE = the logical variable contained in the first location of the EDSIM common block EDSIMZ. It is set by the EDSIM subroutines HEAD, INTO and FROM.

The EDSIM subroutines and functions are grouped according to their purpose, and are defined in the column labelled TYPE as being one of the following:

- SUB : subroutine
- LF : logical function
- IF : integer function

Group	Name	Type	Purpose
Checking	CHKON	SUB	Enables CHECK mode
	CHKOFF	SUB	Enables NOCHECK mode. No EDSIM checking of any kind is performed.
	CHECKD(literal,D)	SUB	The literal and the cells of the named histogram are printed if in CHECK mode.
	CHECKS(literal,S)	SUB	The literal and the members of the named set are printed if in CHECK mode.
	CHECKV(literal,V)	SUB	The literal and the value of the integer variable are printed if in CHECK mode.
Distributions	CLEAR(D)	SUB	The cells of D are set to zero
	TALLY(D,V)	SUB	The tally of the number of observations in the cell of D whose variate value is closest to V is incremented by 1
	SAMPLE(D,V)	IF	The function takes the variate value of a random sample drawn from D. V is used as a seed for the random number generator.
	FREQU(D,V)	IF	The function takes the value of the contents of the cell whose variate value is closest to V
	PRHIST(D,literal-1, literal-2)	SUB	A visual representation of D is produced on the line-printer. The literals are used to label the axes. Literal-1 refers to what is normally the frequency axis, whereas literal-2 describes the variate axis.
	HSTATS(D,NTOTAL, XMEAN,SDEV)	SUB	Returns the number NTOTAL, the mean (XMEAN) and the standard deviation (SDEV) of the entries in D. XMEAN and SDEV are REAL variables. (This information is automatically printed by PRHIST.)
Class	LOAD(E,J,S)	SUB	The set is initialized to contain the entities from 1 to J
	HEAD(E,I,S)	SUB	The set is searched for entity I. If it is found, DONE is set to .FALSE. and no further action taken. If it is not found, DONE is set to .TRUE. and entity I is inserted before the first member of S.

176 Computer Models

Group	Name	Type	Purpose
Class (cont.)	INTO(E,I,S)	SUB	The set is searched for entity I. If it is found, DONE is set to .FALSE. and no further action taken. If it is not found, DONE is set to .TRUE. and entity I inserted after the last member of S.
	FROM(E,I,S)	SUB	The set is searched for entity I. If it is not found, DONE is set to .FALSE. and no further action taken. If it is found, DONE is set to .TRUE. and entity I is removed from the set.
	IN(E,I,S)	LF	The function takes the value .TRUE. if entity I is a member of S, otherwise it is set to .FALSE.
	NOTIN(E,I,S)	LF	The function takes the value .TRUE. if entity I is not a member of S, otherwise it is set to .FALSE.
Set	ZERO(S)	SUB	All members of the set are removed.
	FIRST(S)	IF	The function takes the value of the index of the first member of the set, or 0 if the set is empty
	LAST(S)	IF	The function takes the value of the index of the last member of the set, or 0 if the set is empty
	ANY(S,V)	IF	The function takes the value of the index of a member of the set chosen at random, or 0 if the set is empty. V is used as a seed for the random number generator.
	COUNT(S)	IF	The function takes the value of the number of members in the set, or 0 if the set is empty.
	EMPTY(S)	LF	The function takes the value .TRUE. if the set is empty, otherwise it is set to .FALSE.
Sets	GAINS(S_1,S_2)	SUB	Those members of S_2 which are not already members of S_1 are added to S_1 after the last member
	LOSES(S_1,S_2)	SUB	Those members of S_2 which are also members of S_1 are removed from S_1
	EQUALS(S_1,S_2)	LF	The function takes the value .TRUE. if both sets contain the same members (ordering is not significant), or if both sets are empty - otherwise it takes the value .FALSE.

Group	Name	Type	Purpose
Sets (cont.)	WITHIN(S_1,S_2)	LF	The function takes the value .TRUE. if the members of S_1 are a subset of the members of S_2 (ordering is not significant), or if S_1 is empty - otherwise it takes the value .FALSE.
	APART(S_1,S_2)	LF	The function takes the value .TRUE. if S_1 has no members in common with S_2 (ordering is not significant) - otherwise it returns the value .FALSE. The case of S_1 being empty returns the value .FALSE.
Statistical	RANDUM(V_1,V_2)	IF	The function takes the value of a random number in the range 1 to V_1. V_2 is used as a seed for the random number generator.
	NEGEXP(V_1,V_2)	IF	The function takes the value of a random sample drawn from a negative exponential distribution of mean V_1. V_2 is used as a seed for the random number generator.
	NORMAL(V_1,V_2,V_3)	IF	The function takes the value of a random sample drawn from a normal distribution of mean V_1 and standard deviation V_2. V_3 is used as a seed for the random number generator.
Time	ITIMOK(ITIMES, ITIMCT)	SUB	Checks the time cell declarations for consistency, and initialises all time cells to zero.
	TIMADV(ITIMES, ITIMCT)	SUB	Advances the clock to the next event by finding the smallest positive value in the time cells ITIMES(2) to ITIMES(ITIMCT-1). This value is then subtracted from all the cells in this range, and added to ITIMES(1), i.e. ICLOCK.
	TIMCLR(ITIMES, ITIMCT)	SUB	Clears all time cells to zero.

Use of temporary sets

Suppose we want to select any ship at random from those ships which are in the state 'at sea' and which have a time cell value of less than 10 (remember the time cells were defined so that every ship had an associated time cell). To achieve this in EDSIM we make use of a temporary set and the integer function ANY.

The first step is to select those ships from ATSEA which satisfy the specified conditions, and save them in the temporary set:

```
         CALL ZERO(TEMP)
         ILAST = COUNT(ATSEA)
         DO 10 I=1,ILAST
           J = ATSEA(I)
           IF (TSHIP(J).GE.10) GO TO 10
           CALL INTO(SHIP,J,TEMP)
  10     CONTINUE
```

These instructions access the data portion of the set ATSEA directly and J takes the value of the index of the successive members of the set. The final step is to select an entity at random from the subset now held in TEMP; this is achieved by

```
         IF (EMPTY(TEMP)) GO TO 20
         M = ANY(TEMP,SEED)
```

Reference

1. Clementson, A.T., 'Extended control and simulation language'. *The Computer Journal* 9(3), 215-220, 1966.

Glossary

This list describes terms you may encounter in other books and journals on computer modelling which for reasons of clarity or space we have not used in this book. A brief description of the more commonly-used simulation languages is also included; a fuller description appears in J. E. Sammet's book *Programming Languages: History and fundamentals,* Prentice-Hall, Englewood Cliffs, N.J., from which the original references may be obtained.

Terms not included in this glossary are explained in the text (see Index).

Activity is a period of time during which specified actions are taking place. In the hospital simulation of Chapter 6, an example of an activity is 'operation in progress'.

Algol (*Al*gorithmic Language) is a programming language mainly used in mathematical and scientific disciplines.

Attribute is a quality ascribed to an entity. It is synonymous with 'state'. In the hospital simulation, a person may have the attribute 'undergoing operation'.

Compiler is a complex program which converts a program written in a programming language (e.g. Algol or FORTRAN) into a form which can be run on the computer. (An Algol or FORTRAN program cannot be run directly on a computer - it must first be 'compiled'.)

CSL (*C*ontrol and *S*imulation *L*anguage) is an event-based discrete simulation language. It was the fore-runner of ECSL, on which EDSIM is based.

DYNAMO is a simulation language designed to make easier the modelling of dynamic feedback systems that can be described by a set of suitable equations, e.g. econometric models where interest lies in the time path of the variables. A well-known application of DYNAMO is Forrester's work on industrial systems and world models (see bibliography). A model is specified in terms of a set of equations. Time is advanced in fixed-time increments, and the values of endogenous variables determined at the end of each interval. The values of the variables of the model can be printed in graphical form after each time advancement if desired.

ECSL (*E*xtended *CSL*) provides more powerful set manipulation facilities than are available in CSL. As with CSL a model is described in terms of classes of entities and sets for entities. An ECSL program, which is compiled by an ECSL compiler, is structured as a series of activities. The clock is advanced to the next event, and the activities are then scanned for those which can commence or which have just terminated; appropriate activities - for example, moving entities from one set to another - can then take place.

180 Computer Models

Endogenous ('from within') variables are the output variables of a model, whose values are determined by the interaction between the exogenous variables and the internal variables or parameters of a model.

Entity of a model is the object or thing which is being considered in the model, e.g. person, aircraft.

Event is the instant of time that a change of state occurs in a model. For example, the end of the activity 'operation in progress' is an event.

Exogenous ('from outside') variables are the input variables of a model and are predetermined and independent of the system being modelled. They affect the system, but the system does not act on them.

Flowchart - the pictorial representation of a series of operations performed in a definite sequence. The symbols used to represent the various operations normally conform to some standard in which each symbol has a specific meaning (but it is our opinion that many standards are more complicated than is necessary).

GASP is a method of writing simulation programs in FORTRAN, and bears some resemblance to EDSIM. The entities of a GASP program are called *elements*, which are qualified by means of *attributes*. Elements interact with other elements through events, which in GASP are subroutines written by the user to cause a change to one or more elements.

GPSS (General Purpose System Simulator) is a discrete simulation language which employs *transactions, equipment* and *blocks*. Transactions are the entities (e.g. persons, aircraft) which move through the system and which occupy the physical equipment of the system. A *facility* is any piece of equipment which can be engaged by a single transaction at a time (e.g. runway); a *storage* is a piece of equipment which can be engaged by many transactions at a time (e.g. recovery room). A simulation model is constructed using a block diagram, in which each block represents some basic action (e.g. *originate*: create a transaction; *mark*: note the current clock time on each transaction entering the block). Each block has an associated time indicating the number of time units required for the action of that block. Connections between the blocks indicate the sequence of actions that occur in the system.

Preprocessor (sometimes called a program generator) is a computer program which accepts as input a description of a simulation model, and produces as output an equivalent computer program, written either in a simulation language (e.g. ECSL) or in a general-purpose language (e.g. FORTRAN). For further information see Mathewson, S.C., 'Simulation program generators', *Simulation*, December 1974, pages 181-189.

Probability is a quantitative measure of the likelihood of an event occurring. An event that is certain has a probability of one; an impossible event has a probability of zero.

Random sample - a sample selected in such a way that each individual in the group of entities from which the sample is drawn has an equal chance of being included in the sample.

Sample - a small part (sub-group) of a group of entities (people, numbers) having the same qualities as the entities making up the group.

Simscript is a discrete simulation language built around FORTRAN in which a model is described in terms of *entities* (the objects of the simulation), *attributes* (properties associated with the entities) and *sets* (groups of entities). *Events* modify the status of the system at various instants in simulated time; the clock is advanced to the next event on the event list, and the actions associated with the event, including the addition of further events to the list, are performed.

Simula is a discrete simulation language which is a true extension of Algol - all the facilities of Algol are available in Simula.

Simulation languages (e.g. ECSL, GPSS) are languages specifically developed for implementing simulation models and which incorporate features peculiar to simulation (e.g. set handling facilities, time advancement). An alternative approach to implementing simulation models is to use a general-purpose language such as Algol or FORTRAN - specific simulation facilities are then provided by a library of subroutines (e.g. EDSIM). The latter approach has the advantage that the modeller who already has experience of programming does not have to learn a new language, since the statements he makes are in the language with which he is familiar. The general-purpose languages, particularly FORTRAN, are widely available on different computers (this is not so with simulation languages - none has proved universally popular).

Tracing means 'following the path taken by the computer as it executes a program'. The discussion on program validation in Chapter 4 recommended that the first few entities be modelled both by hand and by computer, and the results compared. The values of the variables, the contents of histograms and the contents of sets at various strategic points in the program can be printed in EDSIM by inserting calls to the respective checking subroutines CHECKV, CHECKD and CHECKS, with the program run in CHECK mode. It is good programming practice to include checking statements *when the program is written*, say at the beginning of each activity in the events section of an EDSIM program, so that a trace can be obtained and its correctness verified. The output from these check statements can be suppressed when no longer needed by running the program in NOCHECK mode. Particularly stubborn errors may necessitate the insertion of more check statements later - the validation practice recommended above should give a clear indication of the best place to insert the extra statements.

Index

Ad hominem argument 1
Advance clock 42, 137
Aggregated models 78
Airport simulation 29
Andreski, S. 7
Attribute 34

Bacon - Maxims of Law 5
Barker, P. 7
Bayes' theorem 75
Bibliography 80
Birth control 78

Causality 5
Central processing unit 168
Channels 26-29
  airport 32
  hospital 127
Checking program 64, 139
Chi-square test 56-62, 66-67
  two-sample 68, 141
Clementson, A.T., 178
Clock advance 42, 137
Closed system 51
Computer
  concepts 168-170
  memory 168
  model 24
  organisation of 168
  stored program 168
Concept
  in human memory 93
  relationships 94-95
Confidence 3-4, 9, 60-61
Confounded experiments 6
Consumption function 23
  Duesenberry 155
  Friedman 155
  Keynesian 153
Context of model 22
Contingent model 76
Continuous model 23
Control unit 168
Corporate business model 50
Costa Rica birth control 78
CPU 168

CSL 171
Cuban missile crisis 77
Cumulative distribution 15

Decision analysis 24
Degrees of freedom 58-60, 68, 141
Deterministic model 23
Discrete model 23
Distributions 165-167
  negative exponential 32, 128, 166
  normal 33-34, 166
  sampling from 13, 16-18, 129
  theoretical 62, 128
  uniform 165
Dominoes 74
Duesenberry consumption 155
Dynamic model 23
DYNKEYNES 151

Economic models 78, 151
EDSIM 171-78
  classes 132, 171
  declarations section 132-134
  histograms 133, 173
  initialization section 134-135
  modes of running 174
  programs 20, 46-48, 57, 145-150
  sets 132, 171
  subroutines 174-177
  temporary sets 172, 177
  termination section 138
  time cells 133, 172
  transitions section 135-138
Endogenous variables 153
Entity 29
Erewhon airport 29, 73
Event-based simulation 26, 41
Execution cycle 169
Exogenous variables 153
Experimenting with model 70-72, 143-145
Explanations 5
Extant models 4-5
Extended CSL 171

Flowchart 19, 38, 40
Ford, J. 7
FORTRAN 169
Forward-linked list 100
Friedman consumption 155
Frijda, N.H. 93
Function 170

Goodness-of-fit
  input distributions 55-63, 141-142
  results 67-69, 142
GPSS 126
Greist, J.H. 75

Histograms 164
Hospital simulation 126

Impersonal models 73
Initial conditions 38, 41, 63-64, 134-135
Instruction sequence register 169
Inter-arrival times 27
  airport 31-32
  hospital 127
IPL 93

Jones, L. 24

Kennedy, J.F. 77
Keynesian consumption 153
Kuzdrall, P.J. 126
Kwak, N.K. 126

Lags, time 78
LIFO list 104
Lindsay, P.H. 74, 93
Links 99
LISP 93

Many-person models 76
Mathematical models 23, 152
Mean 166
Memory
  computer 168
  human 93
Missile crisis 77
Models
  aggregated 78
  computer 24
  Contingent 76
  continuous 23-24
  corporate 50
  deterministic 23
  discrete 23-24
  dynamic 23
  economic 78, 151

Models (cont.)
  extant 4-5
  impersonal 73
  many-person 76
  mathematical 23, 152
  one-person 74
  prescriptive 75
  purpose of 5
  queueing 26-29
  static 23
  stochastic 23
Multipliers 160-161

Negative exponential distribution 32, 128, 166
Network 95
Node 95, 98
Norman, D.A. 74, 93, 97
Normal distribution 33-34, 166
Null state 34

Objectivity 2
Observations, making of 52-55
One-person models 74
Open system 51
Ordering of transitions 38-39, 45, 135
Overstreet, R.E. 76

Pencil-and-eraser method 41-45
Prescriptive model 75
Prisoner's dilemma 76
Probability 3
  distribution 165
Pseudo-random numbers
  generation of 65-66
  testing of 66-67
Purpose of models 5

Queues 26-29
  airport 30
  hospital 127
Queueing models 26-29

Random numbers 64-67
Reduced form 159
Reisman, S. 74
Rumelhart, D.E. 97
Ruritania 9, 73

Sampling
  from measured distribution 16-18, 129
  from theoretical distribution 16-18, 129
Schmitz, H.H. 126

Scientific method 4, 6
Seed 65-67
Sensitivity testing 22, 69-70
Service channel 26-29
  airport 32
  hospital 127
Service time 27
  airport 33-34
  hospital 127-129
Set 34, 132
Simulation
  airport 29
  hospital 126
  journals 80
  rainfall 13
Simultaneous equations 152, 157
  reduced form 159
  solution of 159-163
Smith, R.B. 77
Stack, computer 104
Standard deviation 166
State-transition
  diagram 35, 36, 37, 130
  matrix 34, 36, 37, 130
States 29, 34, 129
Static model 23
Statistical concepts 164-167
Stochastic model 23
Stronge, W.B. 151
Subjectivity 2, 4
Subroutines 169
Suicides 75

Testing model logic 63, 138
Theoretical distribution 62, 128
TIM 98
Time
  lags 78, 153, 160
  path 160
  unit of 39, 133
Transitions 34-38
  ordering of 38-39, 45, 135
Two-sample testing 68, 141

Uniform distribution 165

Validation
  of model 24, 50-51, 79, 138
  of program 24, 139-140
Variance 3
Vertinsky, I. 78

LIBRARY OF DAVIDSON COLLEGE